GOOD TIME COOKING

For Tom, my forever co-host,
who always chooses the perfect wine.

GOOD TIME COOKING

SHOW-STOPPING MENUS FOR EASY ENTERTAINING

ROSIE MACKEAN

PAVILION

AN INTRODUCTION
TO HOSTING

To understand why I have written this book you should probably know a bit about me. First things first – I bloody love to host. Ever since childhood I have been having people to supper, although I must confess my first few menus included cold bowls of mud soup and steak and chips made from plastic blocks. Feeding people has always been my favourite thing to do. The elation of putting a smile on someone's face with food you have made is incomparable and truly addictive, and is certainly what drove me to train as a chef. Cooking itself has always felt more of a reflex to me than anything else. It's something my body does to survive. Happy or sad, busy or slow, I often find myself cooking before I even know what I am doing; it is the thing that soothes, grounds and inspires me most.

Since I started working in food, first as a chef over a decade ago, and then as a food stylist and recipe developer for the last eight years, I have hosted my fair share of dinner parties. I didn't set out to have one of those 'How DO they do it?' moments, but that is literally what my guests would ask me each time they came over. My stock answer would always be 'well I am a chef, I know things'. When the idea for creating a Dinner Party newsletter first came to me in January 2022, I realized I would finally have an opportunity to share those mysterious 'things' that made cooking for crowds easy.

With the newsletter, 'The Dinner Party' I wanted to create a one-stop-shop for people to cook a menu for a dinner party that was cohesive and achievable, and that made them feel confident. One of the first things chefs are taught is that menus need to flow in order for service to flow. You include easy, ingredient-led dishes to give time and space for the more complicated and protracted plates. You do as much prep as possible, even if that just means chopping something up and putting it back in the fridge. You write mise-en-place lists so you can keep track of your prep and make sure it is done in the right order. This is all stuff that is normal in a restaurant but rarely considered in the home kitchen. I think people get hung up on the idea of things being 'freshly cooked' and also simply don't cook often enough to feel confident planning things out. A good restaurant service, and in turn a good dinner party, is a delicate balance between preparation, intuitive cooking and stress-free reheating. With each recipe and menu in this book, my aim is to kit you out with the tools to nail these three key skills and to walk you through them, with my hand on your shoulder, as your friend in the kitchen. A structured menu enables you to wow and please your guests without losing your whole evening to cooking. You can relax and enjoy yourself, drink and be merry. Consider this book a manual for both cooking and hosting.

HOW IT WORKS

Most of the menus in this book contain the recipes for a three-course or four-course dinner party to serve six people; there are a couple that serve two and there are a few that are big sharing meals without 'courses' as such.

Every menu has its own theme, which I mean in the least kitschy way possible. Ever since the newsletter's inception I have tried to write menus that aren't just bland responses to calendar events. Of course, these are sometimes necessary, but so much about cooking for me is a reaction or a mood or even a challenge. For example, there are menus for Valentine's Day and Bonfire Night, but also for when you are working from home and need to prep in between meetings, or for when you only get two hours' notice that you've got a houseful coming. There's an entirely plant-based menu and a menu for when you are having people over to watch sport. There are menus for date nights, for seafood lovers, for cocktail parties. And there menus that simply focus on cuisines – Roman, Bolognese and British food. The dinner parties in this book are the antithesis of stuffy – they are playful and fun.

Each menu comes with its own curated 'Getting Ahead' timeplan and mise-en-place list so that you can organize yourself in the lead up to the event and prepare what you can ahead of time just as a chef would. The dishes work in harmony with each other, both logistically and stylistically, but if you don't want to cook all of them, you don't have to – do what feels manageable. You can also mix and match with other menus and use the information given in the timeplans to intertwine them. In fact, I have suggested six alternative menus pulling together dishes from across the book to show you how easy it is (see page 16). Do not feel limited by the menus – you can play around with combinations and have fun experimenting. Each dish in each menu is a puzzle piece, all you need to do is put it all together in your own home and in your own time, with the calm preparedness of me, a seasoned chef in your ear.

MAKE AHEAD

I have a note on each recipe called 'Make Ahead'. This details which element(s) of the dish can be prepped ahead and how far in advance you can do them. Of course, this is also all included in the Getting Ahead timeplan and Mise-en-Place tables, but if you are only making one recipe instead of a whole menu it is useful to have this information right in front of you.

SUBSTITUTIONS

For every recipe there is a section detailing suitable swaps for ingredients where possible. I truly believe that cooking should be intuitive and recipes should be robust enough to take some kind of twiddling. Otherwise, we would never make discoveries or mistakes and grow as cooks. So I hope my substitutions encourage you to make a recipe your own, if you feel inclined. That said, if a substitution isn't proposed, it probably isn't recommended.

SCALING

The scaling guide for each recipe gives advice on how to reduce or increase quantities of the recipes without losing your mind, and also includes recommendations for any changes needed for smaller or larger batches.

GETTING AHEAD AND
MISE-EN-PLACE TABLES

GETTING AHEAD

The 'Getting Ahead' time plans help you see what you can get done in advance, so that for each course on the day you have at least one, maybe two major parts taken care of. I appreciate that not everyone's weeks are easily peppered with dinner party prep, but if you're hosting after work or on a day where you can't be in the kitchen, getting ahead is going to save your bacon.

Each timeplan starts three days before the big event, giving you the option of spreading your prep into manageable chunks. Where it is possible to prepare a dish or an element in advance that will be just as good a few days old, then the option is always there. For some of the longer recipes in the book, this is indispensable, as spreading the workload for those recipes makes it so much less overwhelming.

MISE-EN-PLACE

This is the fancy name we give to the food prep each section in a restaurant needs to do for their dishes. Breaking down each dish like this should help you to feel organized.

The mise-en-place table breaks down the prep needed for each dish on the day of the party and when to do it, so your thoughts and your space can be organized and calm. Some jobs are best left until closer to kick off and some can be done in the hours before if they haven't been done already.

Use the hour before your guests arrive to organize your space too. I find it helpful to group ingredients by dish so it is all in the same place – little ramekins and tupperwares are really useful for this. I also leave myself notes for anything that needs to stay in the fridge or come out at a specific time.

KITCHEN KIT

There are a few items in my kitchen that I simply cannot live without and that truly make cooking a lot easier in my opinion. These might not seem like the most glamorous or exciting choices but, trust me, they are indispensable. When I am not cooking at home, I take these on every shoot I go to, as well as on holiday.

MICROPLANE
I have at least four of these in varying widths, and they are just the bee's knees. I use them for zesting fruit and grating cheese, but they are also amazing for grating garlic cloves (I'd pick a Microplane over a garlic crusher any day – so much easier to clean!), nutmeg, ginger and shaving frozen things (like jalapeños).

BULLET BLENDER
These were invented for smoothies and healthy things, but I use mine for almost anything (sadly my smoothies now mostly taste like garlic, but it's a price I am willing to pay). The high-powered motor means you can get an amazingly smooth result compared to a food processor, and they are much less bulky.

FOOD PROCESSOR/LARGE BLENDER
That said, I do love a food processor, they make light work of large quantities, are great for making emulsified sauces like mayonnaise and can go in the dishwasher.

METAL TONGS
I use tongs so much, I have six pairs in varying lengths. When cooking meat or long pastas, fish or deep-frying, chances are you will need tongs. These are brilliant for serving too and sure they might not look great, but they are practical and stop your hands getting dirty, so buy some. I prefer metal ends because they last longer, but rubber-ended ones are fine, especially if you are worried about non-stick cookware.

RUBBER SPATULA
A couple of good spatulas are vital, especially for baking or sauce making. The biggest reason I love these so much is the fact that they bend, making it much easier to scoop and scrape every remnant of something you've made out of a vessel. You reduce wastage hugely when you use a rubber spatula.

POTATO RICER
Mashers are dead – use a potato ricer. It's a pretty specific piece of equipment to have, but trust me, you won't look back after you've used it.

CRANKED PALETTE KNIVES AND FISH SLICES
Palette knives and fish slices with cranked handles i.e. where the handle is angled for depth, are such vital pieces of kit. For serving something from a deep container, for flipping delicate things, for spreading large quantities of butter, cream, jam or anything.

BREAD KNIFE
It should go without saying that your knives should always be sharp, for ease and for safety. Having a good, sharp bread knife is particularly important as it can be used for so much more than just bread – carving meat (it's great on crackling), slicing cakes, cutting tomatoes (you lose less juice with a serrated knife). If you cut warm, fresh bread with a crap bread knife, it is a gutting moment and it will create more wastage too.

KITCHEN SPIDER
A large, long-handled wire spoon with a spiderweb-esque design that enables you to remove pieces of food from hot liquids. Essentially, it's a slotted spoon with bigger slots. I use mine all the time; when cooking short pasta, when deep-frying, when blanching vegetables or boiling eggs. The long handle protects you and the bigger slots mean you don't accidentally take lots of liquid out.

HAND-HELD ELECTRIC WHISK
I have tried to make sure that most recipes in this book that require lots of whisking can be made with a hand-held electric whisk. They are so much cheaper and less bulky than a stand mixer.

KITCHEN THERMOMETER
This is just a really useful tool that I really recommend you get if you are hosting a lot. I use mine the most when deep-frying – it means I don't have to use a fryer and can check the temperature of my oil accurately. I also use it when cooking meat to check internal temperatures, when reheating and for caramels.

ESSENTIAL INGREDIENTS

OIL

I mainly make use of three types of oil in the kitchen, and they each have a different purpose:

› Olive oil – great to start the cooking of a dish if it won't require a super high heat and would benefit from the mild aroma.
› Vegetable/sunflower oil – for frying or deep-frying at higher heats, searing meat, for minimal interference flavour-wise in sauces or braises.
› Extra virgin olive oil – for dressings, cold sauces and drizzling. I try to always have a good extra virgin oil on hand to finish dishes.

BUTTER

Unless otherwise specified, I always use unsalted butter so I can be in control of the seasoning of my dishes. I would avoid 'spreadable' butters, as these have been emulsified with vegetable fat and won't give the same flavour or texture as normal dairy butter.

SALT

For seasoning, I always use flaky sea salt unless otherwise specified – I find it to be more mellow and less acrid than fine salt. When seasoning water for cooking (pasta/vegetables), fine salt is best.

CITRUS

When trying to balance a dish with acidity, I often find myself using citrus over vinegars. Lemons are one of my most used ingredients – they provide fragrance, bitterness and sourness. Their zest is divine, too, which is why I usually stick with unwaxed.

SPICES

Spices and spice mixes bring a warmth and depth to dishes in a way that herbs cannot. One thing I am passionate about reminding people is that spices can go out of date. Not in a way that makes them dangerous or toxic, but in a way that makes them lose their flavour. Always check spices are in good condition before using them and chuck anything that smells less potent or fragrant, or in any way different to how it should.

HERBS

I couldn't cook without them – they are in my shopping basket every week and on my plate every single day. Herb preference can be hugely subjective, however, so if at any point I have suggested a herb you don't like, chances are there will be a suggested swap. When I reference herbs in the recipes, I always mean fresh, unless otherwise specified – and when there is parsley, I always mean flat leaf.

GARLIC

By far my favourite allium. I am very picky about garlic – it must have tight skin all over – both the head and the clove. If it has any discolouration or dried out parts, slice those bits off. If it smells at all metallic or sour, then don't use it. When using garlic raw, I tend to prefer smaller cloves so as not to overpower. Garlic powder is great for baking, marinating or curing and dressings.

CHILLIES/CHILLI FLAKES

I really adore heat in my food, from both fresh and dried chillies. Fresh chillies have a perfume that is bright and zingy, whereas dried chillies are a lot more warm and slightly sweet. I tend to use fresh chillies in dressings, sauces and salads and dried ones in recipes that are longer cooks or marinades.

GENERAL NOTE ON INGREDIENTS

MEAT AND FISH

For best results, always buy meat from a butcher who sells meat from ethically and locally reared animals. The difference is so massive, both in the quality of the meat itself and also in environmental terms. Butchers are not always convenient, but there are many brilliant online retailers now selling beautiful British meat.

Similarly with fish, where possible always buy from a reputable fishmonger who sells line-caught fish from the UK.

MY FAVOURITES

ANCHOVIES
Salty, fishy, savoury and SO GOOD. I would put anchovies in most things given the chance. I've had to be a bit more discerning with their application in this book. I always use salted anchovies in oil, usually canned or jarred.

MAYONNAISE
Truly my most-used condiment. Great by itself or an amazing blank canvas for other flavours. Nine times out of ten, I prefer the jarred stuff over homemade, too.

PARMESAN
One of the main reasons I can't be vegan. Parmesan, like anchovies and Marmite (another favourite) contains lots of naturally occurring MSG, which is why it tastes so incredible. I adore MSG, in case that wasn't obvious. Supermarket Parmesan is fine for cooking, but never buy pre-grated. For things like snacking or in salads, I like to buy more expensive 30- or 32-month-old Parmesan from my local Italian deli.

Note on cheeses: For all vegetarian recipes in this book that contain cheese, please substitute any cheeses that are typically made using animal rennet (such as Parmesan, Pecorino, Gruyère and Tallegio), with an equivalent version that is suitable for vegetarians – these tend to be increasingly available in supermarkets nowadays.

NUTMEG
I didn't realize until I wrote this book how much I use nutmeg. I think of this as a creamy spice, meaning that I use it when I want something to taste more creamy, rich and luxurious. It is used a lot in Italian cooking, and that is definitely how I fell in love with it.

OLD BAY
If you don't know Old Bay, get to know. It's an American spice blend full of celery salt and cayenne pepper, and I love using it to jazz up marinades and sauces. It's also great in Bloody Mary's, on pizzas or on scrambled eggs.

QUANTITIES AND GUT FEELINGS

I believe in autonomy in cooking, and so there will always be something in one recipe that another cook would do differently. The recipes in this book are robust enough that you can fiddle with them a bit to suit your palate and they will still come out great. Here is a rough guide on how to approach things:

OIL
Where I have suggested a tablespoon of oil to kick off a pan cook, feel free to eyeball this from the bottle.

SALT
Try and taste your food as much as possible during the cooking process and add small amounts of salt as needed. Don't forget, you can always add but you can't take away! Where I have added salt as a measurement that means it is necessary to the recipe, where I have said salt to taste, then it is at your discretion to season it as much as you wish. That said, a decent pinch of flaky sea salt is always a good idea in my book.

SWEETNESS
In baking recipes, sugar measurements shouldn't be tampered with, but where I've suggested a tablespoon here and there, do adjust according to your palate.

COOKING WATER
Unless otherwise specified, you need to season your water when boiling something – the water penetrates the food it is cooking so you can season it internally, whether it be a vegetable, grain, or pasta. For these, I season the water with fine salt and then taste – it should taste no saltier than any normal food you cook (it should not taste like the sea). Season like you would do a soup – gently but firmly.

PORTION SIZES
I often think it is not worth making something unless you will have leftovers, so I would say the portion sizes throughout the book run on the generous side. Where recipes are to be served at the same time as other dishes in a sharing format, the portions might feel slightly smaller – worth bearing in mind if you are creating your own menu. Use the scaling guide to increase or decrease where necessary.

STYLING –
TRICKS OF THE TRADE

Given that one of my day jobs is a food stylist, it would be remiss of me not to include a breakdown of my tricks of the trade. Some food styles itself, as we say in the business, but sometimes it needs a little help; and it's all a lot easier than you think. I love to lay a jazzy table when I can, and I've shared a few insights into my process for creating a beautiful, relaxed and inviting space for your guests.

My biggest tip for 'styling' food for dinner parties is barely a trick to be honest, but it's an important place to start. When serving a crowd, it is 1000 times easier to plate 'family style' i.e. everything to share. There are, of course, a few exceptions to this, like when recipes result in individual portions, but for the most part this is my golden rule for dinner party food for three main reasons:

FIRSTLY – it is far more generous, inviting and quite frankly, dramatic, to put a few big, heaped dishes down on a table.

SECONDLY – it's a lot less work to plate one dish than six.

THIRDLY – getting people to serve themselves and share things across your table is one of the best things about convivial dining. It relaxes your guests, gets people talking and engaging with the food and leaves you the space to join in and be a part of it, rather than being a glorified waiter.

STYLING A SHARING TABLE

› I love using a selection of oval, square and round plates or platters. These don't always need to be huge, sometimes it's better to do a few medium-size portions to spread across the table rather than ginormous things.

› I tend to always use shallow bowls, as I find deep ones can hide the food, unless I am dealing with something completely liquid that needs depth.

› Serving things in pans or oven trays is FINE – don't feel like it is too informal to put them on the table. As long as you make people aware when something is hot and provide tea towels or protection where necessary. In fact, this is a great way to break up a table and create interest in the overall scene.

› On that note, try and vary the heights across your table – bowls or plates with feet are wonderful, or in their absence you can stack things on boards or upturned bowls.

› If your table is small and you lack the space to have everything on there at the same time, then send dishes around and clear them to a space close by when everyone has served themselves. Don't forget to get someone to serve you too!

› Or if you have the luxury of a secondary table, use that for the food and do some or all of it buffet style.

› Put sauces/accompaniments in several small bowls and dot them around to make sure each end of the table has their own.

MAKING THE FOOD LOOK GOOD

› Always try to leave an empty border on your plate. You want to avoid overfilling plates because the effect of the finished dish can be lost or even worse, spilled. Leaving space means you will be able to see any finishing touches too.

› If in doubt, drizzle with good olive oil. Not only does it taste good, it makes your dish shiny, and drips and pools on the sides of the plate are always sexy – this is why an empty border is important.

› Don't style things that don't need it. Lasagne or pies are good examples of this, some dishes get styled in their making and need only to be cooked and served.

› Neatness is the enemy of gloriously edible food. As I said above, drizzles, drops, sprinkles or smears are evocative and appetizing. That border you have is supposed to get a little messy with all your garnishes.

› Similarly, try and avoid regularity or patterns with your food (unless it's a pissaladière, of course). When plating, let different elements touch and bleed into one another, create piles or heaps and fun shapes. Basically – don't overthink it!!

WHAT TO PLATE ON

› I have a very distinctive style, which I know isn't everyone's cup of tea. I love vintage crockery and glasses, and am a fanatical collector of them. I get all of my stuff from charity shops, flea markets, antique shops and online marketplaces. This does mean I have a lot of options for plating when I am hosting, but I certainly have a few favourite things I always come back to.

› Most food looks good on pastel colours. I tend to gravitate towards blues, greens and pale reds and pinks, which are often patterns on top of cream or white backgrounds. The richer, dark tones in food will really sing when paired with lighter coloured plates.

› I almost always avoid primary colours on crockery as their boldness can wash out the tones of your food. Similarly, I never use brown or black crockery.

› Salads, pastas and risottos are for plates, not bowls! I think you see the texture of these dishes so much better when they are on plates – give it a go and see what you think.

› Using stuff other than crockery to serve on gets a big yes from me. Having a variety of textures i.e. ceramics, metal trays or pans, wooden boards, creates a more lived-in and cosy vibe.

GENERAL TABLE SCAPING

› If you have lots of tablecloth and napkin options, then use them! Like most of my stuff, I hunt for these in charity shops and flea markets. I don't think they are always necessary though, a few jazzy plates will often do the job.

› Another great way of creating height on your table is candles. I always have a few of varying lengths (mismatched, of course), and they create beautiful light for your food too.

› Flowers on the table can be bulky and make it hard to speak to people across from you, but I just adore how they brighten everything up. I like to arrange little posies with only 3–4 stems and spread them down the table – you don't need proper vases – old jam jars, little glasses or empty bottles are fine. Just choose 2–3 different types of flowers from your florist (or supermarket) and play with them – you don't need a huge range to make something pretty.

DIY MENUS

In order to make it easier to mix and match the recipes in this book, here is a list of all the dishes organized by course. I love creating menus, but I would hate for you, my readers, to feel limited by them. My biggest wish for this book is for it to make you feel more self-assured in your cooking, and for dinner parties to feel more achievable. So if that means only doing two dishes, then that's great! When you are inviting people to your home the last thing you want is to feel stretched or uncomfortable, so do what feels good and natural to you. When pulling dishes from different menus together, don't forget to check out how each recipe falls into the timeplans. This way you can create your own timeplan for your dinner party and spread out your workload.

SNACKS AND CANAPÉS

Gildas

Ham, Egg and Romesco Toasts

Dorilocos

Warm French Onion Dip **V**

Mortadella, Ricotta and Pistachio Crostini

Cheese Puffs **V**

Bread, Butter, Anchovies

Olive Ascolane – Deep-fried Olives

Chicory, Taleggio and Roasted Grapes **V**

Zhoug Prawn Cocktail

Egg Mayonnaise and Crisps **V**

Radishes and Tonnato Sauce

Tomato and Butter Bean Crostini **VG**

Lamb and Rosemary Polpette

Wild Garlic Doughballs **V**

Bread and Ham Butter

STARTERS AND SHARING DISHES

Zucchini Alla Scapece **VG**

Baked Onions and Homemade Ricotta **V**

Burrata, Olive Salsa, Aubergine and Bread

Sea Bream Carpaccio, Crab, Green Chilli and Mint

Queso **V**

The Deluxe Cold Starter Medley (Devilled Eggs, Prawn and Avocado Salad, Smoked Trout)

Scotch Bonnet, Honey and Lime Wings

Funghi Sott'Olio with Celery and Parmesan **V**

Roasted Tomatoes with Tarragon and Ricotta **V**

Marinated Feta with Chilli, Lemon and Marjoram **V**

Giant Couscous with Pickled Chillies, Olives and Peppers **VG**

Egg and Avocado Salad **V**

Crab Toasts

Vignarola **VG**

Prawn Aguachile

Clams Bulhão Pato – Clams with Coriander

Fried Asparagus with Anchovy Mayo

Wedge Salad

Grilled Prawns with Mint, Tarragon and Lime

Lamb Arrosticini

Brown Shrimp, Watercress and Iceberg Salad

Tomatoes and Salmoriglio Toast **VG**

Pumpkin with Harissa and Dill **VG**

Radicchio, Apple and Walnut Salad **VG**

Broccoli and Cannellini Beans with Basil and Lemon **VG**

Fritto Misto

White Beans with Leeks, Courgettes and Mint **VG**

Baked Potatoes with Dill, Mustard and Yogurt **V**

Mozzarella with Grilled Cucumber, Fennel and Spring Onion Salsa **V**

Warm Potato Salad with Basil and Pecorino **V**

Coal Roast Aubergine with Tomatoes and Dill **VG**

MAINS

Porcini Tagliatelle **V**

Chicken Milanese, 'Nduja Creamed Peppers, Basil Oil

Braised Merguez with Potatoes and Chickpeas

Roast Chicken with Peppers, Onions and Salsa Verde

Beef Birria

Chicken Tarragon and Chips

Shrimp Po'Boys

Lasagne Alla Bolognese

Pissaladière

Porchetta and Pork Rib Gravy

Vignarola **VG**

Bucatini Alla Zozzona

Proper Fish Pie

Ossobuco, Risotto Milanese

Linguine Alle Vongole and 'Nduja for Lovers

Beef Shin Pie with Colcannon

Rigatoni ai Quattro Formaggi **V**

Courgette, Kale and Potato Pie **VG**

Aglio, Olio and Anchovy Spaghetti

SIDES

White Beans with Leeks, Courgettes and Mint **VG**

Baked Potatoes with Dill, Mustard and Yogurt **V**

Mozzarella with Grilled Cucumber, Fennel and Spring Onion Salsa **V**

Warm Potato Salad with Basil and Pecorino **V**

Coal Roast Aubergine with Tomatoes and Dill **VG**

Wedge Salad

Buttered Leeks and Chilli Oil **V**

Chicken-fat Croutons

Braised Lentils

Chips **VG**

Roast Potatoes with Chilli, Basil and Garlic **VG**

Cavolo Nero, Leek and Brussels Sprout Gratin **V**

Pumpkin with Harissa and Dill **VG**

Radicchio, Apple and Walnut Salad **VG**

Colcannon

DESSERTS

Salted Honey Semifreddo with Peaches and Lemon

Tiramisu

Pear and Almond Tart

Sunday Crumble

Carrot and Horlicks Tres Leches Cake

Trifle

Chocolate Cream Pie

Coffee Panna Cotta with Ginger and Grissini

Sticky Toffee Pudding

Maritozzi

Torta Caprese

Rhubarb Jelly and Cream

Summer Pudding **VG**

Cherry and Mascarpone Mousse

Marmalade Sponge

Raspberry, Orange and Campari Pavlova

Clementine Pudding **VG**

Chilli Oil and Peanut Butter Knickerbocker Glory

V - vegetarian; **VG** - vegan

ALTERNATIVE MENU IDEAS

FOR OUR PLANT-BASED FRIENDS

ANOTHER PLANT-BASED ONE MORE VEGAN RECIPES

Tomato and Butter Bean Crostini

Zucchini Alla Scapece

Vignarola

Summer Pudding

NO BLOATING HERE!

GLUTEN-FREE ONE

Chicory, Taleggio and Roasted Grapes

Brown Shrimp, Watercress
and Iceberg Salad

Braised Merguez
with Potatoes and Chickpeas

Salted Honey Semifreddo with
Peaches and Lemon

COSY AND COMFORTING

A MENU FOR A COLD WINTER'S EVE

Bread and Ham Butter

Proper Fish Pie

Sticky Toffee Pudding

BIG ITALIAN FAMILY LUNCH

AN EASY MENU TO FEED MANY MOUTHS

Tomatoes and Salmoriglio Toast

Burrata, Olive Salsa, Aubergine and Bread

Bucatini Alla Zozzona

Torta Caprese

NEW LEVELS OF SMUGNESS

FREEZER PARTY

Each dish can be made ahead, frozen, and
then defrosted and finished on the day

Olive Ascolane – Deep-fried Olives

Zhoug Prawn Cocktail

Ossobuco, Risotto Milanese

Sunday Crumble

CHEAP AND CHEERFUL

A DINNER PARTY THAT WON'T BREAK THE BANK

Egg Mayonnaise and Crisps

Baked Onions and Homemade Ricotta

Courgette, Kale and Potato Pie

Marmalade Sponge

DRINKS

SERVES 6

freshly squeezed juice of
   2 lemons
freshly squeezed juice of 2 limes
500ml (generous 2 cups)
   ginger ale
400ml (1²/₃ cups) lemonade
120ml (¹/₂ cup) grenadine
450ml (scant 2 cups) white port
100ml (scant ¹/₂ cup) gin
plenty of ice and citrus wedges,
   to serve

SERVES 6

1.5kg (3¹/₄lb) fresh watermelon
   flesh
finely grated zest of 2 limes
freshly squeezed juice of 3 limes
3 tbsp caster (superfine) sugar
good grating of fresh nutmeg
   (around ¹/₄ tsp)
pinch of flaky sea salt
plenty of ice, to serve

SERVES 6

3 ripe peaches
1 thumb of fresh ginger, peeled
   and finely grated
finely grated zest and freshly
   squeezed juice of 2 limes
finely grated zest and freshly
   squeezed juice of 1 lemon
2 tbsp runny honey
600ml (2¹/₂ cups) ginger
   kombucha
1 tbsp apple cider vinegar
plenty of ice, to serve
1 peach, pitted and sliced,
   to serve

WHITE PORT SHIRLEY TEMPLE

A Shirley Temple is typically a non-alcoholic beverage, and that's certainly how I knew them. I would obnoxiously order them wherever I could when I was little, and to be honest I sometimes still do! Nowadays I like them a little stronger, and white port is the perfect foil for the fruity, sherbety flavours, along with a dash of bitterness from Gin. *Pictured on page 100.*

Combine everything together in a large jug (pitcher) and stir well, then chill. Serve over ice with plenty of citrus wedges.

WATERMELON COOLER (NON-ALC)

An iconic non-alc bev that is so deeply refreshing. I love melon juice of any kind, but watermelon is somehow the best. You might be surprised by the addition of nutmeg here but it really works – it somehow makes the watermelon taste more watermelony. On a recent trip to Malaysia, I really loved the nutmeg and sour plum juice that they made out there, and this is a homage to that delicious sweet, sour and fragrant drink. *Pictured on page 109.*

Blitz everything together in a blender, then strain through a fine sieve to remove any seeds. Chill in the fridge before serving over ice.

PEACH AND GINGER SOUR (NON-ALC)

When I am drinking something non-alc at a party, I still want it to taste grown-up. Sour drinks are my absolute favourite thing, and this is wonderfully tart and fiery. If you find yourself wanting to make this when peaches are out of season, it is absolutely fine to use canned. However, you may find that the mixture is a lot thicker and sweeter and might need more citrus and kombucha.

Peel and pit the peaches, then add their flesh to a blender along with the ginger, lime and lemon zest and juice and honey. Blitz to make a purée, then strain through a fine sieve into a jug (pitcher). Pour in the kombucha and add the vinegar. Chill in the fridge for up to 2 hours – just stir again in case the mixture has separated before serving. Pour over ice and garnish with a peach slice.

SERVES 6-8

750ml (3¼ cups) crémant or
    cava, chilled
500ml (generous 2 cups) sweet
    red vermouth – I like Antica
    Formula, chilled
100ml (scant ½ cup) soda water
18 dashes of Angostura bitters
plenty of ice, to serve
1 orange, sliced into wedges
6–8 cocktail cherries with stems

ROSIE VERMOSIE

I really love good red vermouth and am famous for forcing it down anyone who comes by for drinks or dinner. This is a wonderful grown-up cocktail, despite its name, that is spritz-esque in structure but more refined and deeply moreish. It is easy to make in a glass to serve, but it's also great in larger quantities in a jug (pitcher) for a party. *Pictured on page 127.*

In a jug, combine the sparkling wine, vermouth, soda and bitters. Chill in the fridge for a maximum of 2 hours. Pour into ice-filled glasses to serve with orange wedges and cocktail cherries.

SERVES 6

For the olive vodka
200g (7oz) Nocellara olives in
    brine, cheeks removed and
    saved for cooking (see note
    on page 82)
700ml (3 cups) good-quality
    vodka

**For the batch dirty martini
(serves 6)**
450ml (scant 2 cups) olive vodka
    (see above)
80ml (⅓ cup) dry white vermouth
40ml (1½fl oz) still water
4 tbsp olive brine
6 Nocellara olives in brine,
    to serve

BATCH DIRTY MARTINI WITH OLIVE VODKA

Olive vodka is one of those discoveries that I made by accident. Having sliced the cheeks off a pot of Nocellara olives for a recipe, I was left with a handful of olive pits, still with some flesh left on them. I had a half-open bottle of vodka and I thought to myself – I wonder if you can get the vodka to taste like olives? Turns out you can. Use it to make a batch of dirty martinis to serve with The Deeply Retro One menu on page 58. *Pictured on page 68.*

To make the olive vodka, add the olive pits to the vodka and pop it in the fridge. Leave it for 2 weeks before straining to remove the pits (make sure you strain out the olive pits after 2 weeks or it will become bitter). You'll end up with a deliciously funky, saline and buttery vodka. Freeze until needed.

To make the batch martini, combine the olive vodka, vermouth, water and olive brine in a bottle and mix well. Put into the freezer to chill for 4 hours before serving in chilled glasses with olives.

SERVES 6-8

600ml (2½ cups) pink grapefruit
    juice, chilled
400ml (1⅔ cups) pomegranate
    juice, chilled
300ml (1¼ cups) pineapple
    juice, chilled
600ml (2½ cups) dark rum
200ml (generous ¾ cup) freshly
    squeezed lime juice (4–5 limes)
100ml (scant ½ cup) grenadine
plenty of ice, lime and grapefruit
    slices, to serve

PARTY PUNCH

A bowl of punch is a beautiful thing. This is based on a standard rum punch, but it's a little less sweet. Something to sip and savour rather than chug. I love rum and it is important to use a good one for something like this – the smoky notes are great against the fragrant fruit juices. Speaking of which, I recommend using juices that are not from concentrate for best results

Mix everything together in a large punch bowl and serve!

THE BLOODY NICE BIRTHDAY ONE

STARTERS

WILD GARLIC DOUGH BALLS

FRIED ASPARAGUS WITH ANCHOVY MAYO

MAIN

OSSOBUCO, RISOTTO MILANESE

DESSERT

RHUBARB JELLY AND CREAM

This is a 'pushing the boat out' kind of menu for someone you really, really love. It is a mix of dishes that both my partner and I would want to eat on our birthdays. Now that the recipes are handily immortalized in this book, I look forward to him recreating them for me every year (no excuses now Tom).

Ossobuco alla milanese is one of my top ten mains ever, and feels like a fittingly celebratory way to celebrate another trip around the sun. And a big old jelly is SO much easier than cake but gives this menu a delightfully nostalgic end – jelly always makes me think of kids' birthday parties. This one is much more grown up though, I promise...

GETTING AHEAD

	Wild Garlic Dough Balls	Fried Asparagus, with Anchovy Mayo	Ossobuco, Risotto Milanese	Rhubarb Jelly and Cream
Up to 3 days before	› Can make dough balls › Can make butter	› Can make mayonnaise	› Can make ossobuco	–
Up to 2 days before	› Can make dough balls › Can make butter	› Can make mayonnaise	› Can make ossobuco › Can make risotto base	–
Up to 1 day before	› Can make dough balls › Can make butter	› Can make mayonnaise	› Can make ossobuco › Can make risotto base	› Make jelly
On the day	› Make/reheat dough balls › Melt butter	› Make batter › Make mayonnaise › Fry asparagus and lemon	› Chop gremolata › Reheat ossobuco › Finish risotto	› Demould and decorate jelly

MISE-EN-PLACE

	Wild Garlic Dough Balls	Fried Asparagus, with Anchovy Mayo	Ossobuco, Risotto Milanese	Rhubarb Jelly and Cream
Up to 6 hours before	› Can make dough balls and butter	› Can make mayonnaise › Make batter 2 hours before frying	› Can make risotto base	–
Up to 1 hour before	› Bake/reheat dough balls	› Heat oil › Bring mayonnaise to room temperature	› Reheat ossobuco › Chop gremolata › Finish risotto	–
To serve	› Melt butter for hot dough balls	› Dip and fry asparagus and lemon › Serve with mayo	› Plate risotto; top with ossobuco and gremolata	› Demould jelly › Serve with cream and sprinkles

MAKES 24, SERVES 6-8

For the dough balls
240ml (1 cup) lukewarm water
1 tsp caster (superfine) sugar
1 x 7g (¼oz) sachet of fast-
    action dried yeast
200g (1½ cups minus 1 tbsp)
    strong bread flour, plus extra
    for dusting
250g (1¾ cups + 2 tbsp) plain
    (all-purpose) flour
1 tsp fine salt
3 tbsp olive oil, plus extra for
    the bowl

For the wild garlic butter
250g (1 cup + 2 tbsp) soft,
    salted butter
50g (2oz) wild garlic
OR
250g (1 cup + 2 tbsp) soft,
    salted butter
4 garlic cloves, minced
handful of fresh flat-leaf
    parsley

MAKE AHEAD
› The dough balls will keep covered at
room temperature for up to 3 days or
up to 3 months in the freezer.
› The butter will keep for up to
3 days in the fridge or a few months in
the freezer. I always make lots of wild
garlic butter when it is in season and
then freeze it to use all year round.

SUBSTITUTIONS
› If you don't have wild garlic, then
use the recipe I suggest above for a
straight up garlic and parsley butter.

SCALING
› If you wish to halve the recipe, just
use 1 tsp of yeast instead of a whole
sachet. I would keep the recipe the
same, though, and freeze your extra
dough balls for a rainy day.

I don't think my generation will ever recover from the chokehold
that Pizza Express dough balls had on our childhood, and the
dangerous dependency on garlic butter it created... I certainly
haven't. These are entirely modelled on those fluffy soft lumps,
except I've used wild garlic for a slightly grassier flavour (stick
to the usual if you can't find it), and I've melted said butter for
optimal soaking and mopping opportunities.

STARTER

WILD GARLIC DOUGH BALLS

Mix the lukewarm water with the sugar and yeast in a bowl and
leave to sit for 15 minutes until bubbly. Meanwhile, combine both
the flours and the salt in a separate bowl. When the yeast mixture
is nice and foamy, make a well in the centre of the flour and pour
the yeast mixture in along with the olive oil. Stir with a spoon to
form a shaggy dough, then take over with your hands and bring
the dough together to form a ball. Cover the bowl with cling film
(plastic wrap) or a tea towel and let the dough rest for 15 minutes.

Turn the dough onto a clean work surface and knead for about
3 minutes – it should still be nice and soft. Place the dough in
an oiled bowl, cover with cling film and leave to prove at room
temperature for 1 hour 30 minutes until doubled in size.

Tip the dough out onto a lightly floured work surface once more
and then divide it into 24 pieces. I like to weigh the dough, divide
the total weight by 24 and then I know exactly how much each ball
should weigh. Shape each ball by pinching the sides up to meet
and then rolling them in the palm of your hand and on the work
surface. Place the rolled balls onto 2–3 large baking trays lined with
baking parchment, making sure they are well spaced apart. Cover
them with cling film and leave to prove for another hour or until
doubled in size again.

Preheat the oven to 180°C fan (200°C/400°F/Gas 6). Meanwhile,
make the wild garlic butter by pulsing the soft butter with the wild
garlic (or garlic cloves and parsley) in a food processor until finely
chopped and well combined. Uncover the dough balls and bake in
the preheated oven for 10 minutes until they are a very pale gold
colour and puffed up. As soon as they are out of the oven, cover
them with a clean tea towel for 5 minutes to stop a crust forming.

Serve immediately or let them cool on a rack and reheat later
covered tightly with foil in a preheated oven at 160°C fan
(180°C/350°F/Gas 4) for 10–15 minutes. They microwave well, too.
Melt the garlic butter slightly in a pan, then spoon over to serve.

SERVES 6

500g (1lb 2oz) asparagus
1 large unwaxed lemon
50g (⅓ cup) '00' pasta flour
2 tsp fine salt
1.5 litres (6 cups + 4 tbsp)
   vegetable oil, for frying

For the batter
100g (generous ¾ cup) '00'
   pasta flour
100g (⅔ cup) cornflour
   (cornstarch), sieved
1 x 7g (¼oz) sachet of
   fast-action dried yeast
½ tsp caster (superfine) sugar
1 tsp fine salt
220ml (scant 1 cup) water

For the anchovy mayo
1 garlic clove, grated
3 egg yolks
1 tbsp Dijon mustard
4 tbsp freshly squeezed
   lemon juice
50g (2oz) anchovies, drained
100ml (scant ½ cup) olive oil

MAKE AHEAD
› The mayonnaise will keep for up
to 3 days in the fridge.

SUBSTITUTIONS
› If you don't like anchovies, serve
these with a garlicky, herby aioli or
vegan mayo. You can also fry courgette
(zucchini) slices, very thinly sliced
squash or even sliced red onions in
the batter.

SCALING
› This is best made in the batch size
above, otherwise you will be frying
for hours and hours.

This is such a lovely way to use asparagus and a supremely
delicious starter. Anchovies and mayonnaise are pretty high up
on my list of things that I adore, so it wasn't much of a reach to
create an anchovy mayo. It's also amazing with the asparagus and
deep-fried lemon slices, which are the secret hero of this dish.
The yeasted batter makes for a super crisp result that doesn't
overwhelm the delicate spears.

STARTER

FRIED ASPARAGUS WITH ANCHOVY MAYO

To make the batter, mix together the flours, yeast, sugar and salt
in a bowl. Whisk the water in gradually to make a smooth batter.
Cover the bowl with a clean tea towel (kitchen cloth) and leave to
prove at room temperature for 2 hours.

For the anchovy mayo, blend the garlic, egg yolks, Dijon mustard,
lemon juice and anchovies together in a food processor to make a
paste. Then, with the motor running, slowly drizzle in the oil. You
should end up with a thick, glossy and very punchy mayonnaise.

Trim the hard woody ends off the asparagus – or you can bend
them until they snap off. Slice the lemon as thinly as you can and
pick out any pips. Put the lemon slices on kitchen paper (paper
towels) to soak up any excess liquid.

When the batter has proved and is puffy and foamy, mix the 50g
(⅓ cup) of remaining flour and the salt together in a tray. Heat
the oil in a heavy-based pan or a deep fat fryer to 180°C (350°F).

Toss the asparagus spears in the remaining flour, then dip them
in the batter before carefully laying them into the hot oil (you
might want to do this in batches). Try to break the spears up
if they clump together as they cook. Fry the asparagus for 2–3
minutes, then remove and drain the excess oil on kitchen paper.
Once all the asparagus has been fried, dip the lemon slices in the
flour, then the batter and fry in the same way – they will splutter
a bit so be careful.

Serve the fried asparagus and lemon slices with the anchovy mayo.

THIS IS A 'PUSHING THE BOAT OUT' KIND OF MENU FOR SOMEONE YOU REALLY, REALLY LOVE.

SERVES 6

For the ossobuco

6 veal shin pieces, cross-cut with
the bone in the middle (you can
use beef shin if you prefer, but
do note that it will take longer
to cook)

50g (generous 1/3 cup) plain
(all-purpose) flour, seasoned
well with salt and pepper

2 tbsp olive oil, plus extra
if needed

3 tbsp butter

1 carrot, diced

1 onion, diced

2 sticks of celery, diced

200ml (generous 3/4 cup)
white wine

1 litre (1 quart) hot beef stock
(broth)

4 bay leaves

salt and black pepper

For the risotto base

2 litres (2 quarts + 1/2 cup)
hot chicken stock (broth)

0.5g (1/2 tsp) saffron

2 tbsp olive oil

2 tbsp butter

2 banana shallots, very
finely chopped

2 tsp salt

3 garlic cloves, very
finely chopped

500g (1lb 2oz) risotto rice

170ml (3/4 cup) white wine

For the gremolata

15g (1/2oz) fresh parsley leaves

1 garlic clove, peeled

zest of 1 lemon

To finish the risotto

100g (1/2 cup minus 1 tbsp)
cold unsalted butter, diced

100g (3 1/2oz) grated Parmesan
cheese

I realized the value of ossobuco as a dinner party dish when I worked in restaurants, as it's surprisingly easy to do in service. Cooking in advance is key, as is making a par-cooked risotto base so you can finish it off when guests arrive and avoid long periods away from your party. Gremolata is the traditional topping for this dish – the parsley, garlic and lemon provide a little refreshment against the creamy and meatier notes. *Pictured on page 31.*

MAIN

OSSOBUCO, RISOTTO MILANESE

The veal shin pieces have a layer of membrane around them – you don't need to remove it but it's worth making 3–4 deep slits in it, all the way to the flesh, or the membrane will shrink as it cooks and contort the flesh. Dust the shins in the seasoned flour on both sides; set aside. Preheat the oven to 150°C fan (170°C/340°F/Gas 3).

Melt the oil and butter together in a large pan over a medium heat, until the butter is sizzling. Add the veal shins in batches, making sure they get a lovely golden brown colour on both sides. Set the browned meat aside and add the carrot, onion and celery to the pan, along with a little more oil if needed. Brown the veg for around 10–12 minutes, scraping up any golden bits of caramelization on the bottom of the pan with your spoon. Deglaze the pan with the white wine and continue to scrape the golden bits off the bottom of the pan so that they flavour the liquid.

Normally ossobuco is cooked on the stove, but as we are cooking 6 veal shins at a time here I find it much easier to use the oven. Lay the browned shins in the bottom of two deep roasting trays, then pour over the vegetables in their wine followed by the hot beef stock and bay leaves; the stock may not quite cover the meat but that's okay. Cover the trays tightly with foil and then pop them into the preheated oven. Veal shins need around 2 hours, beef shins will need 3–4. You want the meat to be tender but with enough structure that it is still attached to the bones. (If you want, you can scoop out the marrow from the bones and use it in the risotto, I prefer to leave it in for the guests to use later.)

When they are cooked, carefully remove the shins from their broth, cover with foil and set aside. Pour all the cooking liquid into a pan. Pop it over a high heat and bubble for 8–10 minutes until reduced by a third, then pour it back over the veal. If you are making this the day before, let the dish cool completely before chilling in the fridge. If not, cover, leave to cool and then reheat when you're ready.

MAKE AHEAD

› You can make the ossobuco up to 3 days in advance and keep in the fridge until needed.

› The risotto base will be fine in the fridge for 2 days.

› You can also make and freeze both the ossobuco and risotto base up to 3 months in advance. Defrost in the fridge for 24 hours before reheating/ finishing per the recipe method.

SUBSTITUTIONS

› If you want you can make this with lamb shanks, but I really love it just the way it is.

SCALING

› To make more than 6 portions of ossobuco, use 1 veal shin piece per person and increase the recipe by one-third for every 2 people.

› For the risotto, you can allow for about 80g (3oz) of rice per person. You will need roughly 4 times as much stock as rice.

Next, make the saffron stock for the risotto base. Have the hot chicken stock ready in a large pan. Grind the saffron to a powder using a pestle and mortar, then add a spoonful of hot stock and let it sit for 1 minute. Pour the saffron liquid into the stock pan and bring to a simmer, then remove from the heat but keep warm.

For the risotto base, heat the oil and butter in a large, heavy-based pan over a medium heat. When the butter sizzles, add the shallots and salt and let them sweat for 8 minutes until soft. Add the garlic and cook for 1–2 minutes, then add the rice and mix well. Toast the rice, coating it in the fat and moving it all the time to prevent burning, for 4 minutes until it smells intensely ricey. Add the wine and stir well. Keep stirring until the wine has been absorbed and the mix has dried out. Add 2 ladles of hot stock, stir well and set a timer for 14 minutes. You don't have to stir constantly, but keep things moving and each time the stock has been absorbed, add more stock. After 14 minutes, take the pan off the heat, then pour the mixture onto a large tray and spread it out – this helps it cool down quicker. Let it cool to body temperature before covering with cling film (plastic wrap) and chilling in the fridge. Set aside the remaining stock for later.

For the gremolata, finely chop all the ingredients with a very sharp knife (a blunt knife will bruise them and make them too moist). If this is something you don't have time for, don't worry, just briefly blitz the ingredients in a food processor instead.

When your guests arrive, preheat the oven to 150°C fan (170°C/340°F/Gas 3). 30 minutes before you want to eat your main, pop the ossobuco back in a couple of trays with its sauce, cover with foil and put in the oven again to reheat for 20–30 minutes.

When you have eaten your starter, reheat the stock and tip the risotto base into a large pan, breaking up any really solid bits with a spoon. Add a ladle of stock and bring it back up to boiling. Be attentive, the risotto will be thirsty, absorb lots of stock and potentially catch, so add more stock regularly. Continue to add stock (and then water if you run out) until the rice is just tender but still with a little bite; around 10 minutes. Remove from the heat and add the cold butter and Parmesan, mixing hard to 'mantecare' (make it creamy). If the risotto is stiff, add more stock or water – you should be able to shake the pan and see a little wave of risotto form at the edges with the motion – it wants to be saucy.

Check the seasoning, adding salt if needed, and then plate the risotto. It should collapse onto the plate and spread out as you spoon it on – I like to slap the bottom of the plate to help it along. Top with the ossobuco and sprinkle over the gremolata to finish.

SERVES 6-8

For the jelly
900g (2lb) forced rhubarb,
    chopped into 5cm (2in) pieces
200g (7oz) frozen raspberries
peel of 1 lemon
300g (1½ cups) caster
    (superfine) sugar
1.4 litres (1½ quarts) water
12–14 sheets of gelatine
neutral oil, for the mould
    (optional)

To serve (optional)
400ml (1¾ cups) double (heavy)
    cream or squirty cream
lots of colourful sprinkles

MAKE AHEAD
› Please for the love of god make this
ahead! I like to make it the night
before, so there isn't any constant
fridge opening happening while it sets.

SUBSTITUTIONS
› Use the same weight in different
fruits – strawberries, raspberries,
blackberries – have fun! Adjust the
sugar to taste and make sure to weigh
the liquid before you add the gelatine.

SCALING
› As long as you weigh your liquid,
you can reduce/increase the quantities
where necessary. I would avoid trying
to set lots of jelly while using your
fridge for other things, unless you have
several fridges.

Jelly is so satisfying to make yourself and rhubarb is perfect for
it. It has this incredible perfume and acidity which counteracts
the sugary sweetness of the jelly. I also add raspberries for a
great injection of colour. Obviously cake is great and all, but I
remember so clearly eating jelly at all my friends' birthday parties
and I think it's such a fun little dessert to whip out for grown-ups,
too. Plus, it's a wonderful light finish to this menu. Serve it with
double cream if you're feeling classy, or squirty cream if you're
feeling a little bit more loosey goosey. Sprinkles are non-negotiable
either way.

You can either set this in a jelly mould, individual moulds or
bowls. It makes enough for a 1.2 litre (2½ pint) mould.

DESSERT
RHUBARB JELLY AND CREAM

Put the rhubarb into a large saucepan with the raspberries, lemon
peel and sugar and cover with the cold water. Pop the mixture over
a low heat and leave it to come to a simmer. Once simmering, cook
very gently for 10–15 minutes until the rhubarb has softened, then
turn off the heat and leave to infuse for 15 minutes.

Meanwhile, pop your gelatine sheets into a bowl of iced water to
soften; this just helps them dissolve better in the liquid.

Pop a fine sieve over a large bowl or pan and line it with a J-Cloth
(or muslin/cheesecloth). Use a ladle to gently strain the fruit
mixture through the sieve. Do it bit by bit and don't be tempted
to pour as you will likely lose some mix or it will overflow. Discard
the fruit in the sieve or keep it to use in another dish.

When you have strained it, weigh the liquid. You need 4 gelatine
sheets for every 500ml (generous 2 cups) of liquid. Gently reheat
the rhubarb liquid back to steaming. Squeeze out any excess cold
water from the gelatine sheets and then whisk them, one by one,
into the rhubarb liquid. When all the gelatine is incorporated,
pour the jelly into your chosen mould (greased if you are intending
to demould). Cover with cling film (plastic wrap), then pop in the
fridge to set for at least 8–12 hours, or overnight.

To serve, remove the jelly from the fridge and take the cling film
off. If you want to demould, dunk the base in a tray of hot tap
water for about 10–20 seconds, then pop a large plate on top and
invert the whole thing, gently. Remove the mould carefully. Bring
to the table just like that or you can decorate with the cream and
sprinkles if you wish.

THE GAME IS ON ONE

DURING THE FIRST HALF

WARM FRENCH ONION DIP

SCOTCH BONNET, HONEY AND LIME WINGS

HALF TIME

SHRIMP PO'BOYS

DESSERT

CHOCOLATE CREAM PIE

I am an older sister to two brothers, so enjoying watching sport became a necessity from a young age. There is something very wholesome about getting a load of friends together to crowd around a television and observe greatness (or mediocrity, depending on the day). I think our friends across the pond do it particularly well, so the food for this dinner party is heavily USA themed. The menu is designed so that you can prepare as much as possible ahead, do some cooking and eating before kick off, and then again during half time. It's a deliciously relaxed affair to be eaten on sofas with plenty of cold beers and napkins.

GETTING AHEAD

	Warm French Onion Dip	Scotch Bonnet, Honey and Lime Wings	Shrimp Po'boys	Chocolate Cream Pie
Up to 3 days before	› Can caramelize onions	› Can make butter	› Can make remoulade	–
Up to 2 days before	› Can caramelize onions › Can mix with crème fraîche and cream cheese	› Can make butter	› Can make remoulade	› Can make base
Up to 1 day before	› Can caramelize onions › Can mix with crème fraîche and cream cheese	› Can make butter › Can make dip	› Can make remoulade	› Can make base › Can make chocolate filling › Set chocolate filling in base
On the day	› Reheat onions or dip, melt in cheese › Prep serving suggestions › Grill	› Roast wings, coat in butter › Make dip	› Marinade and bread shrimp › Prep fillings › Warm baguette	› Whip cream

MISE-EN-PLACE

	Warm French Onion Dip	Scotch Bonnet, Honey and Lime Wings	Shrimp Po'boys	Chocolate Cream Pie
Up to 6 hours before	› Can caramelize onions › Make dip without cheese	› Can make butter › Make dip	› Can marinade and bread shrimp › Can make remoulade	–
Up to 1 hour before	› Warm in pan; add cheese › Prep serving suggestions	› Roast wings; toss in butter	› Heat oil › Prep fillings › Warm baguettes	–
To serve	› Grill and serve	› Serve wings with dip	› Fry shrimp and serve	› Top with cream; serve (use hot knife)

SERVES 6-8

For the dip
1 tbsp butter
4 tbsp olive oil
2 large onions, finely chopped
200g (generous ¾ cup) full-fat
    cream cheese
300ml (1¼ cups) crème fraîche
    (or full-fat sour cream)
2 tbsp whole milk
100g (3½oz) grated cooking
    mozzarella cheese
100g (3½oz) grated Gruyère
    cheese

Serving suggestions
1 head of celery, cut into
    chunky batons
1 cucumber, cut into
    chunky batons
1 yellow chicory, stalk removed
    and leaves separated
Ritz crackers or water crackers
ridged crisps
toasted bread

MAKE AHEAD
› The onions can be caramelized
and then kept in the fridge for up
to 3 days. Reheat them in a pan before
adding the rest of the ingredients.
› You can make the dip without the
cheeses and chill for up to 2 days
ahead. Reheat the dip, melt in the
cheeses and then grill.

SUBSTITUTIONS
› If you can't get hold of Gruyère, then
replace it with extra mature Cheddar
or comté.

SCALING
› This recipe works well for a group
of 6 about to eat more things, but if
you're looking to serve more then this
recipe is easily doubled. However, I do
suggest splitting the dip into smaller
cooking receptacles before grilling so
you have the option to top up with
more freshly reheated dip rather than
grilling the whole lot and it going cold.

Inspired by the hours and hours of Barefoot Contessa episodes
I watched in my teens (if you're reading this Ina, I love you), I
couldn't conceive a menu based on the land of the free without
a hot dip. This has two of the main ingredients in French onion
soup: deeply caramelized onions and Gruyère, but that's where the
similarity ends. The onions and cheese, along with a litany of other
dairy products, are combined and then thrust under a grill until
bubbling and unctuous. I've suggested a few nibbly bits to serve
with this, but you can very much take the reins and do whatever
you like; this is so good it would even make a pencil sharpener
taste heavenly.

DURING THE FIRST HALF

WARM FRENCH ONION DIP

Put the butter and oil in a large saucepan and set over a low-
medium heat until the butter sizzles. Add the onions and cook
slowly for around 30 minutes, until they are burnished, bronzed,
soft and sweet.

Stir in the cream cheese, crème fraîche and milk until they
are melted in and warmed through. Add all the mozzarella and
70g (2½oz) of the Gruyère and stir to melt. Season well with salt
and black pepper, then pour into an ovenproof dish or bowl.

Preheat your grill (broiler) on a medium heat setting.

Cover the top of the dip with the remaining grated Gruyère and
place under the hot grill for 3–4 minutes until bubbling and
golden. Serve immediately with your chosen accoutrements.

SERVES 6

2kg (4½lb) chicken wings, split at
   the joint into flats and drums
1 tbsp salt
2 tsp black pepper
60ml (¼ cup) vegetable oil
2 chicken stock (bouillon) cubes
   (I like Maggi), crushed

For the Scotch bonnet sauce
250g (1 cup + 2 tbsp) butter
2–3 Scotch bonnet chillies,
   halved and deseeded
1 large thumb-size piece of
   fresh ginger, peeled and
   finely grated
finely grated zest and freshly
   squeezed juice of 2 limes
2 tbsp distilled vinegar
180g (generous ½ cup)
   runny honey
2 tsp all-purpose seasoning

For the dip
6 spring onions (scallions),
   very thinly sliced
340g (1½ cups) sour cream
100g (scant ½ cup) full-fat
   cream cheese
small bunch of fresh dill,
   finely chopped
1 tsp garlic powder
2 tbsp dill pickle juice
1 dill pickle, finely chopped

MAKE AHEAD
› The sauce and dip can be made up to
3 days ahead. Roast the wings on the
day and warm the sauce to serve.

SUBSTITUTIONS
› If scotch bonnets are too hot, you
can swap for 1–2 large deseeded red
chillies. Unfortunately, the only way to
know how spicy a chilli is is by tasting
it, so I cut them in half and then touch
my finger to the inner membrane and
then to my tongue. If it's hot then you
know you've got a spicy one!

SCALING
› If you're cooking this for many more
people I suggest roasting the wings in
batches and keeping warm in the sauce
while you continue roasting more.

As with the dip, I couldn't imagine a menu centred around a
sporting event and American food that didn't include wings.
I wanted a wing that was exceedingly easy but addictive to eat,
and I am thrilled to say I think these hit the spot. If you prefer
to fry your wings before coating them in sauce then by all means
do so, I find roasting them works just as well and is easier for
big quantities. A word on spice – I love the flavour of Scotch
bonnets as much as their heat, hence why I am using them here.
If you would prefer a more mellow spice, switch them for red
chillies and add a few drops of Scotch bonnet hot sauce for a
little bit of the funk instead. It's worth saying, though, that the
creamy dip does level off the bite of the bonnets.

DURING THE FIRST HALF

SCOTCH BONNET, HONEY AND LIME WINGS

Preheat the oven to 180°C fan (200°C/400°F/Gas 6).

Mix the wings with the salt, pepper, oil and crushed stock
cubes. Spread the wings out over two large oven trays lined
with foil or baking parchment. Roast the wings in the preheated
oven for 45 minutes, turning a couple of times during cooking,
until they are golden brown.

Meanwhile, make the Scotch bonnet sauce. Add all the
ingredients to a saucepan and set over a medium heat. Let
the butter melt and the ingredients will start to get to know
each other. Bring the sauce to a simmer and cook gently
for 10 minutes. Remove from the heat and leave to cool for
5 minutes before blitzing in a blender until smooth – take
care when blending this very hot and spicy mixture not to
splash it anywhere.

Combine the dip ingredients, setting aside a few sliced spring
onions to sprinkle on top, and season to taste with salt and
freshly ground black pepper.

When the chicken wings are cooked, toss them in the Scotch
bonnet sauce. They can be served immediately or kept warm
in a low oven covered with foil until needed. Top the dip with
the remaining spring onions and serve with the spicy, buttery
wings, cold beers and plenty of napkins.

THERE IS SOMETHING VERY WHOLESOME ABOUT GETTING A LOAD OF FRIENDS TOGETHER.

SERVES 6

For the prawns

600g (1lb 5oz) large raw tiger
    prawns (shrimp), peeled
    and deveined
3 tsp Old Bay seasoning, or
    1 tsp celery salt
1 tsp chilli powder
3 tsp Cajun seasoning
1 tsp garlic powder
700ml (3 cups) vegetable oil
100g (2/3 cup) cornflour
    (cornstarch)
3 eggs, beaten
200g (4²/3 cups) panko breadcrumbs
3 tbsp cornmeal

For the remoulade

150g (2/3 cup) mayonnaise
1¹/2 tbsp hot sauce, or to taste
1 tbsp American mustard
1 tbsp Dijon mustard
1 tbsp hot horseradish sauce
2 tbsp dill pickle juice
1 tbsp tomato ketchup
1 tsp Cajun seasoning
freshly squeezed juice of 1/2 lemon
1 tsp Worcestershire sauce

To serve

3 medium crusty baguettes
1 small iceberg lettuce, shredded
3 dill pickles, sliced
6 vine tomatoes, sliced

MAKE AHEAD

› The remoulade keeps in the fridge
for up to 5 days.
› You can bread the prawns and leave
in the fridge for up to 2 hours before
frying. Once fried, keep them warm in
a low oven (120°C fan/140°C/275°F/
Gas 1) for up to 15 minutes.

SUBSTITUTIONS

› Swap prawns for oyster mushrooms.
› For vegans, swap the eggs for 100ml
(scant 1/2 cup) plant-based milk, and
the mayo and Worcestershire sauce for
vegan versions.

SCALING

› If you're cooking for two, reduce the
prawns to 200g (7oz) and use 1 egg.
Divide everything else by 3.

A DIY option for a help yourself kind of dinner is a really great choice, as all you have to do is prepare the individual elements and let your guests do the assembly and plating. I travelled to New Orleans a few years ago and ate several hundred Shrimp Po'boys while there, which are baguettes heaped full of crispy fried prawns, salad and Cajun remoulade sauce. The prawns cook incredibly quickly so you can jump up at half time, fry them off and then get everyone to fill their boots. The breading for the prawns isn't entirely traditional, but I found using panko breadcrumbs made them much easier to prepare ahead of time while staying ridiculously crunchy.

HALF TIME

SHRIMP PO'BOYS

Put the prawns in a bowl with the Old Bay, chilli powder, Cajun seasoning and garlic powder. Toss together and leave in the fridge to marinate for 1 hour.

Make your remoulade by mixing all the ingredients together – adjust the heat with extra hot sauce if you want something with a bit more gas.

If your oven isn't already hot from cooking the chicken wings (see page 38), preheat it to 180°C fan (200°C/400°F/Gas 6).

Heat the oil in a large frying pan (skillet) until shimmering; if you stick a chopstick into the oil it should sizzle when it's ready. Pop the baguettes into the oven to warm through for 8–10 minutes.

Prep a breading station for your prawns: lay out one bowl with the cornflour, one with the beaten eggs and one with the panko and cornmeal combined. Start by tossing the prawns lightly in the cornflour, then through the egg and then straight into the breadcrumbs – you may want to use tongs for this. Pop the breaded prawns onto a couple of trays lined with baking parchment ready to be fried.

When you are ready to fry them, carefully drop some breaded prawns in the hot oil and cook for around 2 minutes, turning a couple of times. You will most likely need to do this in batches to avoid crowding the pan, and it will be quicker if you have two pans going. Drain any excess oil from the cooked prawns on kitchen paper (paper towels) and pile onto a plate to serve with the fillings, baguettes warm from the oven and remoulade. I prefer to scoop the middle out of my baguette before filling it with the good stuff.

SERVES 12

For the base

250g (9oz) digestive biscuits
    (graham crackers)
250g (9oz) speculoos cookies,
    such as Lotus Biscoff
5 tbsp caster (superfine) sugar
170g (¾ cup) butter, melted

For the filling

4 egg yolks
175g (¾ cup + 2 tbsp) caster
    (superfine) sugar
40g (scant ⅓ cup) cornflour
    (cornstarch)
500ml (generous 2 cups)
    whole milk
250ml (generous 1 cup)
    double (heavy) cream
200g (7oz) dark (bittersweet)
    chocolate, chopped
pinch of salt
½ tsp instant coffee powder
½ tsp ground cardamom
    (optional)
2 tbsp cold butter, diced

For the topping

300ml (1¼ cups) double (heavy)
    cream
3 tbsp icing (confectioners')
    sugar
1 tsp vanilla bean paste
    (optional)
2 tbsp whole milk

My friend Jess, a gorgeous all-American gal, made me my first ever Chocolate Cream Pie and I was forever hooked. It's basically a cheesecake crust filled with a thick, moussey chocolate custard and then topped with whipped cream. I love how unashamedly indulgent it is. This makes a large pie – enough to do 12 people – but it keeps really well, and trust me when I say you would be sad if you didn't have leftovers. Coffee is great here because it makes the whole thing taste really intensely chocolatey and the cardamom is a lovely background spice to lift and refine the flavours. For slicing this, heat your knife! I dip mine in hot water, then carefully dry it off – this will get you the best clean cuts. *Pictured on pages 44–45.*

DESSERT

CHOCOLATE CREAM PIE

Preheat the oven to 180°C fan (200°C/400°F/Gas 6).

Crush the biscuits and cookies to a fine crumb, either in a food processor or by bashing them with a rolling pin in a sandwich bag (my preferred, stress-relieving method). Mix the crushed biscuits with the sugar and melted butter in a bowl until they are the texture of wet sand.

Take a deep 23cm (9in) springform cake tin and invert the base, then cover it with a circle of baking parchment that is a couple of centimetres (one inch) larger. Close the tin with the covered upside-down base inside it and the parchment sticking out of the sides underneath – this makes it easier to get the dessert off the base when it is finished and easier to remove the paper, too.

Tip nearly all the crumb mixture into the tin, saving 3 tablespoons or so back. Use the back of a spoon to press the mixture into the base of the tin and part-way up the sides – I like the uneven line that you get by doing this. It won't reach all the way to the top but it should make a pretty thick, sturdy base – you want about 2cm (¾in) thickness on the bottom and 1cm (½in) thickness on the sides. Use some of the mix you set aside to help build up the sides if they need it. When you are happy with the state of the base, pop the tin in the preheated oven for 10 minutes to bake, then remove and leave to cool completely.

MAKE AHEAD

› You can make the biscuit base up to 1 day before you fill it.
› You can make the chocolate custard and fill the base up to 1 day before you serve it.
› Whip the cream and top the pie up to 2 hours before serving, keeping in the fridge until needed.

SUBSTITUTIONS

› If you don't want to use dairy, sub out the cream, milk and butter for plant-based alternatives.
› If you don't like the idea of cardamom or coffee, use ground cinnamon or even a splash of amaretto for a nutty finish.

SCALING

› You can halve this recipe for a smaller pie, it will fit well in a deep 18cm (7in) springform tin.

To make the filling, whisk the egg yolks, sugar and cornflour together in a large bowl to make a thick paste. Heat the milk and double cream together in a large saucepan until just steaming, then pour this over the egg-yolk mix, whisking well to combine. Return the hot milk and egg mix to your saucepan over a low-medium heat. The dessert needs your full attention at this point – so do not walk away now! Switch your whisk for a spatula and keep stirring gently, checking there isn't any mixture sticking and overcooking at the bottom of the pan. Eventually all the bubbles on the top will disappear and it will start to thicken; this should take about 10 minutes. As the mixture thickens, switch back to a whisk to avoid any lumps. As soon as the mixture is thick and gently bubbling, remove it from the heat. You just made a crème pâtissière!

Add the chopped chocolate, salt, coffee powder, and cardamom and whisk to combine. The chocolate will melt and turn your crème pat into a glossy, chocolate delight. Finally, beat in the butter until fully melted and combined to make it extra silky. Pour the crème pâtissière into the base of your tin and smooth it out a bit if you like, then cover the surface with cling film (plastic wrap) to prevent a skin from forming. Pop it back into the fridge to set for at least 6 hours. Make sure your fridge doesn't smell before you do this – if your housemate has left half an onion in there uncovered, or you've got some leftover fish curry hanging around, your pie will taste like it – so be very careful to keep your fridge clean and stinky things well contained. Nothing worse than a pudding tasting like old fridge IMHO.

When it's time to serve, gently release your pie from the tin and transfer to a plate, sliding it off the base too (if you're brave), but don't be hard on yourself if you don't – it will still taste and look great! Whip the cream, icing sugar, vanilla and milk together to super soft peaks – you want the cream to just be leaving thick ribbons on its surface, not even peaking really.

Top the pie with the cream, then sprinkle over the leftover biscuit base. Serve immediately!

THE WHEN IN ROME ONE

ANTIPASTI

PANE, BURRO E ALICI — BREAD, BUTTER, ANCHOVIES

VIGNAROLA

MAIN

BUCATINI ALLA ZOZZONA

DESSERT

MARITOZZI

Rome is a city that has captured my soul and my stomach. I have had some of the best meals of my life there, and I am particularly obsessed with the long Roman Sunday lunch, which this menu suits beautifully, just as well as an evening meal.

We are covering a lot of bases with this selection of dishes – a very easy snack, a light and fragrant starter, a rich and hearty main and then a type of cream bun for pudding. If you ask me, we aren't serving cream buns enough these days, so I am happy to provide you all with the tools to do so.

To get the full Roman effect, a few spritzes are required – or you can give your guests a Rosie Vermosie (see page 21) to kick off the fun.

GETTING AHEAD

	Pane, Burro e Alici	Vignarola	Bucatini Alla Zozzona	Maritozzi
Up to 3 days before	–	–	› Can make tomato sauce	–
Up to 2 days before	–	› Can make vignarola	› Can make tomato sauce	–
Up to 1 day before	–	› Can make vignarola	› Can make tomato sauce	› Make dough
On the day	› Prepare butter › Drain anchovies › Assemble	› Make vignarola › Add mint	› Make tomato sauce › Make egg and cheese mix › Cook pasta › Toss together	› Roll and bake buns › Fill with cream

MISE-EN-PLACE

	Pane, Burro e alici	Vignarola	Bucatini Alla Zozzona	Maritozzi
Up to 6 hours before	–	› Can make vignarola	› Can make tomato sauce	› Can bake buns
Up to 1 hour before	› Bring butter out of fridge › Prep anchovies	› Prep mint › Warm/reheat vignarola	› Make/reheat tomato sauce › Make egg mix	› Whip cream and fill buns
To serve	› Slice butter and assemble; serve	› Serve	› Cook bucatini › Toss with sauce and egg › Serve with cheese	› Serve

SERVES 6

200g–250g (7–9oz) good-quality
   unsalted butter, chilled but
   not rock-hard
1/2 fresh white sourdough loaf or
   baguette, sliced into 24 pieces
   or slices
24 good-quality anchovies
   (approx. 3 cans or 2 jars),
   drained

You start most meals in restaurants with bread and butter, so why not at home too? This isn't necessarily an antipasti specific to Rome, but it is one of my favourite dinner party cheats. All you need is fresh bread, good-quality butter and a can of excellent anchovies. You can plate these as canapés, or as a sharing situation for people to build their own. I like to serve these with drinks and then again when people sit down for their vignarola, as they work perfectly together. *Pictured on page 51.*

ANTIPASTI

PANE, BURRO E ALICI — BREAD, BUTTER, ANCHOVIES

Cut the butter into 24 slices, around 0.5cm (¼in) thick. Place a slice of butter on each slice of bread. Top each slice with an anchovy and serve.

Alternatively, you can let the butter soften to room temperature, then beat it until creamy in a bowl. Pile the soft butter attractively on a plate and serve with a plate of the anchovies and a plate of sliced bread to let everyone build their own.

MAKE AHEAD
› Given there is so little to do here and the bread needs to be freshly sliced, I would wait until just before you serve to prep this.

SUBSTITUTIONS
› If your guests are veggie, then a pickled mushroom (see page 150) or a slice of ripe tomato with salt and pepper are both nice alternatives.

SCALING
> This is easy enough to scale up or scale down. The key is having enough fresh bread – 24 pieces will serve 6 with 4 slices each.

ROME IS A CITY THAT HAS CAPTURED MY SOUL AND MY STOMACH.

SERVES 6

4 large Italian artichokes,
   such as mammole or tema,
   or 1 x 400-g (14-oz) can
   of artichoke hearts in
   water, drained

2 lemons (if you are using
   fresh artichokes)

3 tbsp olive oil

1 onion, finely chopped

2 bay leaves

225ml (scant 1 cup) dry
   white wine

600g (1lb 5oz) frozen broad
   (fava) beans

400g (14oz) frozen garden peas

6 sprigs of fresh mint leaves,
   chopped, plus a few extra
   to garnish

your best extra virgin olive
   oil, to serve

MAKE AHEAD

> This is excellent after a rest, so feel free to make it the day before or even 2 days before. I would wait to add the mint when you gently reheat to serve.
> You can defrost and shell the broad beans up to 6 hours ahead and keep them in the fridge until ready to cook.

SUBSTITUTIONS

> Swap any of the veg for asparagus, lettuce, sugar snap peas, roughly chopped runner beans or diced courgette (zucchini).

SCALING

> This recipe is easily doubled or halved – half a recipe would be lovely for 2 people as a main course with crusty bread.

A quintessentially Roman dish that celebrates the arrival of spring. Typically, this is made with the freshest of broad beans and peas in their pods, as well as the most juicy new artichokes. However, I have developed this version with alternatives in mind and kept it meat-free – in Rome it's often made with pancetta. The vegetables are cooked softly and slowly here for optimum flavour, and therefore will never be a verdant bright green. Vignarola made well is a muted pistachio colour.

ANTIPASTI

VIGNAROLA

If using fresh artichokes, fill a large bowl with fresh water, then squeeze the juice of 1½ lemons into it, saving 1 lemon half to rub over the artichokes while you cut them. (Artichoke flesh oxidizes once exposed to the air, so the lemon juice combats this.)

Trim away most of the stem of an artichoke, leaving a 2–3cm (¾–1¼in) stump at the end of the bulb. Pull off all the purple outer leaves to reveal the softer green ones within. There will be a natural ridge about halfway down the length of the leaves, slice along that line to remove the hardy, woody ends of the leaves. Use a knife or peeler to carefully shave away the tough, hairy skin around the bulb and on the remaining stem. Cut the artichoke heart in half lengthways, then use a teaspoon to scoop out the central hairy choke in each half. Cut the halves lengthways again into quarters and drop them into the lemony water. You can rub the lemon over the artichokes at any point, however they will change colour when they cook too – so don't stress. Repeat for the remaining artichokes.

Put the oil in a casserole dish over a low heat, then add the onion. Sweat gently for 12–15 minutes until translucent, then add the fresh or canned artichokes, plenty of salt and the bay leaves. Let them soften for 5 minutes, then add the wine and pop a lid on. Simmer gently for 15 minutes if using fresh or 10 minutes for canned.

Pop the broad beans in a bowl, then under a tepid tap for a minute to defrost them a bit; this makes it easier to tear off the skins – this step is optional, but I much prefer the look and texture. Then stir the shelled broad beans and the peas into the artichokes, then pour in 100ml (scant ½ cup) of water and cover again. Cook for another 20–30 minutes, until the veg are yielding and you have a deeply flavoured braising liquor. Remove from the heat and leave to cool slightly – this is much nicer warm or ambient. Mix in most of the mint, then scatter the top with any remaining leaves and drizzle with your best extra virgin olive oil.

SERVES 6

250g (9oz) guanciale (Italian
  dry cured pork cheek),
  trimmed and diced
6 Italian-style sausages,
  skins removed
2 x 400-g (14-oz) cans of
  cherry tomatoes
800g (1¾lb) dried bucatini
  pasta
9 egg yolks
80g (3oz) Pecorino Romano
  cheese, finely grated, plus
  extra to serve (optional)
2 tsp crushed black peppercorns

MAKE AHEAD

› The tomato sauce can be made up to
3 days ahead and reheated before you
toss it all together.

SUBSTITUTIONS

› If you can't find guanciale, then use
pancetta or thick-cut streaky bacon.
Italian sausages can be swapped for
good-quality butcher's sausages.

SCALING

› If you need to increase the recipe,
you will need to finish it in two pans
to get the best results. If you are
cooking this as a main course with no
other dishes, do 150g (5½oz) of pasta
per person and 3 egg yolks with ½ can
of tomatoes for every 2 people.

I discovered this dish in lockdown while scrolling through Italian Instagram accounts for dinner ideas. This is the secret 5th Roman pasta (the famous 4 are carbonara, gricia, amatriciana and cacio e pepe). Zozzo means filthy, and that is a fairly accurate way to describe this delicious pasta recipe. It is a hybrid of rich, eggy carbonara and tomatoey, meaty amatriciana, with a few sausages in for good measure. It's a lot easier to get the sexy, creamy emulsion with this in a large quantity than with carbonara, as the acid in the tomato sauce helps to coagulate the egg yolks. This is a great pasta main for a dinner party – it's slurpy, fun and absolutely heavenly.

MAIN

BUCATINI ALLA ZOZZONA

Put the guanciale in a cold, deep saucepan. Set it over a low heat for a few minutes, then increase the heat to medium. As the pan heats up, the guanciale will gently render off its fat and become golden and crisp – this will take some time, around 15 minutes. Crumble in the sausage and fry it in the guanciale fat for 5 minutes or so – it doesn't need to brown too much.

Stir in the cherry tomatoes and bring up to a simmer, then leave to cook for 30 minutes. The cherry tomatoes will burst and release their sweet juice into the sauce, which is great with the salty meat.

For the pasta, bring a large pan of water to the boil. Salt it a little less generously than you normally would – there is a lot of salt in some of the other ingredients in this dish. Drop in your bucatini and stir it really well to prevent it from sticking. The pasta will need around 10–12 minutes to cook to al dente.

Meanwhile, mix the egg yolks, Pecorino and black pepper together in a separate bowl to form a yellowy paste. When the bucatini is a couple of minutes away from being al dente, take a small ladle of hot pasta water and whisk it into the egg yolks – this is called tempering the eggs, and it warms them up so that when they go into the hot pasta they don't seize. (It's good to do this when you make carbonara too, FYI.)

When your bucatini is lovely and al dente, set aside your largest mug full of pasta water, then drain the rest. Put the pasta back in its pan and pour in the tomato sauce, mixing it in over a low heat. Remove the pan from the heat, then pour in the egg mixture and a good splash of the pasta water and stir everything together very well. You will instantly see the sauce become creamy and glossy. Add a little bit more pasta water if it is a bit thick, and then you are ready to serve. Sprinkle over extra Pecorino, if you like.

MAKES 12

For the dough (see note)
500g (3²/₃ cups) strong bread
    flour, plus extra for dusting
1 tsp salt
375ml (generous 1¹/₂ cups)
    whole milk
1 x 7g (¹/₄oz) sachet of
    fast-action dried yeast
80g (¹/₂ cup minus 1¹/₂ tbsp)
    caster (superfine) sugar
1¹/₄ tbsp runny honey
70g (scant ¹/₃ cup) soft butter,
    diced
1 egg yolk
finely grated zest of 1 lemon
neutral oil, for the bowl

NOTE: This dough uses a
tangzhong – this is a technique
where you make a sort of roux
with some of the flour and
liquid from the dough to help
keep the buns really soft and
tender. It's super easy and
doesn't take long at all, plus
the results are incredible.

For the glaze
1 egg
1 tbsp whole milk

To fill
400ml (1³/₄ cups) whipping cream
200ml (generous ³/₄ cup) double
    (heavy) cream
120g (³/₄ cup + 2 tbsp) icing
    (confectioners') sugar
1 tsp vanilla bean paste
200g (7oz) apricot jam (jelly)

I couldn't do a Roman menu without honouring this iconic bun. These are such a crowd-pleaser and fun to make, plus they look so beautiful. As with any bread dough, there are a couple of proving periods with this, but luckily the rest of this menu is really easy, so you can give these lots of time. You can keep them classic with a simple sweetened cream, but I like to add a surprise extra filling, apricot jam, which is a common flavour found in other Italian desserts. This recipe makes 12 buns, so you have plenty left for your guests to take home or for you to eat the next day.

For best results, make the dough the night before you want to eat your maritozzi – the prove in the fridge overnight enhances the flavour of the dough and makes it easier to roll the following day. However, I've included instructions for a shorter prove at room temperature if you are pushed for time. You'll need a stand mixer as the dough is too wet to knead it by hand. *Pictured on page 56.*

DESSERT

MARITOZZI

Remove 25g (2¾ tablespoons) of the flour to a bowl for the tangzhong and set aside, then add the salt to the remaining flour in another bowl and set aside.

Put the milk into a saucepan and warm through gently over a low heat. When the milk is just warm to touch (not too hot to handle), pour 250ml (generous 1 cup) of the milk into the bowl of a stand mixer with the yeast and sugar. Mix together briefly and leave the yeast for about 10–15 minutes to get bubbly and foamy.

Meanwhile, make the tangzhong: put the remaining warm milk in the pan back over a medium heat and bring to a simmer. Add the 25g (2¾ tablespoons) of flour you set aside earlier and whisk to combine into a roux – it will start to thicken quickly and look a bit like the beginning of a béchamel sauce. After about 2 minutes of whisking, you will have a thick, smooth paste. Remove from the heat and empty the roux into a bowl to let it cool a bit.

Once the yeast mixture is foamy and the tangzhong is cool enough to handle, you can make the dough. Add the remaining mixed flour and salt, the tangzhong, honey, butter, egg yolk and lemon zest to the stand mixer bowl with the yeast mixture. Using the dough hook attachment, mix on a medium speed until everything is just combined. Stop and let it rest, covered with a clean tea towel (kitchen cloth), for 10 minutes at room temperature.

MAKE AHEAD

› It's really helpful to make the dough the night before and then roll when it is cold.

› The buns are best eaten within 1–2 days, wrap them individually in cling film and keep them at room temperature until you wish to fill them and eat them.

SUBSTITUTIONS

› Instead of apricot jam, you can use any kind you like, or even a spoonful of chocolate spread.

SCALING

› Because this recipe only uses 1 egg yolk it is difficult to reduce, however, you can refrigerate or freeze any excess dough balls after they have been rolled, then bring back to room temperature or defrost before their second prove.

After 10 minutes, put the mixer back on a medium-high speed and mix for 10–12 minutes, until the dough is smooth and elastic. Transfer the dough to an oiled bowl, cover with cling film (plastic wrap) and leave to prove for at least 1 hour 30 minutes at room temperature or, as I prefer, overnight in the fridge until the dough has doubled in size.

When the dough has proved, line two large baking trays with baking parchment. Tip the dough out onto a lightly floured, clean work surface. Divide it into 12 equal lumps – I like to weigh the dough first, then divide that weight by 12 to get perfectly portioned buns. (This dough is a bit sticky, but if you have proved it in the fridge it will be much easier to roll when chilled.) Lightly dust your hands with flour and then shape the balls by pinching the sides up to meet and then rolling in the palm of your hand and on the work surface. Pop 6 dough balls on each lined baking tray, evenly spaced. If the dough has been rolled from chilled, it will need roughly 1¾–2 hours for the second prove. If it has been rolled at room temperature, it will only need 1 hour. The balls should have doubled in size and be jiggly and puffed on their trays before baking.

Preheat the oven to 185°C fan (205°C/405°F/Gas 6).

To make the glaze, whisk together the egg and milk, then when your first tray has had its hour, uncover it and carefully glaze the dough balls. Repeat with the second tray.

Put both trays of dough balls into the preheated oven to bake for 12–15 minutes, until they are risen and a deep, golden brown. Some might cook quicker than others, depending on hot spots in your oven – if you need to rotate, you can do this after the first 12 minutes. Once cooked, transfer the buns to a cooling rack and leave to cool completely.

For the filling, combine the whipping cream, double cream, icing sugar and vanilla bean paste in a bowl and whip to soft peaks.

To fill the buns, use a serrated knife to cut part-way down the middle of each one, keeping them intact at the bottom. Carefully open a bun out slightly and drop in a tablespoon of apricot jam each, followed by 2–3 heaped tablespoons of the cream. Use a small spatula to level the cream off the top, you can put the excess back in the bowl. Repeat to fill the remaining buns. Serve with espresso or a lovely digestivo on ice.

THE DEEPLY RETRO ONE

STARTER

THE DELUXE COLD STARTER MEDLEY — DEVILLED EGGS, PRAWN AND AVOCADO SALAD, SMOKED TROUT AND BROWN BREAD

MAIN

CHICKEN TARRAGON AND CHIPS

DESSERT

TRIFLE

You might look at this menu and wonder, is this *that* retro? And I think that is a fair question. I think what I mean by retro here is a rejection of modernity. These are three dishes that are kind of ageless and yet at the same time, old. They are what you would expect from the dinner parties in the 80s and 90s, I think. It's food that's familiar, comforting and safe in its oldness, but also luxurious and fun. A bit like the restaurant Oslo Court in St John's Wood, North London.

I was introduced to it by my partner who took me there on a surprise date, having eaten there plenty of times with his grandparents. The front of house team are all in black tie, there are trolleys and trays and pouring jugs galore and LOTS of pink. It is known in some circles as the Pink Palace.

Anyway, for me it is the definition of retro and so this menu is wholly inspired by it.

GETTING AHEAD

	Deluxe Cold Starter Medley	Chicken Tarragon and Chips	Trifle
Up to 3 days before	› Can make seafood dressing	–	› Can make raspberry sauce
Up to 2 days before	› Can make seafood dressing	–	› Can make custard › Can make fruit mix
Up to 1 day before	› Can make seafood dressing › Can boil eggs	› Can make chips	› Can make and set jelly › Can make custard › Can make fruit mix
On the day	› Finish devilled eggs › Prep avocados for salad › Butter bread › Chop herbs › Assemble	› Make or reheat chips › Make chicken	› Layer trifle › Whip cream › Decorate

MISE-EN-PLACE

	Deluxe Cold Starter Medley	Chicken Tarragon and Chips	Trifle
Up to 6 hours before	› Make (excluding piping) devilled eggs › Make seafood dressing	› Can make chips › Can prep sauce ingredients	› Prep fruit › Assemble trifle (excluding the cream)
Up to 1 hour before	› Chop herbs › Butter bread › Slice avocado › Assemble devilled eggs on platter › Cut lemons	› Make chicken and sauce; keep warm › Reheat chips › Chop tarragon	› Whip cream and top trifle
To serve	› Chop herbs › Assemble platter; serve	› Warm sauce and chicken; add tarragon › Serve chicken with chips and sauce	› Decorate with strawberries and cherries; serve

SERVES 6, GENEROUSLY

For the devilled eggs
6 eggs
70g (1/3 cup) mayonnaise
good few shakes of Tabasco,
    depending on how spicy
    you like it
1/2 tsp cayenne pepper
1/2 tsp Old Bay seasoning or
    celery salt
pinch of English mustard powder
1/2 tsp Dijon mustard
1 tbsp water
1 tbsp olive oil
small handful of freshly snipped
    salad cress, to serve
small handful of fresh chives,
    finely chopped, to serve

For the prawn and avocado salad
80g (generous 1/3 cup)
    mayonnaise
2 1/2 tbsp tomato ketchup
2 dashes of Worcestershire sauce
1 tbsp hot horseradish sauce
1 tsp your favourite hot sauce
2 large, ripe avocados
freshly squeezed juice of 1 lemon
300g (10 1/2 oz) cooked and peeled
    Atlantic prawns (shrimp) i.e.
    the small ones
3 radishes, topped, tailed and
    finely shredded, to serve

**For the smoked trout and
    brown bread**
400g (14oz) smoked trout
8 slices of brown bread, buttered
    and cut into triangles
4 lemons, cut into wedges

This little selection is based on the food I would be served at dinner with my grandparents, who refused to leave the 70s when it came to cuisine. A medley of delicious smoked fish and prawns, devilled eggs, thickly buttered brown bread and a nod to a salad absolutely slathered in mayonnaise is, to me, heaven. Not only is it easy to prepare but it is also fun to style, with plenty of delicately sliced avocado, ruffles of trout and LOTS of lemon wedges. Plus, being so easy to prep in advance makes this wonderfully hands off, leaving you time to float in and out of the kitchen checking on the chicken and chips. *Pictured on page 68.*

STARTER

THE DELUXE COLD STARTER MEDLEY — DEVILLED EGGS, PRAWN AND AVOCADO SALAD, SMOKED TROUT AND BROWN BREAD

To make the devilled eggs, bring a deep saucepan of water to the boil. When the water is at a rolling boil, carefully lower the eggs into it on a spoon and set a timer for 9 minutes.

While your eggs are boiling, prepare a large bowl of generously iced water. When the timer goes off, use a slotted spoon to move the eggs straight from the pan into the iced water, giving them a little tap to break the shells once they are submerged. Leave to cool for 10–15 minutes.

To peel the eggs, gently tap them on your work surface all over to break the shell, then peel (I find it helpful to keep the eggs submerged in the water while I peel them).

Carefully slice each egg in half lengthways, wiping the knife off between each egg. Scoop the yolks into a bowl. Lay the egg whites out on a tray, cover with cling film (plastic wrap) and refrigerate until needed.

Use a fork to smoosh the yolks up with a couple teaspoons of the mayonnaise to loosen, before transferring to a blender with all the other filling ingredients. Blend until smooth. Check the consistency isn't too thick to pipe – if it is, add a splash more water. Pop into a piping bag fitted with a fluted nozzle (if you have one) and refrigerate until needed.

MAKE AHEAD

› You can boil your eggs 24 hours in advance. Cut open the eggs and make the filling up to 6 hours before, just make sure both are covered and stored in the fridge.
› The seafood dressing can be made up to 3 days ahead but wait to slice the avocado until plating.
› The eggs and indeed the whole platter can be made up and kept covered up to 1 hour before you intend to sir down.
› I recommend keeping the buttered bread under a clean damp tea towel (kitchen cloth) to stop it curling.

SUBSTITUTIONS

› Just do fudgy eggs seasoned with salt pepper, chives and cress if devilling feels like a stretch. Boil the eggs for 7½ minutes and cool them in an ice bath before peeling.
› Crab, crayfish and brown shrimp would be lovely with the avocado.

SCALING

› This is a generous serve for 6–8 people and would do even more if you are hosting more of a canapé affair. If increasing, allow for half an avocado and around 60g (2¼oz) of smoked fish or prawns per person. For the eggs, 1 egg per person is lovely, only reduce or increase the filling quantities if you change the egg amount by more than 2, then up or reduce by a third.

For the salad, mix together the mayo, ketchup, Worcestershire sauce, horseradish and hot sauce to make the dressing. Set aside.

Cut the avocado in half, remove the stone, then peel off the skin. Slice the avocados into quarters, then dress them with the lemon juice and salt and pepper. Arrange the avocado slices over half of a large serving plate. Pop piles of the prawns on top, then drizzle over your dressing. Pop a little heap of shredded radish on top for extra pink pizzazz.

Ruffle the smoked trout onto another plate and arrange the bread triangles and lemon wedges around it.

To plate the devilled eggs, lay the egg-white halves on the same plate as the avocado – if they are really domed and sliding around a bit, I find it helpful to pipe a tiny bit of filling onto the plate for the white to stick to. Pipe some of the filling into the yolk cavity of each egg, you will have more than enough to be generous. Top with your snipped cress and chives and serve. This is wonderful with sparkling wine if you're feeling fancy or an exceptionally dirty and dry martini (recipe on page 21).

SERVES 6

For the chips
1.8kg (4lb) Maris Piper
    (or Yukon Gold) potatoes
150ml (2/3 cup) vegetable oil

For the chicken
2 tbsp butter
1 tbsp olive oil, plus extra
    if needed
8–12 chicken legs, depending
    on size
1 tbsp salt
1 tsp freshly ground black pepper
2 shallots, diced
4 garlic cloves, sliced
2 tbsp plain (all-purpose) flour
200ml (generous 3/4 cup)
    white wine
400ml (1 2/3 cups) chicken stock
    (broth)
20g (3/4oz) fresh tarragon, stalks
    separated and leaves chopped
1 tbsp Dijon mustard
175ml (3/4 cup) double
    (heavy) cream

You might be wondering why I am not calling this tarragon chicken. It's because I'm adopting the gauche trend (also French) of using a postpositive adjective, i.e. Steak Diane, Beef Wellington. Then it feels much more old timey, no? Anyway, I wanted a main for this menu that was a bit more of a brasserie vibe – ageless in its simplicity and deliciousness. And whenever I think of brasserie menus, I think of chicken and chips. The creamy, meaty sauce from the braised chicken is the ultimate foil for my best-ever oven chips. I have approached them in the same way I approach roast potatoes (see page 226) – boiled, cooled, then gently 'oven-fried' in plenty of oil. Just like roasties, they work really well reheated, too. *Pictured on page 68.*

MAIN

CHICKEN TARRAGON AND CHIPS

Peel and cut the potatoes for the chips, making them ideally a width of about 1cm (½in). Keep the cut chips submerged in a large, deep saucepan of cold water to prevent them from oxidizing (use 2 medium-large pans if easier). Season the water well with salt, then bring to the boil. Once boiling, set a timer for 4 minutes. Check a chip after your timer goes off – it should be just cooked but not falling apart. If the potatoes are still a little stiff, cook for another minute. Drain the chips carefully in a colander – I like to use a kitchen spider to get them out of the water rather than tip them, as they can break apart. When the potatoes have drained, spread them out on kitchen paper (paper towels) over a couple of large trays and leave to cool completely.

Preheat the oven to 180°C fan (200°C/400°F/Gas 6).

Pour around the vegetable oil into 2–3 large roasting trays. Heat in the oven for 15 minutes until shimmering and hot, then remove one tray at a time and carefully lay in your chips, taking care not to crowd the trays. Pop back into the preheated oven and roast for 20–25 minutes before removing one tray at a time and turning them over. At this point you are beholden to the potatoes – they don't work for you, you work for them. Keep cooking them in 20-minute intervals and then turning, they will gently crisp (not all at the same time) and become incredibly delicious mini roasties. Remove any that are perfectly golden on all sides and drain excess oil on kitchen paper. When all the chips are cooked, let them cool and spread out over trays again. When you need them, reheat in the oven in a couple of trays while the chicken rests.

MAKE AHEAD

› The chips can be made up to 1 day ahead, they will need to be reheated for slightly longer if coming from the fridge. Make sure to store them spread out if possible. Reheat at 180°C fan (200°C/400°F/Gas 6) for 15–20 minutes until hot and crisp.

› The chicken is best cooked on the day – I like to start to cook the chicken and sauce about 1–2 hours before the guests arrive, then it can just rest until you need it.

› To reheat the recently cooked chicken, cover with a splash of water in the tray, and heat at 180°C fan (200°C/400°F/Gas 6) for 15 minutes. Reheat the sauce separately.

SUBSTITUTIONS

› Bone-in chicken thighs also work well here – 2 to 3 per person.

SCALING

› Reduce the recipe by half to serve 4 people, but use 12 chicken thighs instead and 90ml (⅓ cup) of cream.

For the chicken tarragon, preheat the oven to 180°C fan (200°C/400°F/Gas 6).

Put the butter and oil in a large, wide casserole dish or frying pan (skillet) and set over a medium-high heat. Season the chicken legs with the salt and pepper. When the butter is sizzling, brown the chicken legs in small batches to prevent crowding the pan – place 2–3 legs in the pan at a time, skin-side down, and fry until well browned on all sides. If the pan ever looks like it's getting a bit dark, then add a little bit more oil and turn the heat down slightly. When each leg is browned, set aside in one large or two medium deep roasting trays.

Keep the browning pan(s) over the heat and add a teaspoon of oil if they look at all dry, then chuck in the shallots. Let them soften over a medium heat in all the fabulous golden chicken juices. After about 2 minutes, add the garlic and fry briefly, then stir in the plain flour and cook out for another minute. Pour in the wine and stir really well to release the golden crust from the bottom of the pan and mix well with the flour. Add the stock and bring to the boil, then strain the liquid through a fine sieve. Pour the sauce over the chicken legs in their tray(s). Add the tarragon stalks but not the leaves. Cover the trays with foil and bake in the preheated oven for 20 minutes.

When the chicken legs are cooked, remove them from the sauce and set aside to rest, covered. Pour the cooking liquid into a clean saucepan and bring to the boil. Boil the sauce for about 2 minutes before whisking in the Dijon mustard and adding the cream. Bring back to the boil, then remove from the heat, season with salt and pepper and stir the chopped tarragon leaves through the hot sauce. Serve the chicken draped in the sauce with the chips on the side and dressed watercress.

SERVES 6, WITH LEFTOVERS

For the jelly
300g (10½oz) fresh
    strawberries,
    hulled and halved
100g (3½oz) mixed
    frozen berries
150g (¾ cup) caster
    (superfine) sugar
peeled zest of 1 lemon
6 gelatine leaves (I use Dr.Oetker
    platinum grade gelatine)

For the custard
700ml (3 cups) whole milk
120ml (½ cup) double
    (heavy) cream
1 tbsp vanilla bean paste
6 egg yolks
100g (½ cup) caster
    (superfine) sugar
60g (½ cup) cornflour
    (cornstarch), sifted

For the raspberry sauce
100g (3½oz) frozen raspberries
30g (1oz) raspberry jam (jelly)
1 tbsp caster (superfine) sugar
1 tbsp freshly squeezed
    lemon juice

To assemble
1 x 400-g (14-oz) can of
    peaches, drained
100g (3½oz) strawberries,
    hulled
1 x 400-g (14-oz) can of fruit
    cocktail in juice,
    75ml (⅓ cup) juice reserved,
    the rest drained
40g (1½oz) cocktail cherries
    with stems, plus extra
    to decorate
finely grated zest and freshly
    squeezed juice of ½ lemon
100ml (scant ½ cup) dry sherry
175g (6oz) sponge fingers, or a
    little more or less depending
    on your bowl
400ml (1¾ cups) whipping cream
3 tbsp icing (confectioners')
    sugar, sifted

Bringing a trifle to your table is one of the most satisfying moments a host can have. No matter what century or millennium we are in, people LOVE the drama of a layered dessert. This is my ultimate retro trifle, packed with gloriously luminous jelly, silky custard and tonnes of canned and fresh fruit. A trifle should be a riot of kitsch, so make sure you have plenty of cocktail cherries to hand. This recipe works perfectly in a 2 litre (2 quarts + ½ cup) glass bowl or trifle bowl. *Pictured on page 68.*

DESSERT

TRIFLE

Start the day before by making the jelly. Put the strawberries, frozen berries, sugar and lemon zest in a saucepan with 500ml (generous 2 cups) of water and bring to a simmer over a medium heat. As soon as the liquid starts to bubble, turn the heat down to low and leave to infuse gently for 20 minutes. Meanwhile, soak the gelatine leaves in a bowl of iced water to soften them. After the fruit mixture has infused, strain it through a fine sieve and return to the pan (discarding any seeds or debris) back over a gentle heat. One by one, squeeze out the excess water from each gelatine leaf and whisk into the fruity liquid over the heat. When all the leaves have been added, remove the mixture from the heat, transfer to a jug (pitcher) and leave to cool for 30 minutes. Make sure you have ample and easily accessible space in your fridge to put your trifle bowl (and if your fridge is stinky, clean it!). Pour the jelly into the base of the bowl and put in the fridge to set for at least 8 hours, ideally overnight. Cover with cling film (plastic wrap), if you like, but be sure that it doesn't touch the top of the jelly or it will rip when set.

You can also make your custard and raspberry sauce the day before. For the custard, put the milk, cream and vanilla bean paste in a saucepan and gently heat until steaming. Meanwhile, whisk together the egg yolks, sugar and cornflour in a large bowl – it might seem a bit dry at first but stick with it and it will soon become a thick, pale yellow paste. When the milk mix is steaming, pour it over the egg yolk mix in the bowl, whisking constantly to combine. Return the whole lot to the saucepan and put it back over a medium heat. Whisking gently all the time, cook the custard until it starts to thicken; it will take a few minutes and might feel like it's not working, but a good indicator it's about to get thick is when the foam disappears from the top. It's important to keep whisking, and if you are at all worried about the eggs scrambling then turn the heat down. As soon as the custard starts to boil it will be thick and glossy. Taste it to check there is no residual

MAKE AHEAD

› All elements, apart from the topping cream, can be prepared ahead of time. The jelly is best made a day ahead and the custard will keep in the fridge for 2 days, as will the fruit mix. The raspberry sauce can be made up to 5 days ahead. For best results, only assemble the trifle on the day you will serve it.

SUBSTITUTIONS

› You can avoid the canned fruit and stick to fresh if you prefer and vice versa – fresh peaches and mango are really delicious in this.
› I like sponge fingers because they are traditional, but chunks of Madeira cake are great as well.
› If you don't want to make your own custard you can, of course, buy it, but I find it is often a bit softer so be aware of this.
› Add sprinkles to decorate, if you so wish (and I often do!).

SCALING

› For 6 individual servings in pretty glasses or small bowls, you only need half a recipe.
› For a smaller trifle bowl (around 1 litre/1 quart capacity) to serve 4–6, reduce the recipe by a third.

cornflour – if there is, cook for longer – then remove from the heat and strain through a fine sieve into a clean container. Cover the surface with cling film to prevent a skin from forming, then leave to cool before popping into the fridge until needed.

To make the raspberry sauce, pop all the ingredients into a pan and warm gently until the raspberries have defrosted and are collapsing and juicy. Blitz this in a blender or food processor and then, you guessed it, strain it through a fine sieve to get rid of any seeds and chill until needed.

The next day, when your jelly is set you can prepare to layer your trifle. Cut the canned peaches into chunks and halve or quarter any large strawberries. Set aside a handful of strawberries for the top, then mix the rest with the fruit cocktail, cocktail cherries, peaches and lemon zest and juice. Combine the sherry with the reserved fruit cocktail juice.

For the sponge finger layer, I like to cut around 10–12 sponge fingers in half, dip each one in the sherry mix and then lay them around the edges of the bowl with the cut side sitting on the jelly. I then take 6–8 more fingers, soak them and lay the remaining fingers in the middle of the jelly horizontally, to cover it, cutting them if necessary to fill in any gaps – the amount of sponge fingers you use here will vary slightly depending on the type of serving bowl you are using.

Pop half of the fruit mixture into the centre of the sponge fingers layer, spreading it out so it is around the same level as the upright sponge fingers. Give the chilled custard a good stir to loosen it – as it will have stiffened up overnight – then spoon it on top of the fruit and sponge fingers. Put the remaining fruit on top of the custard and drizzle over half of the raspberry sauce. Softly whip the cream with the icing sugar, pile it on top and then pop back in the fridge until you are ready to serve. Before it goes to the table, decorate with the extra cocktail cherries and the remaining strawberries.

THE FIVE INGREDIENT ONE

ANTIPASTI

ZUCCHINE ALLA SCAPECE

BAKED ONIONS AND HOMEMADE RICOTTA

MAIN

PORCINI TAGLIATELLE

DESSERT

SALTED HONEY SEMIFREDDO WITH PEACHES AND LEMON

One of the best things about Italian food is the minimalism. It is truly ingredient-led, and many of the classic 'recipes' are barely recipes – more like preparations. I adore cooking like this. Often, recipes work to the power of three; the caprese salad is a good example of this. If you take a good tomato, a handful of basil and a couple of mozzarellas, plus tasty olive oil and salt and pepper, it will equal a heavenly plate. That's why it is on menus all over the world. When your ingredients are good it doesn't need to be more complicated than that.

The rule with this menu is that each dish can only have five main ingredients, as well as using the following basic but essential ingredients: oil, butter, seasoning. It is a celebratory feast with plenty of luxurious moments, proving that dinner party food doesn't have to be significantly more expensive than normal. You can still push the proverbial boat out for your pals without breaking the bank.

Serve the dishes all together with plenty of crusty bread and extra olive oil for dipping.

GETTING AHEAD

	Zucchine Alla Scapece	Baked Onions and Homemade Ricotta	Porcini Tagliatelle	Salted Honey Semifreddo
Up to 3 days before	–	–	–	› Can make semifreddo
Up to 2 days before	› Can fry and marinate courgettes	› Can make ricotta	–	› Can make semifreddo
Up to 1 day before	› Can fry and marinate courgettes	› Can make ricotta	› Can make sauce	› Can make semifreddo
On the day	› Shred mint and mix through	› Make ricotta › Bake onions › Warm bread	› Make sauce › Chop parsley › Grate cheese › Cook pasta	› Cut and dress peaches

MISE-EN-PLACE

	Zucchine Alla Scapece	Baked Onions and Homemade Ricotta	Porcini Tagliatelle	Salted Honey Semifreddo
Up to 6 hours before	› Fry and marinate courgettes	› Make ricotta	› Soak mushrooms › Make sauce	–
Up to 1 hour before	› Bring to room temperature	› Bake onions › Bring ricotta to room temperature	› Chop parsley › Grate cheese	› Cut and dress peaches
To serve	› Shred mint and mix through; serve	› Dress ricotta › Halve and garnish onions › Serve with warm bread	› Cook pasta; toss with hot sauce › Add parsley and cheese; serve	› Serve drizzled with honey and sprinkled with salt

SERVES 6

100ml (scant ½ cup) vegetable
   oil, for frying
60ml (¼ cup) good-quality extra
   virgin olive oil, plus extra to
   serve (optional)
4 tbsp white wine vinegar or
   sherry vinegar
1 garlic clove, thinly sliced
3 courgettes (zucchini), sliced
   into thin rounds
large handful of fresh mint
   leaves, shredded
crusty bread, to serve
   (I used ciabatta)

MAKE AHEAD

› You can fry and marinate the
courgettes up to 2 days in advance,
then keep in the fridge. The mint will
probably discolour but it will impart
lovely flavour. If you add it ahead of
time, prep some more to garnish just
before serving. Make sure you serve at
room temperature.

SUBSTITUTIONS

› If courgettes aren't your bag, then
the vegetable here can really be
anything you like – mushrooms,
squash, aubergine (eggplant), fennel,
artichokes, (bell) peppers all work.
› Mint could be swapped for parsley,
basil, marjoram or oregano.

SCALING

› Use 1 large courgette for 2 people,
1 small garlic clove will work just as
well for 2 or for 6.
› For the dressing, it's 1½ tbsp of
oil and 1½ tbsp of vinegar per
large courgette.

The idea behind this classic Neapolitan dish is simple – fry a
vegetable, then marinade it in nice bits. Courgettes aren't famed
for their strong flavour, which is why they are perfect for this
process and, what's more, they are cheap as chips and go a long
way. In frying, they become sweeter and nuttier, which works so
well with the tangy vinegar and fresh mint.

To be served with the Baked Onions and Homemade Ricotta
(see page 74).

ANTIPASTI

ZUCCHINE ALLA SCAPECE

Heat the vegetable oil in a large frying pan (skillet) over a medium
heat to around 170°C (340°F).

Meanwhile, mix the olive oil, vinegar, garlic and a couple of decent
pinches of salt together in a large bowl or dish and set aside. This
will be the marinade.

Working in batches so as not to overcrowd the pan, fry the
courgettes in a single layer in the hot oil until they are lightly
golden on both sides. You will need to turn the slices at least once,
but they won't take more than a couple of minutes on each side.

Drain the excess oil from the courgettes briefly on kitchen paper
(paper towels), before popping them into the bowl of marinade
and stirring well. Continue until you have fried all the courgettes
and they are all well mixed together. Leave to sit in the marinade
for an hour or so at room temperature.

To serve, mix through most of the shredded mint, saving some to
garnish. Drizzle over some more extra virgin olive oil, if needed,
and serve with crusty bread.

SERVES 6

For the ricotta
3 litres (3 quarts + ¾ cup)
   whole milk
4 tbsp double (heavy) cream
220ml (scant 1 cup) freshly
   squeezed lemon juice
   (approx. 5–6 lemons)
good-quality extra virgin
   olive oil, to serve

For the onions
6 small red onions, unpeeled
80ml (⅓ cup) olive oil, plus
   extra to serve
handful of fresh marjoram

MAKE AHEAD
> You can make the ricotta a couple
of days ahead and keep in the fridge,
and it should definitely be made at
least 2 hours ahead of the meal.

SUBSTITUTIONS
> Obviously you can swap the
homemade ricotta process for
400g (14oz) ready-made ricotta.
> White onions work well here too,
of course, but the cooking time might
need to be adjusted depending on size.
> I love marjoram, but it's not always
easy to come by. Its cousin oregano is
a great swap, as is soft young thyme,
lemon thyme or summer savory.

SCALING
> The above ricotta recipe is a great
base amount, I wouldn't be tempted
to make a recipe with less than
2 litres (2 quarts + ½ cup) of milk or
more than 4 litres (1 gallon + 1 cup)
at a time.
> Use 70ml (⅓ cup) of lemon juice
per 1 litre (1 quart) of milk if you are
reducing or increasing the quantity.
> 1 onion per person is plenty here,
you can add another tbsp of oil per
onion if increasing.

This combination is based on a dish I ate a few years ago at
Westerns Laundry restaurant in Islington, North London. You
absolutely do not have to make your own ricotta if you can't be
bothered. I love doing it and wanted to share how easy it is.

To be served with the Zucchini Alla Scapece (see page 72).

ANTIPASTI
BAKED ONIONS AND HOMEMADE RICOTTA

To make the ricotta, pop the milk and cream in a large saucepan
and heat gently. You want to bring the milk to just before boiling
point – around 93°C (194°F) if you are using a thermometer. The
visual cues are steam rising from the milk, just shimmering on the
surface and with the occasional small 'blip blip'. When the milk gets
to this point, pour in the lemon juice. Stir very gently to combine,
and you should see the curds and whey separating straight away.
Take the pan off the heat and leave to stand for 10 minutes.

Line a colander with two clean J-Cloths (or muslin/cheesecloth)
and use a slotted spoon to scoop the curds into the colander. They
should be wobbly and creamy – this is your ricotta! Leave to drain
and cool, then refrigerate until needed.

Preheat the oven to 180°C fan (200°C/400°F/Gas 6).

Trim off the roots and tops of the onions, revealing just a little bit
of flesh at the top. Leaving most of the skin on helps the onions to
keep their shape in the oven. Carve a cross through the top part
and pop them in a roasting tray, root-side down, then season with
the oil and salt and pepper to taste. Roast in the preheated oven
for around 1 hour, turning the onions every so often. They will
most likely fall over when cooking, this is fine.

Meanwhile, plate up the ricotta and bring it to room temperature.
Season generously with salt and pepper and drizzle it with olive oil.

When the onions are tender and caramelized, remove from
the oven. Using tongs to handle them, cut each onion in half
widthways through the middle, then place on a serving plate. Add
a couple of splashes of water to your roasting tray to help scrape up
those pan juices, then pour them all over the onions. Season each
onion with loads of salt, pepper and olive oil. Finally, sprinkle over
the marjoram to serve – its perfume is so delicious mingled with
the sweet and savoury onions and creamy cheese.

WHEN YOUR INGREDIENTS ARE GOOD IT DOESN'T NEED TO BE MORE COMPLICATED THAN THAT.

SERVES 6

60g (2¼oz) dried porcini
    mushrooms
100g (½ cup minus 1 tbsp)
    butter
2 tbsp olive oil, plus extra
    for drizzling
4 garlic cloves, thinly sliced
600g (1lb 5oz) dried egg
    tagliatelle pasta
120g (4¼oz) Parmesan cheese,
    finely grated
60g (2¼oz) fresh parsley,
    finely chopped, plus extra
    to garnish

MAKE AHEAD
› You can soak the mushrooms and
make the mushroom sauce with the
garlic and butter ahead of time if you
wish (up to a day), but it's very little
effort. I would suggest making it
any time on the day of the party
and leaving it out until you need it.

SUBSTITUTIONS
› You can use fresh mushrooms if
you prefer, you will need around
600g (1lb 5oz) of chestnut or shiitake
mushrooms.

SCALING
› Per person, use 10g (¼oz) of porcini
steeped in 75ml (⅓ cup) of boiling
water, 1 garlic clove, 15g (1 tbsp) of
butter and 20g (¾oz) of Parmesan for
100g (3½oz) of pasta.
› If you are making this for more than
6 people, I recommend making the
mushroom sauce, then adding the
butter and combining the sauce, pasta,
cheese and parsley in 2 very large
warm bowls or pans, so you are able
to mix easily and effectively.

Fresh porcini mushrooms are an utter delight, but they are
super expensive because of their short season, so are most readily
available dried. They have a deeply savoury, funky flavour and
I love to pop a couple into a stock base or a gravy, or you can
even make powder with them, which is great for flavouring pie
sauces or a mac and cheese. This pasta dish is a very easy one,
with a glossy sauce that lightly coats rather than anything more
substantial, but it's absolutely stunning in its purity. It reminds
me of pastas I've eaten in trattorias around Umbria and Tuscany,
where porcini are rife. The chefs there know that the way to make
the funghi sing is with fat, a little bit of garlic, parsley and love.
Incidentally, that works for me too.

MAIN

PORCINI TAGLIATELLE

Bring a large pan of water to the boil, and put your kettle on to
boil with at least 400ml (1⅔ cups) of water.

Put the dried porcini in a small saucepan and pour over enough
boiling water from the kettle to cover. Set the pan over a low heat
and simmer the mushrooms very gently for 10 minutes. Remove the
pan from the heat, leaving the mushrooms in their intense stock.

Melt 20g (1½ tablespoons) of butter in a large, high-sided pan. Add
the oil, then the garlic. When the garlic is beginning to sizzle and
become fragrant, add the porcini and their soaking liquid. Bring to
a simmer, season generously with salt and pepper and set aside.

When your large pan of water is boiling, season it with salt as
you would do a soup (taste it!) and then drop in your tagliatelle,
stirring well to avoid it sticking.

When the pasta is close to al dente (after around 7 minutes of
cooking), pop your mushroom stock pan back over a medium heat
and bring it back to a simmer. Add the remaining 80g (generous
⅓ cup) of butter to the stock and swirl it in to emulsify, along
with a ladleful of the pasta cooking water. Using tongs, transfer
the cooked tagliatelle into the mushroom sauce and add two more
ladles of pasta water. Mix the sauce and pasta together well and
allow to simmer for a minute before removing from the heat.

Add the Parmesan, parsley and another ladle of pasta water and
keep tossing until the sauce is thickened – it should be shiny and
coating the pasta, add more pasta water if necessary to loosen
slightly. Season again with salt and black pepper and serve with a
final flourish of more parsley and a drizzle of olive oil on top.

SERVES 6–8

6 egg yolks
130g (generous ¹/₃ cup)
    organic runny honey, plus
    4 tbsp to serve
600ml (2¹/₂ cups) double
    (heavy) cream
1 tsp sea salt flakes, plus
    extra to decorate
3 yellow peaches, pitted and
    quartered
grated zest and freshly
    squeezed juice of ¹/₂ lemon

MAKE AHEAD

› Obviously this needs to be made ahead of time. As long as it's very well wrapped in the freezer, it will keep for up to a month.

SUBSTITUTIONS

› This semifreddo recipe can be used as a base for a million different versions. You could add a biscuit layer, swirl in peanut butter or stir crushed amaretti, chocolate truffles or chopped Toblerone through it – it is super versatile!
› I love this with stone fruit; nectarines, plums or apricots would be delicious too. Or, you could serve with strawberries and black pepper, or raspberries and whisky. Even a hot chocolate sauce would be good.

SCALING

› The loaf tin size above is a lovely, generous size. If making for more people, use 1 egg yolk, 20g (¾oz) of honey and 100ml (scant ½ cup) of double cream per person and make it in 2 tins, or even line freezerproof bowls with cling film and freeze into domes.

A semifreddo is another excellent Italian invention. Not quite a gelato, not quite an ice-cream cake but somewhere in between. Semifreddo literally means 'half frozen', which describes well the creamy, soft texture of this frozen pud. It's not the kind of ice-cream cake that will freeze hard. Honey is divine with ice cream and gives this a gorgeous hint of caramel and a silky finish. I love using salt on sweet things – it works so well here and the honeyed, lemony peaches balance the whole dish beautifully. It's also a make-ahead dream, leave it in the freezer until you need it.

DESSERT

SALTED HONEY SEMIFREDDO WITH PEACHES AND LEMON

Line a 900g (2lb) loaf tin generously with cling film (plastic wrap), using enough to give plenty of overlap to cover the top.

Put the egg yolks into a large bowl and whip them with a hand-held electric whisk at a high speed (this can also be done in an electric stand mixer if you wish, but I don't recommend doing it by hand). Whisk the egg yolks for around 8 minutes until they are very pale and thick. Set aside.

Put the honey into a small saucepan and bring it to the boil, letting it boil for about 20 seconds, then remove from the heat. Carefully pour the hot honey into the whipped egg yolks, whisking constantly with the electric whisk. Continue to whisk until the mixture has cooled down to room temperature – about 5 minutes. It should look glossy, thick and pale and make shiny ribbons on the surface of the mixture when it falls off the whisk.

In a separate clean bowl, use the electric whisk (no need to clean the beaters) to whip the cream and sea salt until softly whipped. Pour the cooled honey mixture into the cream and initially fold it in with a spatula or metal spoon, then use a small balloon whisk to beat out any lumps and get it smooth. Pour the mixture into the lined loaf tin and freeze for at least 12 hours.

Before you serve, mix the cut peaches with 2 tablespoons of honey and the lemon zest and juice in a bowl. Remove the semifreddo from the freezer and leave it to sit for 5 minutes, before turning out onto a serving plate and removing the cling film. Drizzle the semifreddo with the remaining 2 tablespoons of honey, sprinkle with salt and decorate with the dressed peaches. Serve immediately.

THE DATE NIGHT ONE

STARTERS

BURRATA, OLIVE SALSA, AUBERGINE AND BREAD

SEA BREAM CARPACCIO, CRAB, GREEN CHILLI AND MINT

MAIN

CHICKEN MILANESE, 'NDUJA CREAMED PEPPERS, BASIL OIL

DESSERT

TIRAMISU

Over the years I've thought a lot about date cookery (plus have done a fair amount of it), and I think it is an underserved area of occasion-based recipe writing. It really only gets a couple of weeks of attention around Valentine's Day, but the dating game is all year round baby! I think date night food can be really intimidating – it is SO hard to decide what to cook someone, how much to do in advance, how far to push yourself. In my book, a date where you cook for someone at home is usually the third, fourth or fifth date.

You really like each other, you're keen to know more and you also wanna show off. Needless to say, you can also cook this menu for someone with whom you have long been entwined or are even married to; the stakes are a little lower but the love being shown is just the same. This menu strikes the perfect balance of chilled (so it isn't a nightmare sweatfest of a date) but also pushing the boat out. Are you ready for love?

YES I AM.

GETTING AHEAD

	Burrata, Olive Salsa	Sea Bream Carpaccio	Chicken Milanese	Tiramisu
Up to 3 days before	–	–	–	–
Up to 2 days before	–	–	› Can make peppers › Can make basil oil	–
Up to 1 day before	› Can make salsa and roast aubergine	› Can make marinade	› Can make peppers › Can make basil oil	› Make tiramisu
On the day	› Bring everything to room temperature › Tear burrata	› Slice and marinate sea bream › Make crab dressing	› Bread chicken › Cook chicken › Reheat peppers	› Dust with cocoa

MISE-EN-PLACE

	Burrata, Olive Salsa	Sea Bream Carpaccio	Chicken Milanese	Tiramisu
Up to 6 hours before	› Make salsa and aubergine	› Slice and marinate sea bream › Mix crab dressing	› Bread chicken	–
Up to 1 hour before	› Make sure everything is coming to temperature	› Bring fish to room temperature (except the crab)	› Bring oil to room temperature	–
To serve	› Plate up aubergine › Tear burrata › Drizzle with salsa	› Dress fish with crab and chilli › Chop mint and sprinkle over	› Reheat peppers › Fry chicken › Serve with peppers and drizzle of oil	› Dust with cocoa

SERVES 2

For the aubergine
2 aubergines (eggplants)
grated zest of ¹/₂ lemon
1 garlic clove, grated
4 tbsp extra virgin olive oil

For the salsa
100g (3¹/₂oz) Nocellara
    (castelvetrano) olives, cheeks
    removed and then finely
    chopped (see note)
small handful of fresh parsley,
    finely chopped
grated zest and freshly squeezed
    juice of ¹/₂ lemon
2 salted anchovies (from a jar/
    can), drained and finely
    chopped (optional)
1 red chilli, deseeded and finely
    chopped
3 ¹/₂ tbsp extra virgin olive oil,
    plus extra to serve

To serve
1 x good-quality large burrata
    or 2 smaller ones, at room
    temperature
warm, fresh soft bread

MAKE AHEAD
› You can make the aubergine and
salsa 1 day in advance and refrigerate;
bring to room temp before serving.

SUBSTITUTIONS
› If you can't get hold of burrata, good
mozzarella and ricotta will work.
› If you're catering for a vegan, then
leave out the cheese and anchovies,
and use jarred beans or chickpeas
(garbanzo beans) warmed through in
the salsa.
› Nocellara olives are my preference,
but any good green olive will do.

SCALING
› 1 large or 2 small burrata per person.
› The salsa and aubergine can be
doubled or tripled easily, but for larger
quantities you can use ready chopped,
pitted green olives, if you like.

It's burrata, bitch. A low-effort, high reward, ready-to-eat item
is extremely useful when hosting, and a good burrata is a sexy bit
of kit. Please do try and get a good one, though, it makes a big
difference. Employed here with roasted aubergine and a lovely
refreshing salsa, you've got a super seductive plate of food that's
made for sharing.

STARTER

BURRATA WITH OLIVE SALSA, AUBERGINE AND BREAD

Preheat the oven to 250°C fan (260°C/500°F/Gas 10).

Stab the aubergines a few times each with the point of a sharp
knife – this is important as they have a tendency to explode in the
oven if you don't give them a few holes. Pop them in a roasting
tray and onto the highest rack in the preheated oven and roast for
an hour, turning them often. You want the skin to be burnt and
blistered with the inside soft, tender and smoky. Alternatively,
if you have a barbecue (grill) or gas hob, you can char the
aubergine over the flame to achieve a lovely, even smokier flavour.
Meanwhile, take the burrata out of the fridge at least 1 hour before
serving; it will be creamy and silkier at room temperature.

When the aubergines are cooked, slice them open down the middle
and leave to cool for 10 minutes. Scoop the flesh out into a sieve
and leave to drain over the sink for another 10 minutes (there is
a lot of water in them). Finally, roughly chop the cooked, drained
flesh (adding some of the burnt skin too, if you like) and combine
in a bowl with the lemon zest, garlic, olive oil and plenty of salt.
Set aside until needed.

Make the salsa by combining the ingredients in a bowl and
seasoning well with salt and pepper.

Pop the aubergine onto a serving plate and spread it out a bit,
before tearing over the burrata on top. To be fair, you could just
put the ball on there and let your date do the tearing honours, that
could be quite sexy too. In any case, dress with the salsa, a little
drizzle of extra virgin olive oil and some salt and pepper and serve
with warm, fresh bread.

NOTE: To prep the olives, slice 3 cheeks off each one, sliding the knife
diagonally along the pit. Then, pop the pits in a small bottle of good
vodka and steep in the fridge for a couple of weeks. Use this to make the
dirtiest martini of your life (see page 21).

A really luxurious dish that will show your date you mean business, without you stabbing yourself in the wrist attempting to shuck oysters with a butter knife. It's also light, easy and full of flavour. I love the addition of the crab meat in the dressing (any excuse for crab basically), but if you want to leave it out it is just as beautiful without. A must, though, is that your fish needs to be spankingly fresh from a reputable fishmonger.

STARTER

SEA BREAM CARPACCIO WITH CRAB, GREEN CHILLI AND MINT

SERVES 2

2 sea bream fillets, skinned and pin-boned – ask your fishmonger to do this
freshly squeezed juice of ½ lime
1 tbsp extra virgin olive oil
½ tsp sea salt
small handful of fresh mint leaves, shredded

For the dressing
finely grated zest of 1 lime
freshly squeezed juice of ½ lime
100g (3½oz) picked white crab meat
1 green chilli, thinly sliced
2 tbsp extra virgin olive oil

For the toasts
¼ sourdough loaf, thinly sliced into 4 slices
2–3 tbsp olive oil
1 garlic clove, peeled

Take the fillets of sea bream and pop them into the freezer for 10 minutes to firm up – this will make them easier to slice.

Meanwhile, grate all the lime zest into a bowl, then cut the lime in half and squeeze 1 half of juice into the bowl of zest (this zesty juice will be used for the crab later, but it's much easier to zest a whole fruit before cutting it). Squeeze the other half into a separate bowl.

Combine the plain lime juice with the olive oil and sea salt – this will be the marinade for the fish. Remove the sea bream from the freezer and slice as thinly as you can. Lay the fish slices onto a large serving plate and drizzle over the lime juice marinade. Pop into the fridge for at least 15 minutes until ready to serve.

To finish the dressing, combine the crab with the green chilli, lime zest and juice, extra virgin olive oil and salt and chill until needed.

Preheat the oven to 180°C fan (200°C/400°F/Gas 6).

Lay the sliced bread out in an oven tray and drizzle with the oil, turning and smearing both sides of the bread in it for optimum coverage. Toast in the oven for 10 minutes, or until all the toasts are evenly golden. Keep a close eye on it and remove any slices which are getting dark more quickly. When the toasts are done, remove from the oven and immediately rub each hot piece of toast with the garlic, before transferring it to kitchen paper (paper towels) to drain any excess oil.

MAKE AHEAD
› You can slice and marinate the fish up to 6 hours before serving. The crab is best made fresh on the day – add the mint just before serving.
› The toasts can be made up to 3 hours before serving, they are delicious warm or at room temperature.

SUBSTITUTIONS
› Sea bream could be switched for sea bass, pollock, halibut, trout or tuna.
› If you don't want to use crab meat but like the idea of something extra in the dressing, then brown shrimp is a nice swap. Or, some diced fresh apple or fennel would be delicious, too, just do it right before serving or they will oxidize and turn brown.

SCALING
› 1 fish fillet per person is a generous serving here. Using half a fillet per person is also fine to feed more people.

Take the sea bream out of the fridge 30 minutes before you want to serve it. When it's time to eat, dress the plate with the crab and green chilli dressing, then finish by scattering over the shredded mint leaves. Serve with the thin and crispy olive oil toasts.

SERVES 2

2 skinless chicken breasts
1/2 tsp fine salt
pinch of garlic powder
1/4 tsp dried sage
100g (3/4 cup) plain
   (all-purpose) flour
4 eggs, beaten with a pinch
   of salt
200g (4²/3 cups) panko
   breadcrumbs
200ml (generous 3/4 cup)
   vegetable oil
60g (1/4 cup) butter
flaky sea salt, to serve

For the basil oil
25g (1oz) picked fresh
   basil leaves
100ml (scant 1/2 cup) olive oil

For the creamed peppers
60ml (1/4 cup) olive oil
2 red (bell) peppers, deseeded
   and sliced
2 yellow (bell) peppers, deseeded
   and sliced
2 garlic cloves, sliced
2 tbsp 'nduja
120ml (1/2 cup) double
   (heavy) cream

A chicken Milanese is a chic and delicious main course. It is also a great way to make a chicken breast, something I usually avoid, go far and taste excellent. I did debate on whether to include this in the menu for the simple fact that it does have to be cooked to order, but then I decided that actually, one of the fun things about hosting a date is getting to cook together. So my advice is – get everything done in advance, except for the actual cooking of the Milanese, and then do that together, hips grazing at the stove, hands touching as you both reach for the spatula, eyes meeting while sprinkling with salt. It's practically a Richard Curtis movie already. *Pictured on page 88.*

MAIN

CHICKEN MILANESE, 'NDUJA CREAMED PEPPERS, BASIL OIL

To make the basil oil, bring a small pan of water to the boil and prepare a bowl of iced water. Blanch the basil leaves in the boiling water for 10 seconds, then remove and immediately plunge them into the bowl of iced water; this will help them hold their colour.

Take the basil leaves out of the water and squeeze out any excess liquid. Pop the basil in a food processor or bullet blender and add the oil. Blitz until the basil is puréed. Take a small, clean J-Cloth or muslin (cheesecloth) and put it in a sieve over a bowl, then pass the basil mixture through it, so that the bright green oil drains through. Cover the bowl of basil oil and keep in the fridge until needed. You can use the leftover basil mulch in a pasta sauce or pesto or even in a salad dressing.

For the creamed peppers, heat the olive oil in a saucepan over a medium heat. Add the peppers along with a generous pinch of salt and fry gently for around 30–40 minutes, until the peppers are wilted and soft. At this point, add the garlic and fry for a couple minutes, then add the 'nduja and let it melt into the peppers. When the 'nduja is well combined, add the cream and stir, before taking off the heat. Set aside until ready to serve.

To make the chicken, lay each breast between two sheets of baking parchment. Using a rolling pin (or in my case, a cricket mallet), bash each breast out to a thin, even thickness – around 2cm (¾in).

Using a pestle and mortar, crush the salt, garlic powder and dried sage together (if you don't have a pestle and mortar, just mix them) to create a dry brine to season the chicken. Sprinkle it over both sides of each breast and pop them in the fridge for 30 minutes.

MAKE AHEAD

› The peppers and basil oil can be done up to 2 days ahead.
› You can breadcrumb the chicken breasts earlier in the day, and I definitely suggest that you do as it gives you time to clean up the breading station!

SUBSTITUTIONS

› The basil oil process can be ditched in favour of simply chopped basil in good olive oil if you are time poor.
› Leave out the 'nduja and add 1 tsp of smoked paprika instead if you are avoiding pork.
› Chicken breast could also be pork or veal cutlets bashed until thin, if you prefer.

SCALING

› The creamed peppers can be easily increased (30ml/2 tbsp of double cream per pepper), and the basil oil makes enough for at least 6–8 portions.
› The Milanese can be scaled easily by doubling or tripling for larger batches, although you may find you need more fat to cook in so add an extra 100ml (scant ½ cup) of oil per increase.
› If doing chicken Milanese for a crowd, I recommend frying the Milanese ahead in batches and reheating them when needed in an oven preheated to 180°C fan (200°C/400°F/Gas 6) for 10 minutes, turning halfway through. Make sure they are not piled on top of each other in the oven or they will lose their crunch.

Meanwhile, find three dishes or trays each big enough to fit a bashed breast and put the flour in one, the eggs in another and the panko breadcrumbs in the third.

Once the chicken has brined, pat any excess moisture off with kitchen paper (paper towels) and then dip a breast in the flour to give an even coating on each side, dusting off any excess. Next, pop the breast into the eggs and coat liberally on both sides before immediately transferring to the breadcrumbs, which will stick to the egg. (This is a messy process and I like to keep one hand just for the dry ingredients and one for the wet.) Dip the breadcrumbed breast back into the eggs again, coating well, and then the breadcrumbs. This ensures an extra crunchy coating. Put the coated chicken on a piece of baking parchment and repeat the process for the remaining chicken. Cover all the coated chicken with cling film (plastic wrap) and keep in the fridge until needed.

When you are ready to fry, divide the vegetable oil and butter between two frying pans (skillets) and pop them both over a medium heat. When the butter starts to sizzle, gently lay one breast down in each pan and leave to cook for about 4 minutes, then turn over. It won't be fully cooked and golden yet. Cook the other side for 4 minutes, then turn again and cook for another 2–3 minutes, repeating on each side until they are beautifully golden brown and crunchy. This should take about 10–12 minutes total. Transfer the cooked chicken to kitchen paper to drain excess oil.

Reheat the creamed peppers by putting the pan back over a medium heat, adding a splash of water if necessary to loosen. Place each chicken Milanese on a serving plate and top with some peppers, then drizzle over the basil oil and sprinkle with sea salt.

HIPS GRAZING AT THE STOVE, HANDS TOUCHING AS YOU BOTH REACH FOR THE SPATULA.

**SERVES 2, WITH LEFTOVERS
FOR THE MORNING AFTER**

180ml (¾ cup) fresh strong
   coffee of espresso, cooled –
   I like to use espresso powder
   for this
3 egg yolks
80g (scant ½ cup) caster
   (superfine) sugar
350g (1½ cups) mascarpone
1½ tbsp Marsala
2 egg whites
2 tbsp dark rum
175g (6oz) sponge fingers (you
   might not need them all)
2 tbsp dark cocoa powder

MAKE AHEAD

› I STRONGLY recommend you make
this the day before, it will set nicely
and the flavours will mingle together
in the fridge beautifully overnight.
Having said that, here comes my age-
old warning to make sure your fridge
isn't stinky – it can and will affect the
flavour of your pud.

SUBSTITUTIONS

› If you're worried about staying up all
night (for the wrong reason), then use
decaf coffee.
› The booze can be left out completely
or play with it – Kahlua, Frangelico
and amaretto would all go beautifully
with the coffee.

SCALING

› For 4–6 people, double the recipe
and use a 30cm x 20cm (12 x 8in)
dish. For 8–10 people, tripling the
recipe would mean using 1.05kg
(2lb 6oz) of mascarpone, which is
a bit of an annoying amount, so I've
tested it with just 1kg (2lb 4oz) and
it works perfectly. You may need
extra soaked sponge fingers for
the top layer, so increase that by
½ for each doubling of the recipe.

An absolutely golden piece of pub quiz knowledge that I will give
you for free is that tiramisu means 'pick me up' in Italian. And if
that isn't appropriate for a date-night menu then I don't know
what is. It is an iconic pudding because it's impressive but, in the
same breath, kind of low key... It's sponge fingers dipped in cold
coffee and covered with cream cheese at the end of the day. I just
really love a little sexy pudding moment on a date, something
to get the pulse racing and sweeten up that potentially garlicky
breath. Tiramisu is it!

DESSERT

TIRAMISU

Make your coffee or espresso first and then leave it to cool.
Espresso powder is great for this as it has a much stronger flavour.

Pop the egg yolks into a bowl with the sugar and whisk with a
hand-held electric whisk for about 5 minutes until the mix is thick,
glossy and very pale. Add the mascarpone and Marsala and whisk
again until smooth. Give your beaters a little rinse and dry.

In a separate clean bowl, whisk the egg whites to stiff peaks, then
use a metal spoon to fold them into the mascarpone mix. You will
end up with a lovely thick and floofy (a technical term) cream.

Mix the cooled coffee with the rum in a separate dish. Take
each sponge finger and dip it into the coffee mixture for around
4 seconds, then transfer to a 22cm x 16cm (8½ x 6¼in) dish. Lay
the soaked sponge fingers side by side in your dish – you will need
roughly 6 for the first layer. Spoon about half of the mascarpone
cream on top and level out with a spatula.

Using a sieve, dust the top generously with cocoa powder – you
want a nice, thick coverage.

Repeat the layering process with the second round of sponge
fingers, although you might need a couple more this time –
the dish will be slightly wider at the top. Pop the remaining
mascarpone over the top and smooth out again but DO NOT dust
with cocoa yet. The cocoa will bleed too much in the fridge as it
sets and it won't look good when you reveal it. Cover the tiramisu
in cling film (plastic wrap) and pop in the fridge overnight.

When you are ready to serve, remove it from the fridge and dust
with cocoa powder. Use a knife and a spatula to get a couple of
nice wedges out, or don't even bother, just give your date a spoon
and dive in together.

SERVES 12

THE ONE THAT'S A BUFFET

WHITE BEANS WITH LEEKS, COURGETTES AND MINT

BAKED POTATOES WITH DILL, MUSTARD AND YOGURT

PISSALADIÈRE

ROASTED TOMATOES WITH TARRAGON AND RICOTTA

MARINATED FETA WITH CHILLI, LEMON AND MARJORAM

GIANT COUSCOUS WITH PICKLED CHILLIES, OLIVES AND PEPPERS

EGG AND AVOCADO SALAD

Buffet is quite an old fashioned term in many ways, but it's utility is certainly not outdated. This is a menu for when you're hosting something informal, perhaps with lots of people that requires a table filled with food and love. There is a mix of low effort sharing dishes here, along with a couple of big old tarts, which always go down well at a buffet. I think the formula for a good buffet is: 2–3 salads, 3 carby things and lots of dippy, smooshy things to go with bread. You can always make your buffet go further with plenty of bread and crisps, butter and cheeses, cured meats and crudités on ice. Try and vary the height of things on your table too, so nothing gets lost.

GETTING AHEAD

	White Beans with Leeks, Courgettes and Mint	Baked Potatoes with Dill, Mustard and Yogurt	Pissaladière	Roasted Tomatoes with Tarragon and Ricotta	Marinated Feta with Chilli, Lemon and Marjoram	Giant Couscous with Pickled Chillies, Olives and Peppers	Egg and Avocado Salad
Up to 3 days before	› Can make beans	› Can make dill butter	› Can caramelize onions	› Can make ricotta mix	–	–	–
Up to 2 days before	› Can make beans	› Can make dill butter	› Can caramelize onions	› Can make ricotta mix	–	–	› Can boil and peel eggs
Up to 1 day before	› Can make beans	› Can make dill butter	› Can caramelize onions	› Can make ricotta mix	› Can marinate feta	–	› Can boil and peel eggs
On the day	› Make/reheat beans; add chopped mint	› Bake potatoes › Make dill butter › Assemble	› Assemble and bake tarts	› Roast tomatoes › Assemble	› Marinate feta	› Cook giant couscous › Assemble	› Boil and peel eggs › Assemble salad

MISE-EN-PLACE

	White Beans with Leeks, Courgettes and Mint	Baked Potatoes with Dill, Mustard and Yogurt	Pissaladière	Roasted Tomatoes with Tarragon and Ricotta	Marinated Feta with Chilli, Lemon and Marjoram	Giant Couscous with Pickled Chillies, Olives and Peppers	Egg and Avocado Salad
Up to 6 hours before	› Can make dish	› Can bake potatoes › Make dill butter	› Can caramelize onions › Can bake tarts	› Can roast tomatoes › Can make ricotta mix	› Can marinate feta	› Can prep ingredients except for giant couscous	› Can boil and peel eggs
Up to 1 hour before	› Bring to room temperature › Chop mint	› Warm/bake potatoes › Make/reheat butter; add more fresh dill	› Gently warm tarts	› Roast/warm tomatoes › Bring ricotta mix to room temperature › Chop tarragon	› Bring to room temperature	› Cook giant couscous › Assemble salad	› Prep salad
To serve	› Top with chopped mint	› Serve with dill butter, yogurt and aleppo	› Serve	› Serve with tarragon	› Serve with more fresh marjoram on top	› Serve	› Assemble and serve

**SERVES 6 AS A SIDE, OR 10–12
AS PART OF A BUFFET**

80ml (1/3 cup) extra virgin olive
  oil, plus extra for drizzling
2 courgettes (zucchini),
  roughly diced
2 leeks, washed, trimmed and
  thinly sliced
3 garlic cloves, thinly sliced
1.2kg (2²/₃lb) jarred cannellini
  beans (approx. 2 jars), drained
  and liquid reserved
finely grated zest and freshly
  squeezed juice of 1 lemon
1¹/₂ tbsp dried mint
20g (³/₄oz) fresh mint, leaves
  picked and finely chopped

This is one of those brilliant recipes that is very much a formula for a good plate of food and not at all restrictive. Swap the cannellini beans for virtually any pulse and the vegetables for whatever you've got in. I love having something creamy like this on my buffet table – it works as a dip, topping or side and goes with virtually anything. *Pictured on page 100.*

WHITE BEANS WITH LEEKS, COURGETTES AND MINT

Warm the olive oil in a large frying pan (skillet) over a medium heat. Add the diced courgettes, leeks and a good pinch of salt. Cover the pan with a lid and cook for around 10–15 minutes, stirring regularly and re-covering the pan each time. The vegetables shouldn't take on any colour, but they will become transparent and soften.

At this point, add the sliced garlic and stir well. Fry for a couple more minutes before adding the beans, lemon zest and juice, dried mint and a splash of the jarred bean liquid. Simmer gently for about 10 more minutes, then remove from the heat, adding more bean liquid if needed to make it nice and creamy. Add two-thirds of the fresh mint and mix well. Leave to cool to room temperature or serve straight away, warm and drizzled with good olive oil and topped with the remaining fresh mint.

MAKE AHEAD
› This can be made up to 3 days ahead and kept refrigerated, just make sure to warm it up before you serve it.

SUBSTITUTIONS
› You can use butter beans (lima beans), chickpeas (garbanzo beans) or even lentils instead of the white beans. I love courgette here, but squash, peas, broccoli and asparagus would work too.
› If you don't like mint, leave it out and finish with coriander (cilantro), parsley or dill.

SCALING
› This makes a fairly large quantity and would happily serve 6 as a starter or side instead of 12 at a buffet. If you wish to increase quantities, you will need to cook this in two pans.

**SERVES 6 AS A SIDE, OR 10-12
AS PART OF A BUFFET**

1kg (2lb 4oz) new potatoes
120g (1/2 cup) butter
1 large garlic clove, grated
2 tbsp wholegrain mustard
20g (3/4oz) fresh dill, finely
  chopped
50g (scant 1/4 cup) natural
  (plain) yogurt
1 tsp Aleppo pepper or fine
  dried chilli flakes

Baked potatoes are an often overlooked side for a formal gathering but are actually a really easy and cheap way to feed lots of people. I like using new potatoes for this because they take less time to cook and, being small, they allow for more space on the plate, which is crucial in the navigation of a buffet. *Pictured on page 100.*

BAKED POTATOES WITH DILL, MUSTARD AND YOGURT

Preheat the oven to 180°C fan (200°C/400°F/Gas 6).

Spread the potatoes out on a baking tray and bake in the preheated oven for 30–40 minutes until they are soft, then cover in foil to keep them warm if needed.

Meanwhile, melt the butter in a pan over a medium heat and add the garlic. Sizzle for less than a minute before removing from the heat and whisking in the mustard, dill and a good pinch of salt. Keep warm until needed.

To serve, slit open or crush the potatoes and pop them on a couple of plates. Drizzle over the yogurt, then the dill butter. Sprinkle with the fragrant Aleppo pepper or chilli flakes to finish.

MAKE AHEAD
› You can bake the potatoes and reheat them up to 6 hours before serving. The dill butter will keep in the fridge for up to 3 days.

SUBSTITUTIONS
› You can, of course, do 1 normal baking potato per person if you prefer.
› I love using dill in the butter but parsley or tarragon are good alternatives.
› Use non-dairy alternatives for the butter and yogurt to make this vegan.

SCALING
› This recipe is easily doubled or tripled and works well as a canapé – 1/2 a potato per serving, so around 20 potatoes would make 40 bites.

MAKES 2 TARTS

60g (¼ cup) butter
1 tbsp olive oil
1.4kg (3lb) white onions
   (approx. 6–7), peeled
   and thinly sliced
2 x 320g (11½oz) sheets
   of ready-rolled puff
   pastry, chilled
200g (7oz) pitted black olives
120g (4¼oz) good-quality
   jarred or canned salted
   anchovies

MAKE AHEAD
› The onions can be cooked up to
3 days ahead and kept in the fridge.
› You can bake the tart up to 6 hours
before your party and gently warm
it at 120°C fan (140°C/275°F/Gas 1)
for 5 minutes to serve, but it is also
fabulous at room temperature.

SUBSTITUTIONS
› If you prefer to keep this veggie, ditch
the anchovies and make the lattice
with thin strips of drained jarred
chargrilled (bell) peppers.

SCALING
› Divide the recipe in half to work out
the perfect amount for 1 tart and then
go from there if you need to bulk up.
It's best to batch-cook the onions if
you are doing more than 2 tarts.

Traditionally, this is a flatbread but ready-rolled sheets of puff pastry are so just temptingly convenient for a buffet and make knocking up a couple of tarts a walk in the park. The tart is super easy to portion up, so you can guarantee a piece for every guest. This is a delightful Provençal dish that is supremely savoury – our pastry is topped with softened onions, baked to a deep bronze and then topped with punchy anchovies and olives in a pleasing lattice (if you can be bothered). It's so very summery and truly divine with the selection of salads on our table. *Pictured on page 100.*

PISSALADIÈRE

Melt the butter with the oil in a large pan over a medium heat. Add the onions and stir well, then leave to cook slowly for around 25–30 minutes. You don't want to caramelize them too much, just let them gently soften to a lovely blonde colour. Don't be tempted to salt the onions, the addition of olives and anchovies later will add plenty. When the onions are cooked, leave them to cool completely.

Preheat the oven to 200°C fan (220°C/425°F/Gas 7).

Remove your puff pastry from the fridge and unroll the sheets, placing one each on two large oven trays – they can be baked on the baking parchment they come in. Use a small sharp knife to score a border around the edges of each pastry sheet, about 2cm (¾in) wide. Prick the pastry all over with a fork, leaving the border intact. Spread the cooled onions across the two pieces of pastry. Pop them in the preheated oven for 15 minutes, then turn the oven down to 170°C fan (190°C/375°F/Gas 5) and bake for a further 20 minutes until the onions are a deep gold and the edges are puffed and browned.

While the tarts are baking, prep the olives and anchovies. Drain them both very well, patting away any excess oil from the anchovies with kitchen paper (paper towels). I like to carefully slice the anchovies in half lengthways so they are lovely and thin.

When the tarts are ready, remove them from the oven. Create your anchovy lattice on the hot tarts by laying the thin strips of anchovies in diagonal lines across the tart, and then criss-cross with another set of lines going the other way. It is up to you how wide the lattice is, but it's worth remembering the more olives and anchovies that go on the tart, the saltier it will be. I like to leave about 9cm (3½in) of space between my lines. In the middle of the resulting triangles the lattice creates, you can place your olives. Put the tart back in the oven for no more than 5 minutes and then it is ready to serve.

SERVES 6 AS A SIDE, OR 10-12 AS PART OF A BUFFET

500g (1lb 2oz) cherry
    tomatoes on the vine
5 tbsp olive oil

For the ricotta
400g (1¾ cups) ricotta
2 tbsp double (heavy) cream
good grating of fresh nutmeg
small bunch of fresh tarragon,
    leaves picked

A collapsing, wrinkly, juicy roasted tomato is just so evocative, especially if you serve them still on the vine and even more so if their liquor is seeping into something pale and creamy. Here our tomatoes are given a hard roast for a little bit of colour before being piled onto seasoned ricotta that has been floofed up with a bit of cream. The tarragon offers a rounded warmth and somehow makes the tomatoes taste even sweeter. This is also fabulous stirred through pasta or smooshed on toast if you have any leftovers, which you probably won't. *Pictured on page 100.*

ROASTED TOMATOES WITH TARRAGON AND RICOTTA

Preheat the oven to 220°C fan (240°C/475°F/Gas 9).

Lay the tomatoes on their vines in an oven tray and drizzle with the oil. Season generously with salt and black pepper and then roast in the very hot oven for 10–12 minutes until the tomatoes have blistered and lightly caramelized without completely dissolving.

While the tomatoes are cooking, fold the ricotta, cream and nutmeg together and season with salt and pepper. Spread the ricotta onto a plate and then when the tomatoes have cooked, carefully pile them on top. Don't waste any of the divine juices from the oven tray – pour them on top and then scatter over the tarragon leaves and serve.

MAKE AHEAD
› You can roast the tomatoes earlier in the day but keep them on their tray and reheat them before serving.
› The ricotta mix can be made up to 3 days in advance and stored in the fridge.

SUBSTITUTIONS
› Use Greek yogurt instead of ricotta if you need to.
› Tarragon isn't for everyone, so use a classic like basil or mint should you wish to.

SCALING
› This recipe is easily doubled and is, in fact, great to make large quantities of, as it is so easy. For a simple lunch for two, with toast, I would reduce it by half.

SERVES 6 AS A SIDE, OR 10-12 AS PART OF A BUFFET

2 red chillies, deseeded and finely chopped

1 lemon, peeled and the zest finely chopped

1 tbsp dried oregano

large bunch of fresh marjoram, leaves picked

small handful of fresh parsley, finely chopped

60ml (¼ cup) extra virgin olive oil

3 x 200g (7oz) blocks of feta cheese

This is more of a serving suggestion rather than a recipe to be honest. Feta is a bit like olives – it's an excellent addition to most plates of food and is splendid piled high on a buffet table. Here I've shared my favourite way to jazz it up with very little effort but tonnes of reward. Marjoram is the cousin of oregano and is a little bit more delicate and citrusy – I adore it and have long said if someone invented a marjoram perfume I would be all over it. If you can't find it don't worry, you've got plenty of other options. *Pictured on page 100.*

MARINATED FETA WITH CHILLI, LEMON AND MARJORAM

In a bowl, combine the chopped chillies, chopped lemon zest, dried oregano, half the marjoram leaves and all the parsley with the oil.

Drain and dry the feta blocks with kitchen paper (paper towels) and then cut each one into large chunks; you want about 6 chunks per block. Pop the chunks into a large container all in one layer and then cover with the marinade. Leave in the fridge to marinate for at least 1 hour before serving at room temperature with the remaining marjoram leaves sprinkled on top.

MAKE AHEAD

› This can be made up to 24 hours in advance and kept in the fridge, just make sure to bring it to room temperature before you serve it. Don't add the fresh marjoram to garnish until you're ready to serve.

SUBSTITUTIONS

› Use oregano or soft, young thyme instead of marjoram.

SCALING

› 1 block of feta feeds approximately 3–4 people in a buffet setting, so work off that amount to increase or reduce the recipe. Just use the peel of half a small lemon if only doing one block of feta.

MAKE YOUR BUFFET GO FURTHER WITH PLENTY OF BREAD AND CRISPS, BUTTER AND CHEESES.

**SERVES 6 AS A SIDE, OR 10–12
AS PART OF A BUFFET**

300g (10½oz) giant couscous
160g (5½oz) jarred roasted
 (bell) peppers, drained
 and chopped
30–50g (1–2oz) jarred pickled
 chillies, depending on how
 hot you like it, sliced
100g (3½oz) green olives
 with pits, cheeks sliced off
 (see page 82)
1 garlic clove, grated
2 tbsp extra virgin olive oil,
 plus extra if needed
1 tbsp pickled chilli juice from
 the jar
decent handful of fresh parsley,
 finely chopped

This is a far cry from the dry and under seasoned couscous salads that I normally avoid like the plague. Giant couscous is closer in texture to pasta, is a vehicle for flavour and does a wonderful job at staying moist. The clever thing about using lots of pickled products in this is that you don't need to worry about making a separate dressing – it all goes into the bowl together and comes out a triumph.

GIANT COUSCOUS WITH PICKLED CHILLIES, OLIVES AND PEPPERS

Cook the giant couscous in a pan of boiling salted water according to the packet instructions.

While it is cooking, mix together the chopped peppers, chillies, olives, garlic, olive oil and pickle juice in a large bowl. Drain the couscous and then toss it into the bowl with everything while it is still hot, mixing well. Leave to cool for 10–15 minutes.

Mix in the parsley, season with salt and pepper and add more olive oil if the couscous is in any way sticky. Serve at room temperature.

MAKE AHEAD
› This is best made an hour or so before serving, otherwise the couscous can get claggy. If you want to get ahead, mix the other ingredients together up to 6 hours before.

SUBSTITUTIONS
› Don't worry if you need to avoid spice, just add another pepper and a few extra olives instead of the pickled chillies.
› Mint would be gorgeous in this too.

SCALING
› This is easily doubled. If reducing, just use a very small garlic clove so it is not too overpowering.

SERVES 6

6 eggs
4 ripe avocados
finely grated zest and freshly
    squeezed juice of 1 lime
4 tbsp mayonnaise
1 tsp celery salt
1/2 tsp all-purpose seasoning
small handful of fresh basil,
    finely shredded
small handful of fresh chives,
    finely chopped
1 small iceberg lettuce,
    finely shredded

Egg and avocado on toast taking the world by storm was not that surprising given that they have been paired together for bloody ages. Everybody loves them together, so a salad with both makes sense. It also functions as a hybrid dish – something substantial, but also something to smoosh with your bread like a dip, or to create your own little sandwich of the perfect buffet bite. Or is it just me who does that at buffets? Surely not.

EGG AND AVOCADO SALAD

Bring a pan of water to the boil, then carefully lay in the eggs. Boil for 7½ minutes before lifting out the eggs and plunging them into iced water to cool. Peel the eggs and leave them in cold water until needed.

Peel, pit and dice the avocados and place them in a bowl. Dress the avocado with the lime zest and juice, mayonnaise, celery salt, all-purpose seasoning and half of the herbs. Season with black pepper.

Arrange the shredded lettuce over a serving plate, then pile on the dressed avocado. Slice the boiled eggs in half and then pop them on top before sprinkling with the remaining herbs to finish.

MAKE AHEAD
› The eggs can be cooked and peeled and stored in cold water in the fridge up to 2 days ahead. Bring them to room temperature before serving.

SUBSTITUTIONS
› Lemon zest and juice would work in the avocado too.
› A thinly sliced spring onion (scallion) is a fine swap for the chives.

SCALING
› Simply double or halve, 1 egg per person is plenty.

THE FIRST BBQ OF THE SUMMER ONE

MOZZARELLA WITH GRILLED CUCUMBER, FENNEL AND SPRING ONION SALSA

WARM POTATO SALAD WITH BASIL AND PECORINO

GRILLED PRAWNS WITH MINT, TARRAGON AND LIME

LAMB ARROSTICINI

COAL ROAST AUBERGINE WITH TOMATOES AND DILL

DESSERT

SUMMER PUDDING

This is a great menu if you are not super confident with a barbecue (grill) and feel out of your depth doing anything other than burgers and sausages. Fear not! We are going to cook beautiful food that is inventive but quick and easy, too.

With this schedule for a coal barbecue (that takes around 30–40 minutes to get hot) the maximum time you'll spend at the BBQ while guests are in situ is only 10–15 minutes. Perfect.

› 2 hours before guests arrive – light barbecue, make potato salad and leave to cool.

› 1 hour 20 minutes before guests arrive – cook salad veg and aubergine over hot coals.

› 1 hour 30 minutes before guests arrive – leave barbecue and finish up salads.

› 5 minutes before guests arrive – refresh coals.

› When guests arrive – LOTS OF DRINKS.

› 20–25 minutes after guests arrive – new coals will be hot – cook prawns and arrosticini.

› 30–40 minutes after guests arrive – eat!

GETTING AHEAD

	Mozzarella with Grilled Cucumber, Fennel and Spring Onion Salsa	Warm Potato Salad with Basil and Pecorino	Grilled Prawns with Mint, Tarragon and Lime	Lamb Arrosticini	Coal Roast Aubergine with Tomatoes and Dill	Summer Pudding
Up to 3 days before	–	–	› Can make butter and chill	–	–	–
Up to 2 days before	–	–	› Can make butter and chill	–	–	› Can make pudding
Up to 1 day before	–	–	› Can make butter and chill	› Can dice and marinate lamb	–	› Make pudding
On the day	› Grill cucumber and salsa ingredients › Bring mozzarella to room temperature	› Boil potatoes	› Grill prawns › Melt butter	› Thread lamb onto skewers › Make the rosemary salt › Grill	› Grill	–

MISE-EN-PLACE

	Mozzarella with Grilled Cucumber, Fennel and Spring Onion Salsa	Warm Potato Salad with Basil and Pecorino	Grilled Prawns with Mint, Tarragon and Lime	Lamb Arrosticini	Coal Roast Aubergine with Tomatoes and Dill	Summer Pudding
Up to 6 hours before	› Can salt cucumber › Can prep ingredients for grilling	› Can boil potatoes and leave to sit in garlic oil	› Can make butter	› Can marinate the lamb › Can skewer the lamb › Can make the rosemary salt	–	–
Up to 1 hour before	› Can grill cucumber and salsa ingredients › Bring mozzarella to temperature › Assemble salsa	› Can boil potatoes and leave to sit in garlic oil	› Can make butter	› Can marinate the lamb › Can skewer the lamb › Can make the rosemary salt	› Grill aubergines and tomatoes › Assemble	–
To serve	› Tear mozzarella › Chop cucumber › Serve dressed in salsa	› Mix with basil and Pecorino	› Grill prawns › Melt butter › Mix with herbs	› Grill lamb › Serve with rosemary salt and lemon	› Serve	› Serve with double cream and fruit

SERVES 6 AS A SHARING DISH

1 cucumber, peeled
2 tsp flaky sea salt
1 fennel bulb, trimmed,
    quartered lengthways
    and layers separated
10 spring onions (scallions),
    trimmed
small handful of fresh parsley,
    finely chopped
1 large red chilli, thinly sliced
100ml (scant ½ cup) extra
    virgin olive oil
finely grated zest and freshly
    squeezed juice of 1 lemon
4 large good-quality mozzarella
    cheese balls, at room
    temperature, torn into
    bite-size pieces
slices of sourdough or focaccia,
    toasted, to serve

MAKE AHEAD
› I would aim to make the salsa in the
prep hour before your guests arrive, so
your barbecue is nice and free for the
more time-sensitive dishes and so that
you don't have to go inside and chop.

SUBSTITUTIONS
› You can use other herbs than parsley
in the salsa – basil is delicious too.
› I like the fennel for its aniseed
flavour here, but if you don't enjoy
that then leave it out.
› Mozzarella could also be burrata,
stracciatella or ricotta.

SCALING
› Cook 1 fennel and 10 spring onions
for every 4 mozzarella. This would
serve 4–6 as a starter.

Barbecued food doesn't always have to be the main event on a
dish. Sometimes those grilled bits are best used as a condiment or
seasoning, and this recipe is a great example of that. Mozzarella is
a fabulous blank canvas and here I have dressed it in a salsa made
of charred fennel and spring onions and paired it with some smoky
grilled cucumber. Grilled cucumber is INCREDIBLE – it is sweet
and firm and so tasty, it's actually one of my favourite vegetables
to barbecue. *Pictured on page 108.*

MOZZARELLA WITH GRILLED CUCUMBER, FENNEL AND SPRING ONION SALSA

Preheat the barbecue – a coal barbecue will need 30–40 minutes.
Cut the cucumber in half lengthways and use a spoon to deseed it,
discarding the seeds. Sprinkle it with the salt and leave it to sit for
1 hour on a tray. The salt will draw out a lot of the moisture in the
cucumber and make it firmer for barbecuing.

Grill the sliced fennel and spring onions on the barbecue when
the coals are white but the flames have died down. If the fennel
pieces are curved, then press them down to flatten them before
you grill them, so you get more surface area. Turn the veg once
or twice while they cook. The spring onions will cook in under 5
minutes, so keep an eye on them – you want a good char but still
some evidence of green. Remove the spring onions when done and
cover them with a clean tea towel (kitchen cloth) to steam a bit
while you finish cooking the fennel. The fennel itself just needs
some good colour – it is nice if it is still a bit crunchy.

Let the veg cool to a comfortable handling temperature, then
dice up the fennel and finely chop the spring onions. Mix them
in a bowl with the parsley, chilli, olive oil, lemon zest and half
the lemon juice.

Wipe any excess salt off the cucumbers with kitchen paper
(paper towels) and pat them dry. Pop them onto the hot barbecue
to grill for around 8 minutes – you're looking for good bar marks
and a light blackening. Turn them once or twice for an even
grill. Remove from the heat and squeeze over the juice from the
remaining lemon half.

To serve, arrange the torn mozzarellas on a platter, then drizzle the
fennel and spring onion salsa on top. Slice the cucumber into bite-
size half moons and dot them around the plate. Serve with plenty
of toasted/grilled bread.

SERVES 6-8 AS A SHARING DISH

1.5kg (3lb 5oz) white potatoes,
    such as Désirée or King Edward
2 garlic cloves, grated
grated zest and freshly squeezed
    juice of 1 lemon
250ml (generous 1 cup) olive oil,
    plus extra to serve
70g (2½oz) Pecorino cheese,
    shaved
50g (2oz) fresh basil leaves, torn

I also call this Airbnb salad, as I first made it on holiday in Italy staying in self-catering accommodation with not much kitchen kit but a decent wood grill for plenty of fresh fish and meat. Potato salad is a must at a barbecue, but being in Italy I didn't want to slather my potatoes in mayonnaise when I had beautiful oil, basil, garlic and cheese. Plus, it was one of the only things I could make with such a sparsely equipped kitchen. It was a huge hit and has become a firm family favourite, much requested whenever I am with my brothers. It's great for kids, too, as the flavour is essentially that of pesto, without actually having to make pesto. I like to peel the potatoes because they absorb the dressing better, but if you don't have time don't worry at all.

WARM POTATO SALAD WITH BASIL AND PECORINO

Peel and chop the potatoes into chunks, the same size as if you were making roast potatoes. Put them in a large saucepan and cover them with cold water. Season the water generously with salt and bring it up to a rolling boil. Cook the potatoes for around 10–15 minutes over a medium heat until they are just tender.

Meanwhile, mix the garlic with the lemon zest and juice, olive oil and salt and pepper to taste in a large bowl. Drain the potatoes when they are cooked and then pour them straight into the garlicky oil and mix well. The hot potatoes will drink up the dressing and become deliciously flavourful as they cool.

When the potatoes are room temperature, mix in two-thirds of the Pecorino and basil, saving some for the top. Plate the potatoes, drizzle with more oil and sprinkle with the remaining torn basil leaves and shavings of Pecorino cheese.

MAKE AHEAD
› This is best served on the day it is made, but feel free to boil your potatoes and dress them a few hours in advance of your meal. Just keep them covered at room temperature until you need them.

SUBSTITUTIONS
› Pecorino can, of course, be swapped for Parmesan, and mint or dill would both be great instead of the basil.

SCALING
› Allow for 200g (7oz) of potatoes per person to scale up or down.

SERVES 6

100g (½ cup minus 1 tbsp)
    salted butter
2 garlic cloves, grated
finely grated zest and freshly
    squeezed juice of 1 lime
3 sprigs of fresh tarragon, leaves
    picked and finely chopped
4 sprigs of fresh mint, leaves
    picked and finely chopped
600g (1lb 5oz) raw tiger prawns
    (jumbo shrimp), shell on

Prawns are a great thing to elevate a barbecue spread, plus they are no work for you to prepare – all the gloriously messy shelling and head sucking is done by the happy eater. They certainly need something for dipping, and this herbal, refreshing yet rich butter is excellent with the sweet and smoky prawn flesh. You can keep the butter warm in a pan on the barbecue and pour it right on top of the just-grilled prawns, too, so you don't even have to go inside to plate up. *Pictured on page 108.*

GRILLED PRAWNS WITH MINT, TARRAGON AND LIME

Preheat the barbecue – a coal barbecue will need 30–40 minutes.

Melt the butter in a saucepan and add the garlic and lime zest – keep the lime for squeezing later. When it just starts to bubble, remove it from the heat and stir in the chopped herbs.

Grill your prawns on a screaming hot barbecue – they should instantly start turning pink and their shells will start to blacken. They need just under 2 minutes on each side. You can grill the cut lime halves too. Put the prawns straight on a plate, squeeze over the lime juice and drizzle over the pungent butter. Heaven.

MAKE AHEAD
› The butter can be made up to 3 days in advance, but I would advise simply mixing the ingredients with softened butter, rather than melting it. Then chill it and melt when you need it.

SUBSTITUTIONS
› The butter will work with any grilled seafood or meat; it would be fabulous on squid, scallops or even chicken wings.

SCALING
› I like to serve 2–3 prawns (shrimp) per person, so check with your fishmonger when you buy them how many you have and go from there.

SERVES 6-8

1.2kg (2²/₃lb) lamb shoulder,
   diced into even 3cm
   (1¹/₄in) cubes
4 tbsp extra virgin olive oil
1 tsp garlic powder
1 tsp dried chilli flakes
5 sprigs of fresh rosemary,
   leaves picked
2 tsp flaky sea salt
1 lemon, cut into wedges

12–15 x 25cm (10in) skewers,
   if using bamboo, soak in water
   for at least 30 minutes first

Lamb is probably my favourite meat to barbecue; grilled lamb just has this absolutely incredible flavour and don't even get me started on the crispy charred fat. Arrosticini hail from Abruzzo in Eastern Italy and are delightfully easy. The lamb shoulder (great marbling) gets a simple marinate and then is threaded onto skewers and cooked on a blistering grill. Lamb shoulder is normally associated with slow cooking but, here, cooked very quickly, it is wonderfully tender and has a superlative depth of flavour compared to the more expensive cuts. Serve these with your favourite hot sauce or chilli oil – they are killer. *Pictured on page 108.*

LAMB ARROSTICINI

Mix the lamb shoulder cubes with the olive oil, garlic powder, chilli flakes and a good pinch each of salt and black pepper in a bowl. Leave to marinate in the fridge for a couple of hours, then bring out to come to room temperature about 30 minutes before you wish to eat.

Preheat the barbecue – a coal barbecue will need 30–40 minutes – and soak your skewers (if using bamboo).

Thread the lamb cubes onto the skewers – you want to have around 10cm (4in) left on the end of each one for easy handling.

Using a pestle and mortar, bash the rosemary leaves and sea salt together to make a green rosemary salt.

Carefully lay the arrosticini on the hottest part of the grill of a lovely hot barbecue. They will need about 2–3 minutes on each of the 4 sides until deeply golden all over and slightly charred.

Once they are cooked, pop them onto a plate with the lemon wedges, squeeze over a bit of lemon, sprinkle over the rosemary salt and serve.

MAKE AHEAD
› You can marinate the lamb overnight, if you wish.

SUBSTITUTIONS
› Diced lamb leg, pork shoulder or chicken thigh would also work well, although you would need to cook the pork and chicken through a little bit more carefully.

SCALING
› Allow for 200g (7oz) of meat per person. If reducing the recipe, halve the seasonings.

SERVES 6

3 large aubergines (eggplants)
300g (10½oz) fresh plum
   tomatoes, left whole
   for grilling
3½ tbsp extra virgin olive
   oil, plus extra to serve
1 garlic clove, grated
1 tsp ground cumin
20g (¾oz) fresh dill,
   finely chopped

This is a great salad-dip for a summer party. I love chucking aubergines into the white coals when I am barbecuing as they take on amazing flavour from the charring of their skin and involve hardly any prep. While the aubergines cook, it's nice to softly roast some tomatoes in foil to mix with them – their sweetness balances out any bitterness. Chuck a bit of dill in there and, well, with very few ingredients you've created something extremely delicious! Such is the magic of the barbecue.

COAL ROAST AUBERGINE WITH TOMATOES AND DILL

Preheat the barbecue – a coal barbecue will need 30–40 minutes.

Stab each aubergine in 3–4 places with a knife (this prevents them from exploding as they cook). Tuck them into the hot coals while you barbecue. They will take around 25–30 minutes to cook through. When you see a side becoming particularly charred, then rotate it to make sure they cook evenly.

Meanwhile, create a little tray out of a few sheets of folded foil. Put the tomatoes on the tray and then onto the grill and pop the lid on the barbecue for 10 minutes or so. They will char and blister as they cook, but the tray of foil stops them from melting into nothing. When the tomatoes are bubbling, remove them carefully and leave to cool slightly.

MAKE AHEAD
› I prefer to make this earlier on the day of the barbecue when you are in your prep-grilling stage.

SUBSTITUTIONS
› A couple of charred and finely chopped red (bell) peppers would be delicious instead of the plum tomatoes, and you could coal roast courgettes (zucchini) instead of the aubergines.
› I love dill in this, but coriander (cilantro) would be divine too.

SCALING
› This quantity is great for a sharing spread but you can increase it if you want it to serve more – use 1 aubergine for 2 people as a guide.

Carefully excavate the aubergines from the coals when they are completely soft and their skin is blackened. Pop them on a tray, open them up with a knife and scoop all of their insides out with a spoon. They will release a fair amount of liquid, so put the flesh into a sieve over a bowl or the sink to drain slightly.

Roughly chop the warm tomatoes and put their flesh and juice into a mixing bowl. Finely chop the warm aubergine flesh and unite it with the tomatoes. Stir in the oil, garlic, cumin, salt to taste and half of the dill. Spoon the dip onto plates, drizzle with some extra olive oil and scatter over the rest of the dill to finish.

SERVES 6-8

1kg (2lb 4oz) mixed frozen
    berries
320g (1½ cups + 1 tbsp)
    caster (superfine) sugar
1 tsp vanilla extract
2 strips of fresh lemon peel
2 strips of fresh orange peel
8 slices of soft white bread,
    crusts cut off
200g (7oz) mixed fresh berries,
    to serve
double (heavy) cream, to serve

MAKE AHEAD
› It is vital that you make this
pudding at least a day ahead, but
2 days works, too!

SUBSTITUTIONS
› If you would prefer to make up
your own mix of berries by all means
do, just as long as the frozen weight
is 1kg (2lb 4oz).
› Use plant-based cream to serve
if you'd rather.

SCALING
› Don't try and make a larger single
pudding as your bread slices won't
accommodate a bigger recipe – they
are only long enough for this quantity.
I would just make 2 puddings instead.

My mum rolled this out for dinner parties all the time when I was
growing up and it sounds really strange on paper but it is such a
good pud. It is really easy to make, super cheap and cheerful and
it looks really beautiful in a very retro way.

DESSERT

SUMMER PUDDING

Pop the frozen berries into a large saucepan, then stir in the sugar,
vanilla, lemon and orange peels. Add to a low heat and slowly and
very gently defrost the berries, letting them release their juices.
When the berries have totally defrosted and are just warm, remove
from the heat. Some will have disintegrated slightly – that's fine!
Remove and discard the peels. Drain the berries in a fine sieve for
at least 20 minutes, reserving the juice and the berries separately.

Line a 1 litre (1 quart) pudding bowl or glass bowl with cling film
(plastic wrap), so that there is plenty of overlap; it helps if the
bowl is a bit damp – the cling film sticks better. Take 6 slices of
bread and cut them in half lengthways slightly on the diagonal,
so each piece is a wonky, not very pointy triangle. Dip a piece of
bread into the berry juice briefly, shake off any excess and then lay
it so the thinner end is at the base of the bowl and the thicker end
is towards the top. Take another piece and repeat, but this time
overlap the bread slightly with the first, pressing the edges together
to seal. Continue like this until the whole bowl, apart from the
base, is covered in soaked bread. Take the penultimate slice and cut
it to fit (with overlap) the base. Dip it in the juice and press it into
the base of the bowl, sealing with the bread that is already in there.

Carefully spoon the drained berries into the bread bowl, pressing
gently to fill. There should be a gap between the surface of the
berries and the top of the bread. Soak the final piece of bread in
the berry juice and then lay it over the top of the berries. Fold over
the ends of the bread around the edge and press them down onto
the top piece to seal. Drizzle with 4 tablespoons of berry juice and
cover with the cling film overlap. Weigh down the pud using a
plate that fits in the bowl, topped with 2 cans of beans (or anything
heavy you have to hand). Pop in the fridge to set overnight, or for
at least 8 hours. Chill the remaining berry juice in the fridge too.

When you are ready to serve, remove from the fridge and unwrap
the top layer of cling film, gently loosening the sides. Invert the
bowl onto a serving plate, give it a little tap and it should come
loose. Remove the bowl and cling film and drizzle with a few
spoons of the reserved berry juice. Garnish with fresh berries
and serve in slices with plenty of double cream.

THE TWO HOURS' NOTICE ONE

STARTER

TOMATO AND SALMORIGLIO TOAST

MAIN

RIGATONI AI QUATTRO FORMAGGI

DESSERT

RASPBERRY, ORANGE AND CAMPARI PAVLOVA

Occasionally we can find ourselves put in the position of last-minute hosting. In this instance, I personally think it's perfectly acceptable to just do a cheeseboard and open eight packets of crisps, but *sometimes* it's nice to surprise people too. This dinner party is a toolkit for hosting on the fly, with flair.

Our starter is a speedy classic 'stuff on toast' and requires only a few minutes of work. Our main dish is, of course, everyone's favourite quick meal – cheesy pasta but better. And

our pudding is a showstopping cheat's pavlova, using shop-bought meringue to great effect. The menu is entirely achievable in less than 2 hours – all the preparation it requires is a trip to the shops for anything you might not have. To facilitate this further, I have provided a shopping list so your brain can focus on stealth. As we are doing this in under 2 hours, our 'getting ahead' and mise-en-place tables look a little different too.

ON YOUR MARKS PEOPLE.

SHOPPING LIST

Fruit and Veg	Dairy	Dry Goods and Condiments	Bread	Frozen
1 packet of fresh oregano	100g (3½oz) Gruyère cheese	200ml (generous ¾ cup) extra virgin olive oil	1 large ciabatta	280g (10oz) frozen raspberries
1 packet of fresh rosemary	180g (6¼oz) Gorgonzola Dolce or soft blue cheese	80g (6½ tbsp) caster (superfine) sugar		
1 lemon	180g (6¼oz) Taleggio cheese	flaky sea salt		
1 small packet of fresh parsley	100g (3½oz) Parmesan cheese	700g (1½lb) dried rigatoni pasta		
600g (1lb 5oz) ripe cherry tomatoes	400ml (1¾ cups) double (heavy) cream	black pepper		
1 head of garlic	500g (2 cups) crème fraîche	fresh nutmeg		
1 packet of chives	300ml (1¼ cups) whipping cream	Campari		
2 oranges		50g (generous ⅓ cup) icing (confectioners') sugar		
200g (7oz) fresh raspberries		vanilla bean paste		
		10 meringue nests		

MISE-EN-PLACE

	Tomato and Salmoriglio Toast	Rigatoni ai Quattro Formaggi	Raspberry, Orange and Campari Pavlova
When you get home from the shops	› Make the salmoriglio	–	› Make the coulis
Up 1 hour before guests arrive	› Slice bread › Soften tomatoes in salmoriglio	› Weigh and grate the cheeses › Put water on to boil › Chop chives	› Segment oranges
To finish	› Toast bread, rub with garlic and top with tomatoes and salmoriglio	› Cook pasta and make cheese sauce; toss together › Serve with chives	› Whip cream › Assemble pavlova; serve

SERVES 6

For the salmoriglio
200ml (generous ¾ cup) extra
    virgin olive oil, plus extra
    to serve
10 sprigs of fresh oregano,
    leaves picked and roughly
    chopped
6 sprigs of fresh rosemary,
    leaves picked and finely
    chopped
finely grated zest of 1 lemon
1 tsp caster (superfine) sugar
1 tsp flaky sea salt
large handful of fresh parsley,
    finely chopped

To serve
600g (1lb 5oz) small, ripe
    cherry tomatoes
1 large ciabatta, cut into
    12 slices at an angle
1 garlic clove, peeled

MAKE AHEAD
› You can make the salmoriglio and
tomatoes as soon as you get home from
the shops and let them sit. Just gently
reheat for the toasts when needed.

SUBSTITUTIONS
› If you can't find good-looking ripe
cherry tomatoes but there are plum
tomatoes available, then use them
instead. Cut them into quarters before
gently poaching in the salmoriglio.
› Use thyme instead of oregano or
rosemary, if you need to.

SCALING
› This would also do 20–30 small
toasts as a canapé. If you wish to
reduce or increase, allow for 2 slices
of bread and 100g (3½oz) of tomatoes
per person.

Tomatoes on toast has long been my favourite quick lunch, always
with one riff or another, using up other bits I find in my fridge.
This version is a little bit smarter, a little bit more vibey for a
dinner party but still in its essence a 10-minute dish. Salmoriglio is
a marinade-come-condiment of sorts from Sicily, typically used on
grilled meat and fish. It makes use of hardy herbs like oregano and
rosemary that really perfume its other prerequisite, good olive oil.
I like to use it here almost like a confit for our tomatoes. Warming
them in the salmoriglio makes them tender, sweet and fragrant.
It's an unexpectedly impressive dish, and perfect for when you are
pushed for time.

STARTER

TOMATO AND
SALMORIGLIO TOAST

To make the salmoriglio, mix all the ingredients, apart from the
parsley, together in a saucepan, then add the tomatoes. Put the pan
over a low heat and cook gently for 5 minutes. As the oil heats up,
the tomatoes will soften and the ingredients will become fragrant.

After 5 minutes, turn the heat up and bring the mixture to a gentle
simmer – take care as there may be some spluttering. Cook for
another 2 minutes before removing from the heat. Set aside.

Preheat the grill (broiler) for the bread. Toast the ciabatta slices
under the hot grill on both sides until golden, then while they are
still hot, rub them with the garlic clove.

Stir the parsley into the tomatoes and then pile them onto the
toasts. Drizzle with some more extra virgin olive oil and serve.

THIS DINNER PARTY IS A TOOLKIT FOR HOSTING ON THE FLY, WITH FLAIR.

SERVES 6

400ml (1¾ cups) double
   (heavy) cream
700g (1½lb) dried
   rigatoni pasta
180g (6¼oz) Taleggio
   cheese, rind removed
   and roughly cubed
180g (6¼oz) Gorgonzola
   Dolce cheese, rind removed
100g (3½oz) Gruyère
   cheese, finely grated
100g (3½oz) Parmesan
   cheese, finely grated
1 tsp freshly ground
   black pepper
good grating of fresh nutmeg
large handful of fresh chives,
   finely chopped, to serve

MAKE AHEAD
› Don't make this ahead! You can
prep your cheese, though, if you like.

SUBSTITUTIONS
› Switch up the two funky, creamy
cheeses with whatever other funky,
creamy cheeses you like. Gruyère
could be swapped for mature Cheddar
if you can't find it.

SCALING
› This is the maximum quantity for
one large pan, any more and you will
need to split this over two pans. For
the sauce, you will always need 1.4
times as much cheese as the cream, so
for two people do 100ml (scant ½ cup)
of cream to 180g (6¼oz) of total cheese
and 220g (7¾oz) of pasta.

This is as close as you will get to macaroni and cheese in Italy.
Four-cheese pasta is, quite clearly, delicious every day, but when
you are in a rush it's a spectacular way to feed a crowd. You need a
fair whack of cheese for it, granted, but doesn't nearly everything?
I love the ease of this sauce – no roux needed! You simply melt the
cheese into the double cream and the pasta water does the rest of
the work. Sublime.

MAIN

RIGATONI AI QUATTRO FORMAGGI

Make sure all your cheeses are grated/chopped and ready to go
before starting to cook this dish, as this all needs to come together
fairly quickly.

Bring a large pan of water to the boil for the pasta and season it
well with salt.

Meanwhile, put the double cream into another large saucepan
(that is big enough to stir your cooked pasta in) and set over a
medium heat.

When the cream is just steaming and the water for the pasta is
boiling, you can begin. Drop the pasta into the boiling water and
stir well so that it doesn't stick. It will need around 9 minutes.

Add the Taleggio to the cream, stirring it in gently, until
melted and combined. Add the Gorgonzola and let it melt in
too – take care not to let the mixture boil at any point and turn
the heat down if needed. Stir in the Gruyère next, then finally
the Parmesan. You should have a thick, creamy cheese sauce.
Season the sauce with the black pepper and nutmeg – it will
probably be salty enough.

By the time you've done this, your rigatoni should be perfectly al
dente. Reserve a large mug of pasta water, then drain the pasta in a
colander before transferring it into the pan of cheese sauce. Mix it
in really well, adding just a small splash of pasta water at first. The
sauce will thicken slightly from the starch of the pasta and become
even creamier. Add more pasta water if it needs loosening slightly.
Pile your serving plates high with the cheesy pasta and top with a
sprinkling of chopped chives for freshness.

SERVES 6

For the coulis
280g (10oz) frozen raspberries
5 tbsp caster (superfine) sugar
finely grated zest of 1/2 orange
4 tbsp Campari liqueur

For the cream
500g (2 cups) crème fraîche
300ml (1¼ cups) whipping cream
finely grated zest of 1 large
    orange
50g (generous 1/3 cup) icing
    (confectioners') sugar, sifted
1 tsp vanilla bean paste

For the pavlova
10 shop-bought meringue nests
2 oranges, peeled and segmented
    (you can use the ones you
    zested above)
200g (7oz) fresh raspberries

MAKE AHEAD
› You can make the coulis any time
before your guests arrive.

SUBSTITUTIONS
› Strawberries or blackberries would
be lovely here.
› If you don't have Campari, a red
vermouth or Aperol will work instead.

SCALING
› You can make cute individual
pavlovas if you prefer, with one
meringue nest per person.

Shop-bought meringue is nothing to be ashamed about. In fact, I think it is one of the best inventions of the late-20th century. Don't get me wrong, a beautiful homemade meringue is great, but it just isn't always feasible. This pav is proudly made with shop-bought meringue and it looks absolutely STUNNING, tastes incredible and is the work of mere moments to prepare. Pavlovas can be a little sweet sometimes, but the Campari in the raspberry coulis and the orange segments do a good job of neutralizing that.

DESSERT
RASPBERRY, ORANGE AND CAMPARI PAVLOVA

To make the coulis, place the raspberries, sugar, orange zest and Campari into a bowl and mix well. The Campari will help defrost the raspberries pretty quickly. When the raspberries have softened, blitz the mixture in a blender until smooth, then pass it through a fine sieve to get rid of the seeds. You should be left with a thick, smooth coulis. Set aside.

In a bowl, whip the crème fraîche, whipping cream, orange zest, icing sugar and vanilla together very softly to create soft, barely holding peaks. I like to keep half the cream plain, then gently swirl a couple of tablespoons of the coulis into the other half in 2–3 stirs – no more or the cream will over-whip!

To build the pavlova, create a bottom layer of 4 meringue nests on a serving plate. Add a couple of dollops of each cream, then a few orange segments and fresh raspberries and a good drizzle of coulis. For the next layer, do 3 meringue nests, more of both creams, more fruit, more coulis. Make sure the layer of meringue is securely pressed into the cream. Next do 2 meringues and repeat. When you get to the final meringue and cream layer, make sure you have some fresh raspberries left for the top. Drizzle over a little more coulis and serve with a Campari digestivo alongside.

THE WFH ONE

STARTERS

GILDAS

HAM, EGG AND ROMESCO TOASTS

MAIN

BRAISED MERGUEZ WITH POTATOES AND CHICKPEAS

DESSERT

PEAR AND ALMOND TART

This was one of the most requested menus from friends of mine when I was brainstorming dinner party ideas. Being a freelancer, traditional work-from-home (WFH) set-ups with multiple online meetings and 9–5ish hours aren't something I am actually that familiar with, so I needed some guidance when it came to how this menu could work. I was told that the recipes should be easy to stop and start, or be okay to be left alone should an urgent email come in. They needed to be fridge-friendly, use plenty of ready-made ingredients and have quick stages that can be completed on lunch breaks or just before the guests arrive.

So, this is what I landed on. You can, as usual, start your prep 3 days before, but this menu is totally achievable in one working day too. You'll notice that this menu has a Spanish and Middle Eastern lilt to it; it's dynamic, simple yet chic, and lets the ingredients do the work for you. The hardest bit is getting the shopping done.

GETTING AHEAD

	Gildas	Ham, Egg and Romesco Toasts	Braised Merguez	Pear and Almond Tart
Up to 3 days before	–	› Can boil eggs	› Can make the braised merguez	› Can make the frangipane
Up to 2 days before	–	› Can boil eggs › Can make romesco	› Can make the braised merguez	› Can make the frangipane
Up to 1 day before	–	› Can boil eggs › Can make romesco	› Can make the braised merguez	› Can make the frangipane
On the day	› Assemble gildas	› Toast bread	› Prepare toppings	› Assemble tart › Bake the tart

MISE-EN-PLACE

	Gildas	Ham, Egg and Romesco Toasts	Braised Merguez	Pear and Almond Tart
Up to 6 hours before	› Can assemble the gildas	› Can boil eggs › Can make romesco › Can make toasts	› Can make the braised merguez	› Can assemble tart and bake tart
Up to 1 hour before	› Can assemble the gildas	› Can boil eggs › Can make romesco › Can make toasts	› Prepare toppings	› Can bake tart
To serve	› Serve with crisp dry beverages	› Assemble › Top with jamón and serve	› Serve with toppings	› Serve with clotted cream

SERVES 6

18 good-quality pitted
   green olives
18 good-quality canned or jarred
   anchovy fillets, drained
12–18 pickled jarred guindilla
   chillies, depending on their
   size, tops left on

18 cocktail sticks (toothpicks)

A mainstay on bar menus across the country, so why not in our homes? A gilda is a traditional pintxo from the Basque Country, which entails three of the world's most delicious things – anchovies, olives and pickled chillies. They look so elegant and delightfully retro intertwined on their cocktail sticks, are the work of minutes and taste sensational. Plus, they are the perfect drinking food to get the evening started.

STARTER

GILDAS

You can honestly assemble these any which way, but this is how I prefer to arrange them.

Take each olive and thread it onto a cocktail stick widthways. Next, thread the tip of one anchovy, followed by the tip of a chilli underneath the anchovy. Wrap the anchovy over the other end of the olive, followed by the chilli to envelop it completely.

Serve with extremely cold beverages.

MAKE AHEAD
› These can be assembled up to
6 hours ahead and kept covered
in the fridge until 30 minutes
before serving.

SUBSTITUTIONS
› If you're not a fan of chillies,
a gherkin works nicely instead.

SCALING
› Easy peasy, 1 of everything per
person x by how many you think
your guests will eat, unless your
pickled chillies are massive.

SERVES 6

3 eggs, at room temperature
12 slices of fresh bread, each
    about the thickness of your
    little finger – I like sourdough
    baguette for this
2 tbsp olive oil, plus extra
    to serve
100g (3½oz) jamón serrano,
    slices torn in half

For the romesco
20g (¾oz) stale bread
2 tbsp flaked (slivered) almonds
1 small garlic clove, peeled
1 red chilli
½ tsp smoked paprika
200g (7oz) roasted red (bell)
    peppers from a jar, drained
    well and roughly chopped
1½ tbsp extra virgin olive oil
1 tsp sherry vinegar

MAKE AHEAD
› The eggs can be boiled up to 3
days ahead and kept in the fridge.
› The romesco can be made up to
2 days ahead and kept in the fridge,
just bring it to room temperature
before using.

SUBSTITUTIONS
› If your guests are veggie, this is
just as nice *sans jamón*. You could use
slices of grilled aubergine (eggplant),
asparagus or courgette (zucchini).
› If you don't have almonds, walnuts
or pecans would work here too.
Alternatively, if a guest has a nut
allergy, leave the nuts out and
double the bread quantity.

SCALING
› This romesco recipe makes more
than enough, but if you want to make
around 20, then simply double the
recipe, apart from the garlic. Use a
large clove instead of a small one.
› For perfect yolked slices of egg,
you will need to cook more than you
need, as the ends of the egg are just
white. Allow for an extra egg for every
5 toasts, 2 would do 10 but 3 is better.

I've long said the starter for my death row meal would be a 'toast buffet', where all the possible toasts and their toppings that I could ever want would be available for me to pillage. Toast is a simple thing, but so, so good and an absolute workhorse of a dinner party dish. These are an excellent little starter that takes minutes to put together with prep that can be scattered throughout the working day. Boil your eggs when you have your breakfast, blitz up the romesco while you make lunch, toast the bread when your last call is done. Then all you need to do is open a packet of good jamón and pile them up.

STARTER

HAM, EGG AND ROMESCO TOASTS

Bring a saucepan of water to a rolling boil, then carefully lay in the eggs and boil them for 7 minutes. This should get you some nice, fudgy, but on the side of a harder boil, eggs – perfect for slicing. When the eggs are cooked, immediately transfer them to cold water to chill down. Peel and set aside in the fridge until needed.

To make the romesco sauce, preheat the oven to 160°C fan (180°C/350°F/Gas 4).

Tear the stale bread into small pieces and place on an oven tray with the almonds. Pop into the preheated oven for 8 minutes until the bread is crunchy and the almonds are browned. Keep an eye on them and if the almonds are colouring too quickly, remove them earlier. Let the bread and almonds cool before blitzing them up in a food processor with the remaining ingredients, adding salt to taste. Set aside.

When you're ready to make the toasts, preheat the oven to 180°C fan (200°C/400°F/Gas 6).

Drizzle the fresh bread slices generously with olive oil, then toast them in the preheated oven until just golden, around 10 minutes.

When you are ready to serve, slice each egg into 5–6 slices down the middle. Dollop a tablespoon of romesco onto each piece of toast, then top with a slice of egg. Take a half slice of jamón and drape it over the egg – try and arrange your toppings so you can see a bit of everything, the egg and jamón can be at slightly jaunty angles. Drizzle with a touch more olive oil, then season with salt and pepper and serve.

SERVES 6

For the braise
2 tbsp olive oil
12 merguez sausages
2 onions, thinly sliced
4 garlic cloves, thinly sliced
1 large red chilli, thinly sliced
1 tbsp baharat spice mix
800g (1¾lb) waxy potatoes,
    peeled and thickly sliced
1 x 400-g/14-oz can of plum
    tomatoes, crushed
400ml (1⅔ cups) lamb stock
    (broth)
1 x 660-g/23-oz jar of chickpeas
    (garbanzo beans), drained

For the toppings
½ large cucumber, diced
3 ripe plum tomatoes, deseeded
    and diced
1 small red onion, diced
generous pinch of salt
200ml (generous ¾ cup) natural
    (plain) yogurt
1 garlic clove, grated
small bunch of fresh mint leaves,
    finely chopped
small bunch of fresh parsley
    leaves, finely chopped

MAKE AHEAD
› The braise can be made up to 3
days ahead and will improve with age.

SUBSTITUTIONS
› If you can't get merguez, use a good-
quality butcher's sausage and add an
extra tbsp of baharat to your braise.
› The toppings here are very flexible,
try avocado or diced red (bell) pepper
in the salad, swap in dill or coriander
(cilantro), and crumble over feta
instead of yogurt.

SCALING
› This recipe is easily reduced by half,
allowing for at least 2 sausages per
person. If making a larger quantity,
prep the braise in 2 pans and place
in 1 or 2 large oven dishes to cook at
160ºC fan (180ºC/350ºF/Gas 4) for
40–50 minutes, if that relieves your
hob for a bit.

Sausages are a huge time saver. Their meat is seasoned and primed,
they are already perfectly portioned, they don't take long to cook
and they perfume everything that cooks around them. A sausage
like merguez, spiced and rich, is brilliant here cooked slowly with
potatoes and chickpeas, all in one pot with very little fussing. A
glorious, cocklewarming dish that is hugely gratifying to make and
serve. I've added a couple of easy toppings, too, for a bit of glam,
which you can leave scattered across the table for a bountiful feast.

MAIN

BRAISED MERGUEZ WITH POTATOES AND CHICKPEAS

Put the olive oil into a large, wide saucepan or casserole dish over
a medium heat. Add the sausages and brown them off; you may
need to do this in batches depending on the size of your pan. When
all the sausages are lightly browned on all sides, set them aside on
a plate. You will be left with the divine merguez fat in the pan.

Add the onions to the pan and fry them for around 10–12 minutes,
until they are just starting to get golden edges. Add the garlic,
chilli and baharat spice mix and cook for another 4–5 minutes
until the garlic is beginning to turn golden, then add the potatoes
and stir well to coat. Pour in the tomatoes, lamb stock and
chickpeas. Bring to a simmer, season well with salt and pepper,
then nestle the sausages back into the pan. Turn the heat down
low to bring the mixture to a gentle bubble, then cover with a
piece of baking parchment on the surface of the stew (the paper
lets the sauce reduce a bit more than using a lid, but it won't
completely dry out). Cook gently for 40–50 minutes until the
potatoes are tender and the sauce is slightly thicker.

To make the toppings, combine the cucumber, tomatoes and
red onion with the salt in a bowl. Mix the yogurt with the garlic
and another pinch of salt to taste.

Serve the hot stew in two deep platters for the table, topped
with the salad and mint and parsley with the garlic yogurt for
your guests to dollop themselves.

SERVES 6-8

2–3 ripe pears
freshly squeezed juice of
   1/2 lemon
1 tbsp demerara/raw cane sugar
1 x 320g (11½oz) sheet of
   ready-rolled puff pastry
1 tbsp flaked (slivered) almonds
1 tbsp icing (confectioners')
   sugar, sifted
clotted cream, to serve

For the frangipane
100g (½ cup minus 1 tbsp)
   soft butter
100g (½ cup) golden caster
   (superfine) sugar
2 eggs
2 tbsp plain (all-purpose) flour
100g (1 cup) ground almonds
pinch of salt
25g (⅓ cup) desiccated
   (dried shredded) coconut

MAKE AHEAD
› The frangipane will keep in the fridge for up to 5 days. Bring it to room temperature before using.
› You can prep the tart as a whole and leave it in the fridge, ready to bake, up to 6 hours before, just give it an extra 5 minutes in the oven at 180°C fan (200°C/400°F/Gas 6).
› You can bake the tart up to 6 hours before and warm it in the oven at 160°C fan (180°C/350°F/Gas 4) for 10 minutes before serving.

SUBSTITUTIONS
› Swap pears for apples, poached quince or rhubarb, sliced pineapple, any stone fruit or strawberries, blueberries and raspberries.
› Pine nuts or pistachios are a delicious topping, and you could use ground pistachios in the frangipane.

SCALING
› If cooking for more, scale your quantities according to how many sheets of puff you will use. For a smaller tart, the frangipane is easily divisible by half, just use 1 tbsp of coconut instead and you may find mixing by hand easier.

When we were little this is a pudding my mum would always let us help her make; that's how easy it is to do. There's nothing new here, all the flavours are deeply comforting and familiar and that's what I love about it. Sheets of puff pastry are really a magnificent invention, as is frangipane – together with pears they are unstoppable. Plus, once you have the frangipane and the pastry covered, the fruits and additional toppings are very interchangeable. I love a recipe that is also a blueprint, and this is certainly one of those.

DESSERT
PEAR AND ALMOND TART

Start by making the frangipane. Cream together the butter and sugar for a couple of minutes until pale – it's not a huge amount to work with so this can be done by hand or using a hand-held electric whisk or in a stand mixer. Beat in the eggs, one at a time, adding 1 tablespoon of the flour with each egg. Fold in the ground almonds, the salt and the coconut to make a smooth, thick batter (I love sneaking in the coconut here, it's not enough to overpower or affect the texture but it gives such a lovely fragrant hum of old-fashioned baking).

Preheat the oven to 180°C fan (200°C/400°F/Gas 6).

Peel, core and slice the pears, then coat them in the lemon juice and demerara sugar in a bowl. Gently unroll your sheet of puff pastry onto an oven tray (on its paper). Dollop the frangipane onto the pastry, spreading it all over but leaving a 2.5cm (1in) border of plain pastry round the edges. Arrange the pear slices all over the top in a single layer – you might not need all of them. Pop into the preheated oven to bake for 20 minutes, then turn the heat up to 200°C fan (220°C/425°F/Gas 7) and bake for another 20 minutes. When there are 10 minutes of cooking time left, quickly whip out the tart, sprinkle over the flaked almonds and return to the oven.

When the tart is a deep golden colour and the nuts are toasted, remove from the oven and leave to cool slightly – this can be served warm or at room temperature. Dust with the icing sugar and serve with heaped spoonfuls of clotted cream.

THIS MENU HAS A SPANISH AND MIDDLE EASTERN LILT TO IT; IT'S DYNAMIC, SIMPLE YET CHIC.

THE ALTERNATIVE ROAST ONE

TRIMMINGS

BUTTERED LEEKS AND CHILLI OIL

CHICKEN-FAT CROUTONS

BRAISED LENTILS

MAIN

ROAST CHICKEN WITH PEPPERS, ONIONS AND SALSA VERDE

DESSERT

SUNDAY CRUMBLE

Roast dinners are a quintessential British meal, and rightly so. I, however, don't often have mine in the quintessentially British style. I love the principle of the meal – a piece of meat and tons of sides for sharing – but the repetitive, restrictive nature of it just drove me bonkers. Roast chicken is still my favourite, but I want vibrancy, I want texture and I want each mouthful to sing in perfect balance. I think that is what a roast dinner is all about – the perfect mouthful. And my mouth wants to be wowed.

When hosting and roasting, trying to get everything done at the same time while also looking after your guests is tricky. Freeing yourself from the notion that the potatoes and carrots and whatever else has to be ready at exactly the same time as the bird is part one of unlearning the roast dinner. I love to do veg that cooks under the bird. I mix up my carbs, and make a sauce in the blender rather than having to wait to make a last-minute pan gravy.

GETTING AHEAD

	Buttered Leeks	Chicken-fat Croutons	Braised Lentils	Roast Chicken	Sunday Crumble
Up to 3 days before	–	–	› Can make lentils	–	› Can make crumble topping
Up to 2 days before	–	–	› Can make lentils	› Can prep veg for tray	› Can make crumble topping
Up to 1 day before	–	› Can make croutons	› Can make lentils	› Can prep veg for tray › Can make salsa verde	› Can make crumble topping
On the day	› Cook leeks	› Make croutons	› Make lentils	› Prep chicken › Roast veg › Make salsa verde	› Make and bake crumble

MISE-EN-PLACE

	Buttered Leeks	Chicken-fat Croutons	Braised Lentils	Roast Chicken	Sunday Crumble
Up to 6 hours before	› Can make leeks	› Can make croutons	› Can make lentils	› Can prep veg › Can make salsa verde › Spatchcock chicken	› Can make crumble topping and fruit base
Up to 1 hour before	› Can make leeks	› Gently warm croutons in the oven	› Gently reheat lentils	› Roast chicken and rest	› Assemble and bake crumble
To serve	› Reheat leeks and serve with the chilli oil	› Serve with chicken	› Serve with chicken	› Carve chicken and serve	› Serve with custard

SERVES 6 AS A SIDE

90g (¹/₃ cup + 2 tsp) butter
90ml (¹/₃ cup) water
1kg (2lb 4oz) leeks, washed,
    trimmed and sliced into 2cm
    (³/₄in) medallions – I like to
    cut them on the bias
1–2 tbsp chilli oil, depending
    on how hot you like it

I have a medical addiction to leeks and I don't understand why they seem to be so neglected as a hero vegetable. They are sweet, unctuous, a vehicle for all fat and a perfect roast accompaniment, especially as they don't need much help. In this case, butter and water are all you need to get things going and the final, optional, flourish of your favourite chilli oil just brightens and lifts what is already very delicious.

TRIMMINGS

BUTTERED LEEKS AND CHILLI OIL

Put the butter and water into the bottom of a wide saucepan or casserole dish, along with the leeks (in one layer if possible) and a generous pinch of salt. Pop the lid on, then place over a medium heat. Bring to a simmer, then turn the heat down slightly and leave to gently steam and soften for 20–25 minutes, checking every so often and turning them. The leeks will release their own liquid and will soften and become tender in the butter. Check they are cooked by piercing them with a butter knife, there should be no resistance.

Serve in their cooking juices, drizzled with your favourite chilli oil.

MAKE AHEAD
› You can cook the leeks a couple of days before but they are more likely to lose their shape. They will hold well if cooked on the day and kept covered until needed.

SUBSTITUTIONS
› Leave out the chilli oil, if you prefer, or use a bit of mustard in the butter if you would like a more subtle heat.

SCALING
› Roughly half a leek per person is a good amount for a side.
› If doing a larger quantity, make sure to use more than one pan, it is important that the leeks are not piled up as they won't cook evenly.

SERVES 6 AS A SIDE

chicken fat from the cavity
of the bird
80ml (1/3 cup) vegetable oil
1 garlic clove, bashed
3 slices of stale sourdough
bread, diced

Roast potatoes are God tier but they require a lot of attention and a lot of oven opening and shuffling, both of which are less than ideal while hosting and trying to cook a chicken perfectly. Another thing that is God tier is bread. Some people eat roast poultry with bread sauce, which I actually don't go a bundle on, but bread sauce 'reversed' (or not quite, but sort of) is chicken-fat croutons. And they are bloody great. *Pictured on page 142.*

TRIMMINGS
CHICKEN-FAT CROUTONS

Pop the chicken fat into a large frying pan (skillet) and place over a low heat. As the pan warms, the fat will start to render and melt. Leave this to slowly sizzle for 10–15 minutes, until you have at least 1–2 tablespoons of molten fat in the pan.

Turn the heat up to medium and add the vegetable oil. Add the garlic and fry for a couple of minutes before adding the bread cubes. Fry the bread gently in the fat on all sides until it's crisp and golden – around 10 minutes. Remove the bread from the pan and drain any excess oil on some kitchen paper (paper towels). Season with salt and pepper and keep warm until needed.

MAKE AHEAD
› The croutons can be made up to 1 day ahead and kept at room temperature in a sealed container. Simply reheat them in the oven as it cools after the chicken has roasted.

SUBSTITUTIONS
› Ciabatta also works well instead of sourdough bread.

SCALING
› To make more croutons than this, it may be worth purchasing some extra chicken thighs and harvesting their fat from the skin and periphery. I do this and then freeze the thighs for a curry another day.
› This recipe is easily doubled or halved, just keep the garlic the same even if doing less.

SERVES 6 AS A SIDE

8 smoked streaky bacon
    rashers, diced
3 tbsp olive oil
1 onion, finely chopped
1 carrot, peeled and finely
    chopped
2 sticks of celery, finely chopped
100ml (scant 1/2 cup) dry white
    vermouth
2 fresh bay leaves, torn
200g (7oz) dried Puy lentils or
    green lentils (French lentils)
800ml (3 1/3 cups) chicken stock
    (broth)

MAKE AHEAD

› This dish can be made up to
3 days in advance. Gently reheat
on the hob before serving.

SUBSTITUTIONS

› Leave out the bacon if you prefer.
› Fennel bulb is a lovely addition
here, along with a pinch of dried
chilli flakes.

SCALING

› This recipe serves 6 as a side, but
it would serve 4 as a more substantial
accompaniment. If you reduce the
recipe quantites, keep the soffritto
(aka the veg), bacon and wine
amounts the same, just reduce the
lentils and the stock; you will need
roughly 4 times as much stock as
lentils and around 30–50g (1–2oz)
of lentils per person.
› If you want to increase the recipe,
double the whole thing to serve at
least 12 people as a side.

A pulse is a gorgeous swap for a traditional roast accompaniment.
I love lentils with roast chicken, and lentils and salsa verde go
together like a wink and a smile, so this is truly a sublime trio.
Plus, these can be prepared days ahead, will only improve with
time and feed a crowd exceptionally easily. AND, if I haven't sold
you on it already, they will go great in a leftover chicken soup.
Pictured on page 142.

TRIMMINGS

BRAISED LENTILS

Put the bacon into a large, heavy-based saucepan set over a medium
heat. As the pan heats up, the bacon fat will render, but add some
of the olive oil if you need it. Fry for 10–12 minutes until crisp, then
add the onion, carrot and celery (your classic soffritto base) and
any remaining oil. Cook the soffritto and bacon together until the
vegetables have started to soften – another 10 minutes or so.

Pour in the vermouth and scrape up any crispy bits from the base
of the pan, then simmer for 1–2 minutes until reduced by half.

Stir in the bay leaves, lentils, chicken stock and a generous pinch
of salt and bring up to a simmer. Cook gently for 40 minutes over a
medium heat, until the lentils are just tender and most of the liquid
has been absorbed. If you need to add more liquid during cooking,
just top up the pan with a little water. Season again with salt to
taste and keep warm until needed.

SERVES 6

For the chicken

1 large free-range chicken,
    approx. 2–2.5kg
    (4¹/₂–5¹/₂lb), ask your butcher
    to remove the wishbone and
    spatchcock it for you
    (or follow the steps below and
    spatchcock it yourself)
2 onions, thinly sliced
3 red (bell) peppers, deseeded
    and cut into chunks
3 yellow (bell) peppers, deseeded
    and cut into chunks
6 garlic cloves, unpeeled
60ml (¹/₄ cup) extra virgin
    olive oil
2 tbsp flaky sea salt, plus extra
    for seasoning
1 tsp freshly ground black
    pepper, plus extra for
    seasoning

For the salsa verde

1 tbsp capers
1 garlic clove, peeled
2 canned or jarred anchovy
    fillets, drained
1 tsp Dijon mustard
30g (1oz) fresh parsley leaves
20g (³/₄oz) fresh tarragon leaves
10g (¹/₄oz) fresh dill leaves
10g (¹/₄oz) fresh mint leaves
100ml (scant ¹/₂ cup) olive oil
squeeze of fresh lemon juice

This is honestly my favourite way to cook a roast chicken, and it is one of my most requested dishes from loved ones. The onions and peppers under the chicken get charred and also almost confit, so they create the most intensely delicious condiment for your bird. The chicken itself is juicy and crisp-skinned, and cooks in under an hour. The salsa verde is the perfect refreshing, piquant and savoury foil for the rich dish, and so easy to make. Not to mention that these things make an absolutely killer sandwich if you have leftovers. Ideally, use a free-range and ethically reared chicken. *Pictured on page 142.*

MAIN

ROAST CHICKEN WITH PEPPERS, ONIONS AND SALSA VERDE

Remove the chicken from the fridge 30 minutes before you want to cook it.

Preheat the oven to 220°C fan (240°C/475°F/Gas 9).

Remove the large fat deposits from inside the cavity of the chicken and set them aside for the chicken-fat croutons (see page 138). If your chicken is already spatchcocked, you can skip the next step; if you are doing it yourself, follow these steps:

Flip the bird over on a chopping board so it is breast-side down, with the parson's nose (bottom) closest to you. Take a pair of good kitchen scissors, or even some very clean garden secateurs, and using the sides of the parson's nose as your guide, cut down either side of the chicken's spine to remove it completely. Do this carefully, the bones are brittle but might need a bit of force to crunch through them. When the spine is removed, flip the bird over and use the heel of your hand to press down hard in the middle of the breast bone to flatten the bird. The advantage of preparing the chicken like this is that it levels it out, making sure the legs and breasts cook at the same time in the oven.

Find a roasting tray that is large enough to accommodate your spatchcocked bird and put the onions, peppers and garlic into the bottom, along with half of the extra virgin olive oil and plenty of salt and pepper. Mix it all together well.

MAKE AHEAD

› The peppers, onions and garlic can all sit prepped in the tray in the fridge for up to 2 days before being cooked, just make sure to season them only just before roasting.

› The salsa verde can be made up to 24 hours before it's needed, but is best made fresh on the day.

SUBSTITUTIONS

› Use courgettes (zucchini), red onions or fennel in your veg mix instead, if you like.

› The salsa verde herb ratios can be adjusted if you have more of one herb than the other, just make sure the total weight of leaves is the same. Basil is good, too, but it can be a bit overpowering.

SCALING

› If you are cooking for less than 6 people, reduce the pepper quantity by 1 per head, but keep the onions the same unless cooking for only 2, in which case just use one. You can use a 1.6kg (3½lb) chicken for 4 people.

› If you are cooking for more than 6 people, you will need to do 2 birds. Divide the peppers and onions between the two roasting trays.

› It will take longer to cook 2 birds in the same oven, as the one on the lower rack will not crisp up as much as the higher one. Keep rotating them during cooking and cook for 1 hour and 10 minutes in total before resting.

Lay the chicken on top, breast-side up but opened out like a book, so the legs are completely exposed too. Drizzle over the remaining olive oil, sprinkle over the sea salt flakes and black pepper and rub it all into the skin, taking care to get inside any creases. Place the chicken tray on the highest rack and roast in the preheated oven for 50 minutes, turning the tray round once or twice to ensure the skin is evenly golden.

Remove from the oven and leave to rest for 15 minutes.

To make the salsa verde, place all the ingredients in a blender, adding salt to taste, and blitz until relatively smooth.

When the chicken has rested, pop it onto a board. I like to portion the chicken ahead of taking it to the table – doing so is much easier if the butcher has already removed the wishbone and if you have a properly sharp knife. First, run a knife between the breast and the thighs, then pop the thigh bones out to completely release them. Find the hinge between the drumstick and the thigh and cut through it to separate them. Run the knife down the side of the breast bone to release the breast on each side. Take your time and try to keep the knife as close to the breast plate as possible. Release each breast and slice it into 4–5 thick slices. Finally, remove the wings and arrange all the chicken pieces on a platter, either with the delicious peppers and onions or the crispy chicken-fat croutons (page 138). Serve with the salsa on the side for guests to drizzle over.

SERVES 6

For the crumble topping
350g (2²/₃ cups) plain
    (all-purpose) flour
200g (³/₄ cup + 2 tbsp) cold butter,
    diced
220g (1 cup + 1 tbsp) golden caster
    (superfine) sugar
½ tsp ground cinnamon
75g (2²/₃oz) chopped nuts of your
    choice – pecans are delicious
1 tsp baking powder
½ tsp flaky sea salt
custard, to serve

For the fruit filling
3 Bramley apples (or Granny
    Smith apples), peeled,
    cored and roughly chopped
3 ripe Conference pears
    (or Bosc pears), peeled,
    cored and roughly chopped
250g (9oz) frozen or fresh
    blackberries
120g (²/₃ cup minus 1 tbsp) golden
    caster (superfine) sugar
1 tbsp cornflour (cornstarch)
1 tbsp vanilla bean paste
finely grated zest and freshly
    squeezed juice of 1 lemon
freshly squeezed juice of 1 orange

MAKE AHEAD
› You can make the crumble topping
up to 3 days ahead and keep tightly
sealed in a bag or container in the
fridge until needed. Simply blitz
again in the food processor to loosen.
› You can bake and reheat the crumble
when needed, but it may lose its
juiciness a bit – be warned.

SUBSTITUTIONS
› Apples and pears could be swapped
or joined by peaches and plums,
or even some very ripe rhubarb.
Blackcurrants, raspberries and
strawberries are also lovely.

SCALING
› This recipe is easily halved or
doubled. If baking 2 crumbles at a
time, allow up to 20 minutes extra
cooking time. Don't forget to rotate
the crumbles in the oven as they cook.

I call this Sunday crumble only because growing up, we would
most often eat crumble on Sundays, regularly making use of
whatever was left in the fruit bowl. Crucially, our crumble would
have almost double the recommended amount of topping. Mine
and my mum's favourite bit of a crumble is the bit of slightly
claggy crumble dough that is underneath the uppermost crunchy
layer and just above the fruit. If a recipe is sparse on topping, then
this bit is sacrificed and we simply will not allow it. Here I've
combined apples and pears and blackberries, because I love the
pear's fragrance against the apple's sharpness.

DESSERT

SUNDAY CRUMBLE

To make the crumble topping, blitz the flour and butter together
in a food processor until the mix resembles breadcrumbs. Add
the sugar, cinnamon, nuts, baking powder and salt and blitz again
briefly to combine. Keep the mixture in the fridge while you make
the fruit filling.

In an ovenproof crumble dish, mix the apples, pears and
blackberries with the sugar, cornflour, vanilla and fruit zest
and juice. Leave to marinate in the dish until needed.

Preheat the oven to 180°C fan (200°C/400°F/Gas 6).

Cover the top of the fruit in the dish with the crumble topping,
making sure it is completely enveloped. Pop into the preheated
oven for around 50 minutes, until the top is golden brown and
crisp. Remove and leave to stand for 5 minutes before serving
with hot or cold custard.

I WANT VIBRANCY, I WANT TEXTURE AND I WANT EACH MOUTHFUL TO SING IN PERFECT BALANCE.

THE ONE FROM BOLOGNA

ANTIPASTI

MORTADELLA, RICOTTA AND PISTACHIO CROSTINI

FUNGHI SOTT'OLIO WITH CELERY AND PARMESAN

MAIN

LASAGNE ALLA BOLOGNESE

DESSERT

COFFEE PANNA COTTA WITH GINGER AND GRISSINI

This menu is dedicated to my favourite city in Italy – Bologna. Affectionately known as 'La Grassa' or 'The Fat One', for its rich culinary traditions and fairly rich food.

There are many amazing dishes from this fabulous city's cuisine that would be perfect for a dinner party, but none more famous than lasagne alla bolognese. This is a bit of a process to make but so very worth it.

The feeling of setting down a perfectly executed and stunningly delicious lasagne on a table full of friends is like getting the deciding question in a pub quiz right and winning the trophy – it's unbeatable.

If the lasagne does feel like too much to do, then I highly recommend making the bolognese ragù in any case and serving it with some fresh tagliatelle.

GETTING AHEAD

	Mortadella, Ricotta and Pistachio Crostini	Funghi Sott'olio with Celery and Parmesan	Lasagne Alla Bolognese	Coffee Panna Cotta with Ginger and Grissini
Up to 3 days before	–	› Can pickle mushrooms	› Can make bolognese › Can make béchamel	–
Up to 2 days before	–	› Can pickle mushrooms	› Can make bolognese › Can make béchamel	› Can do coffee infusion
Up to 1 day before	–	› Can pickle mushrooms	› Can make bolognese › Can make béchamel › Can make pasta and assemble lasagne	› Do coffee infusion › Set panna cottas
On the day	› Toast bread › Top with ricotta and mortadella	› Slice celery; shave Parmesan; chop parsley; bring mushrooms to room temperature	› Make pasta and assemble lasagne › Bake	› Chop stem ginger › De-mould panna cottas

MISE-EN-PLACE

	Mortadella, Ricotta and Pistachio Crostini	Funghi Sott'olio with Celery and Parmesan	Lasagne Alla Bolognese	Coffee Panna Cotta with Ginger and Grissini
Up to 8 hours before	› Can toast bread	–	› Can make pasta › Can make/reheat béchamel › Reheat ragù › Assemble lasagne	› Can chop stem ginger; leave at room temperature
Up to 2 hours before	› Bring ricotta to room temperature › Chop pistachios	› Bring mushrooms to room temperature › Shave celery and Parmesan › Chop parsley	› Bake lasagne; leave to stand	› Chop stem ginger; leave at room temperature › Crush grissini
To serve	› Top crostini with ricotta, mortadella and pistachios	› Assemble salad and serve	› Revel in the glorious moment of setting this lasagne down on your table	› Dip moulds in hot water to de-mould › Serve with stem ginger and grissini

MAKES 12 CROSTINI

1 small ciabatta, sliced into
    12 thin slices
2–3 tbsp olive oil, plus extra
    to serve (optional)
1 garlic clove, peeled
250g (9oz) ricotta cheese
100g (3½oz) sliced mortadella
1 tbsp shelled pistachios,
    roughly chopped

MAKE AHEAD
› You can toast your ciabatta slices
earlier the same day and leave them
to cool before transferring to a lined,
airtight container.

SUBSTITUTIONS
› Mortadella can be swapped with
literally any good, thinly sliced
Italian salumi – prosciutto, parma
ham, fennel salami, etc. If you want
to reduce your meat intake or have
veggie guests, use grilled marinated
artichokes or aubergines (eggplants)
instead and a sprinkling of chopped
parsley, if you like.
› Ricotta is lovely here because it is
so divinely creamy and easy to eat,
but if you can't get hold of it then
mascarpone or mozzarella would
work very well.

SCALING
› One small ciabatta sliced into 12,
serves 6; so the easiest way to increase
this recipe is to double it or use a
larger baguette to serve more. Add
40g (2 tbsp) of ricotta and 15g (one
slice) of mortadella per person.

Crostini, or rather 'things on toast', are literally a gift to a party
menu. Everyone wants to eat them, they look great and they
are easy as hell, especially if you build them using ready-to-eat
ingredients. Mortadella is Bologna's most famous cured meat, and
I adore it. This combination with ricotta and pistachios is by no
means original, but it is very, very good and incredibly quick to
put together. *Pictured on page 151.*

ANTIPASTI

MORTADELLA, RICOTTA AND PISTACHIO CROSTINI

Preheat the oven to 180°C fan (200°C/400°F/Gas 6).

Lay the sliced bread onto an oven tray and drizzle with the olive
oil, turning and smearing both sides of the bread in it for optimum
coverage and crispness.

Toast the bread in the preheated oven for 10 minutes, or until all
the toasts are evenly golden. Keep an eye on them and take any out
that are getting darker more quickly; ovens often have hot spots
and this can happen. When the toasts are out of the oven, rub each
one with the garlic clove – the hot bread will suck up that garlic
flavour. Transfer the toasts to some kitchen paper (paper towels)
to drain any excess oil and cool.

When you are ready to serve, season the ricotta with salt and
pepper and then use a spoon to dollop it onto the toasts. If your
mortadella is in large slices, then you may need to tear it up into
smaller pieces. Drape your mortadella in glorious meaty pink
ruffles on top of the crostini. Finally, sprinkle each toast with
some chopped pistachios and a drizzle more olive oil, if you like.

CROSTINI, OR RATHER 'THINGS ON TOAST', ARE LITERALLY A GIFT TO A PARTY MENU.

SERVES 6

For the pickled mushrooms

200g (7oz) shiitake mushrooms,
    cut into small pieces
200g (7oz) baby button
    mushrooms, quartered
300g (10½oz) chestnut
    mushrooms, sliced
300ml (1¼ cups) white
    wine vinegar
6½ tbsp caster
    (superfine) sugar
2 tsp fine salt
10g (¼oz) dried porcini
    mushrooms
2 tsp black peppercorns, crushed
200ml (generous ¾ cup) extra
    virgin olive oil
8 fresh bay leaves
peel from 1 lemon
2 garlic cloves, bashed
1 red chilli, halved lengthways
small handful of finely chopped
    fresh parsley

For the salad

6 sticks of celery, shaved or
    very thinly sliced
70g (2½oz) 24–30 month-old
    Parmesan cheese, shaved

MAKE AHEAD

› The mushrooms literally HAVE to
be made ahead, so do that then don't
worry about the rest until it's dinner
time! The mushrooms keep for up to
1 week in the fridge.

SUBSTITUTIONS

› Feel free to swap celery for a mix of
rocket (arugula) and sugar snap peas.
› I love the mushrooms on a dollop of
good ricotta – the creaminess works
well with the piquant pickle.
› Mix up the mushrooms! Enoki and
pioppini are so lovely pickled, as well
as girolles or chanterelles if you can
get your hands on them.

SCALING

› I like to double the recipe and save
half to have with scrambled eggs or on
pizza. If you want to reduce the recipe,
it may be worth using just one type of
mushroom as the quantities are small.

September in Italy is when porcini season is in full swing, and
you can find in most restaurants a delicious salad of raw porcini,
celery and Parmesan. Porcini are expensive and hard to come by
over here, but I've got a great swap. It might sound bizarre, but
the funky mushroom is balanced spectacularly by the refreshing
shaved celery and salty, brazen cheese. Funghi sott'olio are lightly
pickled mushrooms that are then preserved 'under oil', and they
work just as well here with the celery and Parmesan providing a
savoury, sour kick and a ready-made dressing. Moreover, they are
much better after a few days in the fridge, meaning you don't have
much to do for your guests on the night. Make sure you get lots of
good bread for mopping up the delicious juices.

ANTIPASTI

FUNGHI SOTT'OLIO WITH CELERY AND PARMESAN

Use a clean, damp cloth or some kitchen paper (paper towels)
to clean any muck off your mushrooms and trim any soily feet.

In a large saucepan, combine the vinegar, sugar, salt, dried porcini
and peppercorns with 700ml (3 cups) of cold water and bring to
the boil. When the pickling liquid is boiling, tip in the cleaned,
fresh mushrooms and simmer for 7 minutes over a medium heat.

Remove from the heat and drain the mushrooms, reserving a
couple of tablespoons of the pickling liquid. In a clean container
large enough to fit all the mushrooms inside, mix the reserved
pickling liquid with the extra virgin olive oil, bay leaves, lemon
peel, garlic cloves and chilli and then add the mushrooms. Cover
the container with a lid and chill in the fridge for at least 24 hours.

Before you want to serve the mushrooms, make sure to bring them
to room temperature. Remove the bay leaves, lemon peel, garlic
and chilli and mix in the chopped parsley. Spread the mushrooms
out over a couple of plates and then tuck in pieces of shaved celery
and a few shavings of Parmesan. Finish with plenty more Parmesan
shavings on top. I love to eat this with warm focaccia.

**SERVES 6, WITH LOTS LEFTOVER
FOR BREAKFAST THE NEXT DAY**

For the ragù bolognese

1 onion, peeled

1 large carrot, peeled

3 sticks of celery

3 tbsp olive oil, plus extra
   for lasagne sheets

160g (5½oz) sliced cured meat
   such as mortadella, salami,
   prosciutto or a mix

100g (3½oz) sliced pancetta

500g (1lb 2oz) minced (ground)
   beef, 20% fat

400g (14oz) minced (ground) veal

500g (1lb 2oz) minced (ground)
   pork, 20% fat

2 fresh bay leaves

1 Parmesan rind

600ml (2½ cups) tomato passata
   (strained tomatoes)

200ml (generous ¾ cup) red wine

175ml (¾ cup) whole milk

500ml (generous 2 cups) beef
   stock (broth)

salt and black pepper

For the béchamel sauce

110g (scant ½ cup) butter

1.3 litres (5½ cups) whole milk

110g (¾ cup + 1½ tbsp) plain
   (all-purpose) flour

½ tsp freshly grated nutmeg

salt and black pepper

For the spinach pasta

400g (scant 3¼ cups) '00' pasta
   flour, plus extra for dusting

60g (2¼oz) baby spinach leaves,
   dried well if at all damp

2 eggs

fine semolina, for dusting

To assemble

600g (1lb 5oz) fresh lasagne
   sheets (see pasta recipe above
   or you can use shop-bought)

125g (4½oz) Parmesan cheese,
   finely grated

Large, deep roasting tin or dish
   – at least 35cm x 25cm
   (14 x 10in) or 40cm x 28cm
   (16 x 11in)

For spinach pasta, you will need
   a powerful bullet blender and
   a pasta machine

This is my version of a traditional Bolognese lasagne – simply ragù, béchamel, fresh spinach pasta and Parmesan. It is a bit of work and a two-day process, but the result is truly sublime. If you don't have a pasta machine, you can just buy fresh lasagne sheets and blanch them as per the method. You'll still achieve the show-stopping layers – an absolute dinner party winner. *Pictured on pages 154–155.*

MAIN

LASAGNE ALLA BOLOGNESE

Cook the bolognese at least a day in advance to intensify and unify the flavours. For the ragù, pulse the onion, carrot and celery in a food processor until finely chopped. Heat the oil in a large casserole dish over a medium heat and add the mixed chopped vegetables. Cook gently for 15 minutes until soft, sweet and lightly golden. Meanwhile, pulse the cured meat and pancetta in a food processor until it is roughly the same texture as your minced meat. Once the veg is soft, add in the meat products one at a time (cured, pancetta, beef, veal, pork), breaking down any big lumps and stirring each addition very well. Once all added, cook for 15 minutes to evaporate any liquid in the pan (we don't want to brown the meat here, just dry it out a bit). Add the bay leaves, Parmesan rind, passata, wine, milk and stock and bring to a simmer. Season generously with salt and pepper, cover with a lid and leave to simmer over a low heat for 3½ hours, stirring and checking every so often. Once cooked, it should be a uniformly soft, unctuous and deeply savoury sauce. Leave to cool and chill in the fridge overnight.

For the béchamel sauce, melt the butter in a large saucepan over a medium heat. Warm the milk in another pan. When the butter is sizzling, whisk in the flour to make a roux. Cook for a couple of minutes, then add your first ladle of warm milk and whisk into the roux to make a thick, smooth paste. Once it is just about bubbling again, whisk in a bit more milk. Repeat until all the milk is added in. Bring to a gentle simmer and cook for 5 minutes. Remove from the heat, season very generously with salt, pepper and fresh nutmeg. Cover the surface of the béchamel with cling film (plastic wrap) to stop it from getting a skin and then set aside until needed.

For the spinach pasta, ensure your leaves are dry (pat them with kitchen paper if needed). For best results, blitz half the flour and half the spinach together in your blender to make a bright green powder. Pass the mix through a fine sieve, discarding any big lumps of stalk. Repeat with the remaining spinach and flour, and combine both batches in a bowl. Beat the eggs in another bowl with 4 tablespoons of water. Make a well in the flour mix and pour in the eggs. Use a fork to bring together the flour and eggs, then

MAKE AHEAD

› The ragù and béchamel can both be made up to 3 days ahead. The lasagne itself can be assembled the day before and cooked on the day.

SUBSTITUTIONS

› If you prefer to avoid veal, then make up the weights with more beef. If you don't eat pork, then make up the weight of the pork mince, cured meat and pancetta with more beef once again.

› If you want to make a simple egg pasta instead of the spinach pasta, just omit the spinach and add an extra egg to the flour – there's no need to blend anything, just mix, knead and rest.

SCALING

› If you want to make a smaller lasagne, I would advise still cooking a whole recipe of bolognese and then freezing it for a rainy day/another lasagne. Everything else is easily halved, although if making spinach pasta, then do a half recipe with 1 egg and 1 egg yolk.

use your hand to form a dough. Transfer to a clean surface and knead for 3 minutes, then cover with cling film and leave to rest for 10 minutes. Knead for a further 8 minutes, until you have a smooth and springy ball of dough. Cover tightly with cling film and rest at room temperature (or in the fridge if it's a hot day) for at least 1 hour.

To roll the pasta in a pasta machine, make sure you have plenty of clean space to lay out your lasagne sheets. Divide the dough into two, keeping one half tightly covered. Use a rolling pin to roll the dough into a rough oblong that is just smaller than the width of the mouth of your machine (if it's wider, it'll tear when you roll it). Run the pasta through the thickest setting on your machine twice, then slowly decrease the settings as you roll it through twice each time. Dust the pasta dough with flour if it's a bit sticky. Once you have reached the thinnest setting, only run it through once. Cut your sheets to the width of your lasagne dish and dust them on both sides with semolina (I use 2–3 sheets of lasagne per layer, and make them a tiny bit wider than my dish for a little bit of overlap). Lay the sheets out on a little bit more semolina to dry – wooden surfaces are great for this as they suck up excess moisture from the pasta. Repeat with the other half of the dough and leave to dry for about 10 minutes. Meanwhile, reheat your béchamel and ragù to make them easier to spread into layers (add a drop of milk to the béchamel if it has really thickened up) and bring a large pan of well-salted water to the boil for the pasta. Prepare a bowl of iced water and a tray of kitchen paper ready for blanching.

To assemble the lasagne, spread one ladle of hot ragù in the base of your dish. Cook 2–3 sheets of lasagne (enough for the first layer) in the boiling water for 1 minute, then use a kitchen spider or slotted spoon to remove them and plunge into the iced water. Briefly dry the sheets on the kitchen paper before laying them into the dish. For the next layer, add another generous ladle of bolognese followed by a ladle of béchamel drizzled all over and a small handful of Parmesan. Blanch another set of lasagne sheets, drain, lay on top and repeat to make a 6–7 layer lasagne (blanching as you go avoids a situation where lots of cooked lasagne sheets get stuck together). For your final layer, oil the lasagne sheets after they are blanched so they get extra crispy in the oven. Top with ragù, béchamel and the remaining Parmesan. You can cook this straight away or leave it to cool and chill in the fridge overnight. If you are chilling it, then cover the top with a piece of baking parchment and then cling film. To cook the lasagne, preheat the oven to 180°C fan (200°C/400°F/ Gas 6). Remove the lasagne from the fridge 30 minutes before cooking if it has been chilled. Remove any parchment and cling film, cover the dish with foil and bake for 30 minutes. Then uncover and bake for a further 40 minutes for a divine bronzed top. Leave to rest for at least 25 minutes before serving to ensure it isn't too sloppy and you can see those lovely defined layers.

SERVES 6

300ml (1¼ cups) whole milk
700ml (3 cups) double
    (heavy) cream
130g (⅔ cup) light brown
    soft sugar
225g (8oz) coffee beans
3 gelatine leaves (I use
    Dr. Oetker platinum
    grade gelatine)

To serve
3 grissini
2 stem ginger balls in
    syrup, diced
2 tbsp stem ginger syrup

6 dariole moulds or glasses

MAKE AHEAD
› The panna cottas ideally need to
be made the day before the dinner
party to make sure they set in time.
I recommend making the coffee
infusion 1 day before making the
panna cottas for the flavours to
impart overnight or for a minimum
of 6 hours beforehand.

SUBSTITUTIONS
› Chopped/crushed almonds,
pistachios or even walnuts would
also be lovely on top.

SCALING
› To reduce the recipe, divide by a
third per 2 people and increase in the
same way. For a large party, I would
certainly suggest setting these in
bowls to avoid the fiddly de-moulding
process which could slow you down.

This is a sublimely decadent end to a meal as it delivers that coffee
hit you so often need but in the form of a silky, wibbly wobbly
pud. It does involve a little bit of advance prep but I have found
that the best coffee flavour comes from a long infusion with coffee
beans, so it had to be done. You can set these in moulds and then
de-mould just before serving, but if that sounds stressful, then set
the mix in glasses or small bowls instead – they will taste just as
good and that's all that matters.

DESSERT

COFFEE PANNA COTTA WITH GINGER AND GRISSINI

Preheat the oven to 160°C fan (180°C/350°F/Gas 4).

Combine the milk, cream and sugar in a saucepan and warm
through gently over a low heat. Meanwhile, spread the coffee beans
out on a tray and pop into the preheated oven for 5 minutes – you
don't want to roast them any more, you are simply warming them
through so they are ready to release even more fragrance. When the
beans have had their time, pop them into the cream mixture and
stir well. Heat the mixture until it's steaming, then remove from the
heat and leave to cool completely before refrigerating. The beans
need to infuse for a minimum of 6 hours, but can also sit overnight.

After the mixture has had a lovely long rest, soak the gelatine leaves
in a bowl of iced water for 5 minutes to soften them. Pass the cream
mixture through a fine sieve to get rid of the coffee beans, then pop
back over a low heat in a pan until just steaming. Take each gelatine
leaf and squeeze it gently to get rid of any excess moisture before
whisking into the coffee cream. Once all three leaves are in, remove
from the heat, pour into a jug (pitcher) and leave to cool for
15 minutes. Pop your moulds or glasses onto a tray, then pour and
divide the mixture between the vessels. Cover the whole tray with
cling film (plastic wrap) and place in an easily accessible, flat space
in your fridge. Leave to set for at least 6 hours or ideally overnight.

Before serving, crush the grissini lightly, and chop the stem ginger
and mix with its syrup. If your panna cottas are in moulds, prepare
a tray of hot water (from the tap is fine). Take each mould and
dip it carefully into the water, making sure the water level isn't
higher than the lip of the mould. Let the panna cotta soften in the
water for around 60–90 seconds, then remove from the water and
invert onto your chosen plate. Give the top of the mould a tap and
remove it. Pop a teaspoon of the stem ginger on each panna cotta
and then top with the grissini.

THE ONE THAT'S A SEAFOOD FEAST

STARTERS

PRAWN AGUACHILE

CLAMS BULHÃO PATO — CLAMS WITH CORIANDER

MAIN

PROPER FISH PIE

DESSERT

TORTA CAPRESE

Here is a menu to make the pescatarians in your life feel special. I simply adore fish and seafood, and a whole dinner party celebrating it is my idea of a perfect meal. I think the versatility of it is what I love the most, and I have tried to demonstrate that here.

Our snack and starter are both bright, light and super fragrant, whereas our main is rich, lush and comforting. Fish and seafood dishes are not always easy things to 'get ahead' on, but I have tried to find ways to get around this and create something that is relaxed and delicious in equal measure.

Sensibly, it is not custom to eat fish for dessert, so instead we have one of my all-time favourite flourless chocolate cake recipes – torta caprese.

GETTING AHEAD

	Prawn Aguachile	Clams Bulhão Pato	Proper Fish Pie	Torta Caprese
Up to 3 days before	–	–	› Can make sauce › Can make mash	–
Up to 2 days before	–	–	› Can make sauce › Can make mash	› Can make torta caprese
Up to 1 day before	› Can prep prawns and store in fridge	–	› Can make sauce › Can make mash	› Can make torta caprese
On the day	› Make aguachile › Prep cucumber and onion	› Prep ingredients › Purge clams › Cook clams	› Warm mash › Warm sauce › Prep fish › Assemble › Bake	› Make torta caprese

MISE-EN-PLACE

	Prawn Aguachile	Clams Bulhão Pato	Proper Fish Pie	Torta Caprese
Up to 6 hours before	› Can make aguachile and keep in fridge up to 3 hours before › Prep garnish	› Can prep ingredients › Purge clams	› Can make mash › Can make sauce › Assemble pie	› Can make torta caprese
Up to 1 hour before	› Bring to room temperature	› Warm bread	› Remove from fridge	› Bring to room temperature if in fridge
To serve	› Top with jalapeño, cucumber and onion › Serve with tortilla chips	› Cook clams; pile into bowls › Serve with warm bread	› Bake for 35–45 mins; leave to stand for 5 mins › Serve	› Serve with crème fraîche or cream

SERVES 6 AS A SNACK

350g (12oz) peeled fresh king prawns (jumbo shrimp)
3 fresh jalapeños or green chillies
100ml (scant ½ cup) lime juice (approx. the juice of 5 limes)
40g (1½oz) fresh coriander (cilantro)
1 tsp flaky sea salt
1 small cucumber, peeled
1 small red onion, ½ finely diced, ½ thinly sliced
tortilla chips, to serve

An aguachile is a wonderful thing – it is a dish from Sinaloa in Northern Mexico, similar to ceviche, that is made with fresh green serrano chillies and lime juice. Mine is by no means authentic, not least because I can't get serrano chillies, but also because it is an attempt at recreating the best one I've ever had, which was at a restaurant called Contramar in Mexico City, nowhere near Sinaloa. I've used jalapeños as I can get them fairly easily where I live, but feel free to use green chillies if that's all you can find. This is supposed to have a nice kick but not be overly spicy, so definitely test your chillies before you blend them in case they are extremely hot for you. You can serve this with tortilla chips as a snack or double the recipe and serve it as an elegant and easy starter.

STARTER

PRAWN AGUACHILE

Slice the prawns in half lengthways, scrape out their veins, pop them into a bowl and set aside.

Put 2 of the jalapeños or chillies in a high-powered blender with the lime juice, coriander, salt and half the cucumber and blend to a purée. Pour the purée over the prawns, then add the finely diced red onion. Mix well and leave to marinate in the fridge for 2–3 hours.

To serve, thinly slice the remaining jalapeño and cucumber. Spread the marinated prawns out on a large plate with their sauce and garnish with the sliced jalapeño, cucumber and red onion. Serve with good-quality tortilla chips and cold beers.

MAKE AHEAD
› The aguachile is best made no more than 3 hours ahead, but it can then sit in the fridge until you need it.

SUBSTITUTIONS
› Use thinly sliced tender white fish like sea bass, sea bream, pollock or even scallops instead of prawns.

SCALING
› This amount is good for 2–3 people as a starter and can be easily doubled if needs be.

SERVES 6

1.2kg (2²/₃lb) fresh clams*
1 tbsp fine salt, for purging
    the clams
70g (scant ¹/₃ cup) butter
3 tbsp olive oil, plus extra
    to serve
9 garlic cloves, thinly sliced
1 tsp dried chilli flakes
60g (2¹/₄oz) fresh coriander
    (cilantro),
    stalks and leaves separated
    and both finely chopped
250ml (generous 1 cup) dry white
    wine – a Portuguese vinho
    verde is perfect
freshly squeezed juice of 1 lemon

*Make sure you store your clams
in the fridge covered in a damp
cloth or newspaper – do not store
them in water or they will die.

MAKE AHEAD

› This is best made fresh but you can
prep most of your fresh ingredients
earlier in the day and keep them
covered in the fridge – purge and
drain the clams, chop the garlic, pick
the coriander but don't chop it until
nearer the time.

SUBSTITUTIONS

› For my coriander haters, this is your
worst nightmare. Switch the coriander
for parsley, although I would also
reduce the quantity by half as it can be
quite strong. A mix of parsley and dill
would be lovely here too.
› Mussels work well prepared exactly
the same way. Make sure the shells are
cleaned and debearded too, though.

SCALING

› Allow for approximately 200g (7oz)
of clams per person with bread for a
starter portion.

Clams were the gateway drug into my deep obsession with
molluscs and crustaceans as food. And it was this dish that did
it – on a family holiday in Portugal when I was about seven years'
old, Dad ordered bulhão pato and I never looked back. This has
been (somewhat unofficially) voted the best seafood dish in the
world, and I tend to agree. The clams are cooked with tonnes of
garlic, coriander and white wine and the result is an unbelievably
tasty broth that I would happily drink by itself. Oh, and it is
obligatory to serve these with plenty of crusty bread for dipping.

STARTER

CLAMS BULHÃO PATO — CLAMS WITH CORIANDER

To clean the clams, give them a rinse under cold running
water in a colander. Pop them into a bowl, then cover with
fresh water and add the fine salt. Discard any clams that are
open or broken. Mix well and leave the clams to sit in the salted
water for 30–60 minutes in the fridge – they will expel and
purge themselves of any sand inside. After they have purged,
pour away the dirty water. Wash the clams once more in clean
water and drain them through a colander one last time.

Melt the butter with the olive oil in a large saucepan over a
medium-high heat. When the butter is sizzling, add the sliced
garlic, chilli flakes and the chopped coriander stalks. Fry for a
minute or two until fragrant and lush, then tip in your clams
and white wine. Stir well and leave to simmer, uncovered, for
around 5–8 minutes, or until all the clams have opened. Throw
away any clams that do not open.

Take the pan off the heat, add the lemon juice and chopped
coriander leaves and adjust the seasoning if necessary – the
clams will be salty already so may not need anything. Serve
immediately with toasted bread drizzled with good olive oil.

SERVES 6-8

For the filling

300g (10½oz) smoked
   haddock fillets
2 fresh bay leaves
600ml (2½ cups) whole milk
60g (¼ cup) butter
1 leek, washed, trimmed and
   thinly sliced
60g (scant ½ cup) plain
   (all-purpose) flour
200ml (generous ¾ cup)
   double (heavy) cream
2 eggs (optional)
handful of fresh parsley,
   finely chopped
small bunch of fresh dill,
   finely chopped
120g (4¼oz) frozen peas
300g (10½oz) skinless pollock
   fillets, cut into chunks
180g (6¼oz) raw peeled tiger
   prawns (jumbo shrimp)
finely grated zest of 1 lemon

For the mash topping

1kg (2lb 4oz) Maris Piper
   potatoes (or Yukon Gold
   potatoes), peeled and cut
   into even chunks
100g (½ cup minus 1 tbsp)
   butter
120ml (½ cup) whole milk
50ml (scant ¼ cup) double
   (heavy) cream
2 garlic cloves, grated
70g (2½oz) Cheddar cheese,
   finely grated
20g (¾oz) Parmesan cheese,
   finely grated
good grating of fresh nutmeg

Fish pie is a hug in a bowl for me – it's creamy and rich and just washes all my blues away. It seems to be a fairly uniquely British dish, like many potato-topped pies. It is excellent for a dinner party as it can be prepped well in advance and left in the fridge until you need it, plus it's super warming and soaks up all manner of libations. The fillings are certainly flexible and I think it's important to honour the preferences of your household. What is not flexible is that it MUST be topped with buttery, cheesy, garlicky mash.

MAIN

PROPER FISH PIE

To make the filling, put the smoked haddock in a saucepan with the bay leaves and cover with the milk. Put the pan over a medium heat and bring slowly up to a simmer. As soon as it starts to steam, take the pan off the heat and set aside for 15 minutes – this method is a really gentle way of poaching the haddock while also getting loads of its flavour into the milk. After 15 minutes, take the haddock out of the milk and remove the skin while flaking the fish into a bowl. Keep an eye out for any stray bones, removing them as you go. Cover the bowl of fish with cling film (plastic wrap) and set aside. Keep the pan of warm poaching milk and discard the fish skin and bay leaves.

Meanwhile, melt the butter in a separate saucepan and add the leek. Sweat for 8–10 minutes over a gentle heat, avoiding getting any colour on the leek. When the leek is soft, add the flour and stir well to make a roux, letting it cook out for a minute or so. Add a ladle of the warm haddock poaching milk and beat into the mixture until smooth. Add more milk, bit by bit, beating until smooth each time and allowing it to come back to the boil before each addition. Continue until all the milk has been added and you have a smooth leek béchamel sauce. Simmer gently for 5 minutes before removing from the heat. Add the double cream and season generously with salt and pepper. Pour into a large dish, cover the surface with cling film and leave to cool.

To make the mash, put the potatoes in a large saucepan and cover with cold water. Season the water well with salt and put over a high heat. Bring to the boil and cook for 15–20 minutes until completely soft in the middle. Drain immediately into a colander.

Heat the butter, milk and cream gently in a saucepan until just warm and the butter is melted while you mash the drained potatoes – I highly recommend a potato ricer for this. It is

MAKE AHEAD

› The sauce (minus the raw fish) and mash can both be made up to 3 days in advance. Store the sauce in the dish you will cook the pie in so you can simply dot the raw fish and prawns in it when you wish. It will be easier to apply the mash if you gently warm it first. You can assemble the pie on the day you want to cook it and keep it in the fridge until an hour before you're ready to cook it.

SUBSTITUTIONS

› You can absolutely switch up the fish combinations here, I would keep the haddock, though, for its excellent flavour. Halibut, ling, trout, brown shrimp, even brown crab meat or lobster would be divine in this if you want to make it even more special.

SCALING

› Halve the recipe for a main course for 4 people with sides. For 12 people, double the recipe and make in 2 or 3 large dishes.

important to mash the potatoes while they are still hot, as that will ensure they won't go gluey. (Similarly, we are heating the butter, milk and cream so they don't bring the temperature down either.) When the potatoes are mashed, pour in the hot butter, milk and cream and gently combine with a spatula. Add the garlic, cheeses and nutmeg and season generously with salt and pepper. Set the mash aside until needed.

I love boiled egg in my fish pie, as that's how my granny used to make it, but these are entirely optional. If you want to add the eggs, now is a good time to cook them in boiling water for 7½ minutes until fudgy, then cool in iced water and peel.

Preheat the oven to 180°C fan (200°C/400°F/Gas 6).

When the leek béchamel sauce has cooled to at least body temperature, mix in the flaked haddock, parsley, dill and frozen peas. Transfer your mixture to a large ovenproof vessel – a 32cm (13in) cast-iron pan or 30cm x 37cm (12 x 14½in) baking dish. Pop your pollock pieces and prawns in a bowl, then season generously with salt, pepper and the lemon zest. Cut the boiled eggs into quarters. Stud the fish pie mixture with the raw prawns, pollock and eggs, getting an even distribution across the dish. Cover the top of the dish with the mashed potato – it is a generous coating I assure you. You can either drag a fork across the top for crispy ridges, or do as I like to do and use the back of a teaspoon to create a fish scale pattern in the mash. Put on a high shelf in the preheated oven and bake for 35–45 minutes (it will take longer if it has been in the fridge) until the top is golden and the filling is bubbling (you may experience a bit of bubbling over and that's no bad thing, just put a baking tray underneath the pan/dish to stop it from burning in your oven). Leave to stand for 5 minutes before serving with more peas if you like, or wilted spinach.

SERVES 8-10

200g (7oz) 70% dark (bittersweet)
   chocolate, chopped
200g (¾ cup + 2 tbsp)
   butter, diced
200g (2 cups) ground almonds
20g (¾oz) hard amaretti
   biscuits, crushed (or you can
   add an extra 20g/¾oz ground
   almonds instead if you wish)
200g (1 cup) golden caster
   (superfine) sugar
2 tbsp dark cocoa powder, sifted
1 tsp fine salt
6 eggs, 2 whole and 4 separated
1 tbsp icing (confectioners')
   sugar, sifted
crème fraîche or whipped
   cream, to serve

MAKE AHEAD
› This cake is absolutely sensational
eaten the day it is made, but it also
holds up really well in the fridge, so
it's completely up to you, 2 days later
it is just as delicious as long as it hasn't
been cut. I would recommend (as
always, I am a broken record) bringing
it to room temperature before serving
if it has been previously chilled.

SUBSTITUTIONS
› If you want the cake to be dairy-free,
then swap the butter for vegetable fat.
› Instead of amaretti, you could add
1 tsp of almond extract or 1 tsp of
amaretto, if you like.

SCALING
› This recipe is easily doubled if you
need to make more than one cake. I
wouldn't bother reducing it though,
it's so good you might as well make
a big one.

This is a bloody wonder of a cake. Originally from the gloriously
chic island of Capri that sits in the Gulf of Naples, this dessert
has been described in Italian as one of history's most fortunate
mistakes. The myth goes that a Caprese baker forgot to add flour
to a cake he was making and discovered the ethereal fudginess
you get from a nut-based, flourless cake. This is a really easy
recipe, with a quick cook time and it keeps brilliantly. I like
using the crushed amaretti biscuits here because they have a
beautiful almondy caramel flavour, but feel free to omit.

DESSERT

TORTA CAPRESE

Preheat the oven to 150°C fan (170°C/340°F/Gas 3). Grease
and line the base of a 23cm (9in) springform cake tin with
baking parchment.

Pop the chocolate and butter in a heatproof bowl and melt
together – you can do this either over a pan of gently simmering
water (making sure the base of the bowl doesn't touch the water),
or in short bursts in the microwave. When the chocolate is
completely melted, mix together with the butter and set aside
to cool slightly.

In a large bowl, use a spatula to combine the ground almonds,
amaretti (if using), sugar, cocoa powder, salt, 2 whole eggs and
4 egg yolks. The mixture will be very thick. Add the melted
chocolate to the almond batter and stir well to combine.

In a separate, large and very clean bowl, use a hand-held electric
whisk (or a stand mixer if you have one) to whip the egg whites
to stiff peaks. Using a metal spoon, take a large spoonful of the
egg whites and beat it hard into the chocolate mixture – this will
loosen up the stiff batter enough to incorporate the rest of the egg
whites softly. Add a quarter of the remaining whites at a time and
use the spoon to fold them in gently. Continue until all the whites
are in and folded evenly through – be patient with your folding
and don't rush it, it's worth taking the time over. Transfer the
batter to the lined tin and pop the cake into the preheated oven
for 28–30 minutes; go for the shorter time if your oven runs hot,
or slightly longer if you think your oven runs a bit cooler. Remove
from the oven and leave to cool completely before removing from
the tin. The cake will be fudgy and slightly gooey in the middle.

When the cake is completely cooled and you are ready to serve,
transfer it to a plate. Dust with the icing sugar and slice with a
sharp knife, serving with crème fraîche or whipped cream.

THE BEST OF BRITISH ONE

STARTERS

BREAD AND HAM BUTTER

BROWN SHRIMP, WATERCRESS AND ICEBERG SALAD

MAIN

BEEF SHIN PIE WITH COLCANNON

DESSERT

MARMALADE SPONGE

I suppose you could also call this menu, 'the pub food one', as it is certainly a selection of things I would 100% order in a pub. This dinner party is a celebration of food from our beautiful British isles – hearty, rustic grub that is soothing and soulful.

Our centrepiece is a majestic beef shin pie, and it is truly a recipe I have doted over. Pie is a quintessentially British dish, and something I think we all love to make as much as eat, even though it can take a while. After working on a project about British food a couple of years ago, I was reminded of its brilliance and decided it needed its very own menu here, full of rich and sumptuous cooking and, of course, a stunning hot pudding (a dessert category in its own right).

A large part of this menu can be prepped ahead, too, because if there's one thing we Brits know how to do – it's utilize a fridge.

GETTING AHEAD

	Bread and Ham Butter	Brown Shrimp, Watercress and Iceberg Salad	Beef Shin Pie with Colcannon	Marmalade Sponge
Up to 3 days before	› Can make butter	› Can make shrimp dressing	› Can make pie filling	–
Up to 2 days before	› Can make butter	› Can make shrimp dressing	› Can make pie filling	› Can make sponge
Up to 1 day before	› Can make butter	› Can make shrimp dressing	› Can make pie filling › Can make colcannon (apart from bacon)	› Can make sponge
On the day	› Bring butter to room temperature	› Make shrimp dressing › Assemble salad	› Make pastry › Assemble pie and chill in the fridge › Make/finish colcannon › Bake pie	› Make sponge or reheat

MISE-EN-PLACE

	Bread and Ham Butter	Brown Shrimp, Watercress and Iceberg Salad	Beef Shin Pie with Colcannon	Marmalade Sponge
Up to 6 hours before	› Can make butter	› Can make shrimp dressing	› Make pastry › Assemble pie and chill in the fridge › Can make colcannon	› Can make sponge
Up to 1 hour before	› Bring butter to room temperature › Warm bread	› Prep salad › Chop chives	› Bake pie › Reheat colcannon and crispy bacon	› Reheat sponge › Warm custard
To serve	› Serve with bread, pickles, mustard	› Assemble and dress salad	› Serve with colcannon	› Serve with custard

Truthfully, I first made ham butter in an attempt to sidestep having to make rillettes, which I love but take forever. So, initially this recipe was sort of French in style. However, the more I have made it, the more I have found it to be quintessentially British. Ham butter is exactly as described – it's a compound butter made with shredded ham hock, spiced with good things like nutmeg and cloves and loosened with wholegrain mustard. Sound familiar? Yes, it is a lot like the base of a good British ham, but in butter form. So now I like to serve it a bit like a pared back ploughman's (this is just a little snack after all). Plate this with good, soft, fresh white bread and a few of your favourite British condiments – English mustard and pickled onions are essential for me, but go with what you like.

**SERVES 6 AS A SNACK,
WITH BREAD**

For the butter
150g (5¹/₂oz) cooked and
    flaked ham hock
125g (¹/₂ cup + 1 tbsp)
    softened butter, cubed
pinch of ground nutmeg
pinch of ground cloves
¹/₄ tsp ground ginger
¹/₄ tsp smoked paprika
¹/₂ tsp ground white pepper
1 tbsp wholegrain mustard
dash of Tabasco

To serve
good-quality, soft, white bread
pickles of your choice
English mustard

STARTER

BREAD AND HAM BUTTER

Put all the butter ingredients together in a bowl and use a spatula to beat it all together. You will end up with a chunky pink butter – it's not supposed to be super smooth so don't worry about that.

Serve the butter at room temperature with some lovely bread and all your favourite accompaniments.

MAKE AHEAD
› The butter can be kept in the fridge for up to 5 days.

SUBSTITUTIONS
› If you can't get ham hock, use high-quality cooked ham and finely chop it or pulse until shredded in a blender.

SCALING
› If you're planning on making this as more of a starter or lunch plate, then the butter recipe is easily doubled or tripled. Where pinch is given as a measurement, increase to ¹/₄ tsp.

A CELEBRATION OF FOOD FROM OUR BEAUTIFUL BRITISH ISLES — HEARTY, RUSTIC GRUB THAT IS SOOTHING AND SOULFUL.

SERVES 6 AS A STARTER

For the brown shrimp
120g (1/2 cup) mayonnaise
1 tsp freshly grated horseradish,
    or 1 tbsp hot horseradish
    sauce
1 tsp Dijon mustard
finely grated zest of 1 lemon
freshly squeezed juice of
    1/2 lemon
small handful of finely chopped
    fresh chives
140g (12oz) brown shrimp

To serve
2 large iceberg lettuces,
    outermost limp leaves removed,
    cut into chunks
90g (3 1/4 oz) watercress
2 sticks of celery, thinly sliced
    at an angle

MAKE AHEAD
› The shrimp dressing can be made
up to 3 days ahead, just give it a mix
before you dress the salad as it might
have separated a bit.

SUBSTITUTIONS
› Crab meat is also delicious in this
dressing, but if you're looking to make
it cheaper, then small Atlantic peeled
prawns (shrimp), like the ones you
get in prawn cocktail sandwiches, are
good too.
› You can use baby gem instead of
iceberg, and rocket (arugula) instead
of watercress if needed.
› Chervil or tarragon would be great
instead of, or alongside, the chives.

SCALING
› This quantity would work for a
sharing spread for 8–10. To reduce,
allow for ¼ iceberg lettuce per person
and around 60g (2 ¼ oz) of shrimp.

St. JOHN restaurant in Farringdon, East London, has informed a lot of the inspiration for this menu for its faithfulness to British cookery. This salad is inspired by their utterly delicious brown shrimp and cabbage salad. It is ingenious to pair the sweet, salty brown shrimp with a plain leaf like cabbage or, in this case a personal favourite of mine, iceberg lettuce. I wanted to pay homage to my grandparents here too, as it was at their house I first ate brown shrimp and loved it. My grandpa, like me, was medically addicted to mayonnaise and so I've included it in a creamy, zingy sauce that works beautifully with the shrimp. Peppery watercress and celery offer tart balm to the sweet, fatty dressing. It's a divine, elegant and light little starter – a perfect preamble for pie.

STARTER

BROWN SHRIMP, WATERCRESS AND ICEBERG SALAD

Whisk together the mayonnaise, horseradish, Dijon mustard, lemon zest and juice and half of the chives until smooth, then fold in the brown shrimp and check the seasoning, adding salt and black pepper to taste.

I like to arrange the iceberg, watercress and celery on a large platter, then drizzle over the shrimp dressing. Sprinkle over the remaining chives to finish.

SERVES 6

1 x 6–8cm (2½–3in) cleaned beef
    shin marrow bone, unsplit
    (ask your butcher, optional)
3 tbsp vegetable oil
1.5kg (3¼lb) beef shin off
    the bone, cut into 4–5cm
    (1½–2in) chunks
1 tbsp flaky sea salt
2 onions, diced
1 large carrot, diced
2 sticks of celery, diced
70g (½ cup + ½ tbsp) plain
    (all-purpose) flour
400ml (1⅔ cups) beef stock
    (broth)
40g (1½oz) beef yeast extract,
    such as Bovril
1 x 440ml (15fl oz) can of Irish
    stout, such as Guinness
1 tbsp English mustard
2 tbsp Worcestershire sauce
1 tbsp hot horseradish sauce
2 tsp black peppercorns, crushed

For the pastry

400g (3 cups) self-raising flour,
    plus extra for dusting
200g (7oz) beef suet
1 tsp salt
½ tsp freshly ground
    black pepper
240ml (1 cup) water
butter or oil, for greasing
1 egg
1 tbsp whole milk

For the colcannon

1.2kg (2⅔lb) Maris Piper
    (or Yukon Gold) potatoes,
    peeled and cut into even
    medium chunks – about the
    size of roast potatoes
110g (scant ½ cup) butter
160g (5½oz) Savoy cabbage,
    shredded (approx. 1 small
    cabbage)
6 spring onions (scallions),
    thinly sliced
160ml (scant ¾ cup) double
    (heavy) cream
good grating of fresh nutmeg
100g (3½oz) smoked streaky
    bacon, diced
large handful of fresh chives,
    finely chopped

30cm x 37cm (12 x 14¼in)
    deep pie dish

A proper beef shin pie is just the most glorious thing, but it does require some effort. I find the whole process very therapeutic, though – the braising of the beef, making the pastry (suet pastry is so easy), the crimping and the glazing. I also like to do a classic marrow bone chimney, but if it feels a touch macabre, then don't worry about leaving it out. *Pictured on pages 176–177.*

MAIN

BEEF SHIN PIE WITH COLCANNON

Start the pie filling the day before. If you are using the marrow bone, preheat the oven to 200°C fan (220°C/425°F/Gas 7).

Put the bone in an oven tray and roast in the preheated oven for 25 minutes, then remove and scoop out the marrow from the centre while the bone is still hot. Pour off and reserve any fat to fry the beef with later. Set the marrow and bone aside to cool and turn the oven down to 140°C fan (160°C/325°F/Gas 3).

Heat the vegetable oil in a large casserole dish, adding any beef fat from the bone, if you have it. Season the beef shin chunks with the sea salt, then add them in batches to the casserole dish and brown over a high heat. When all the beef has browned, with good colour on all sides, remove it from the casserole and set aside.

Add the onions, carrot and celery and turn the heat down to medium. Let the vegetables caramelize for 10–12 minutes. Add the flour and stir it in well. Slowly pour in the beef stock, mixing well to avoid lumps, then stir in the beef yeast extract and stout. Mix in the mustard, Worcestershire sauce, horseradish sauce and black pepper and bring to a simmer. Return the browned meat to the pan, cover with a lid and put in the preheated oven to slow-cook for 3½–4 hours until the meat is meltingly tender and unctuous, and the gravy glossy. Chop the cold marrow (if using) and stir it in. Leave the mix to cool to room temperature, then chill overnight.

To make the pastry, combine the flour, suet, salt and pepper in a bowl. Slowly pour in the water and stir to make a shaggy dough. Turn it out onto a work surface and gently bring it together, adding an extra splash of water if it feels too dry or a dusting of flour if it feels overly wet. You will be able to see large chunks of suet in the pastry and this will act like butter when the pastry cooks and make a flaky, crispy crust. Wrap the pastry in cling film (plastic wrap) and leave to rest for an hour in the fridge.

MAKE AHEAD

› The pie filling can be made up to 3 days ahead.
› I would recommend making the pie earlier in the day so it can chill before you bake it.
› The colcannon can be made up to 24 hours ahead, just wait to do the crispy bacon on the day.

SUBSTITUTIONS

› Use the same quantity of vegetable suet if you don't like the stronger beefy flavour of beef suet or need a halal option.
› Beef cheeks would also work well here, as well as short rib and oxtail.
› Any brown ale can work instead of stout.

SCALING

› Increase or decrease the pie (filling and pastry) by a third to serve more or less – 2kg (4½lb) of beef is enough for 8–10, 1kg (2¼lb) is enough for 4–6.

After an hour, grease your pie dish with butter or oil. Divide the pastry into two – roughly two-thirds for the base and a third for the pie top. On a lightly floured work surface, roll out the larger piece of pastry until it is slightly wider than the size of your pie dish and about 0.5cm (¼in) thick. Carefully lay the pastry into the dish, making sure it sits evenly on all sides. Mix the egg and milk together and brush the edges of the pastry with this. If using the bone, position it in the centre of the pie. Fill the dish with the braised beef in an even layer. Roll out the second piece of pastry to the same thickness. If using the bone, cut a 5cm x 5cm (2 x 2in) cross in the middle of the pastry; if not, you don't need to. Lay the pastry on top of the pie filling, fitting the top of the bone through the cross. If you are not using the bone, cut a small cross in the middle of the pastry and insert a pie chimney if you have one, or leave the cut as it is. Use your thumb or the back of a teaspoon to crimp and seal the pastry edges on all sides, then trim any excess pastry away. Brush the pastry all over with the egg and milk to glaze, then chill in the fridge for at least an hour.

For the colcannon, put the potatoes into a large pan and cover with cold water. Season well with salt, then place over a high heat and bring to the boil. Cook the potatoes for about 15 minutes until they are tender and starting to fall apart.

Meanwhile, heat 3½ tablespoons of the butter in a medium pan until sizzling. Add the cabbage and spring onions, let them sweat for 2–3 minutes over a medium heat, then cover. Cook, checking every so often, for 8–10 minutes until soft but still a lovely green.

Heat the remaining butter and cream together in another saucepan over a low heat until the butter has melted. When the potatoes are cooked, drain them and use a potato ricer to get a smooth mash. Return the potatoes to the same pan over a medium heat. Add the melted butter and cream and beat it in. Stir in the cabbage, spring onions, nutmeg and lots of salt and pepper. Cover and set aside.

Preheat the oven to 180°C fan (200°C/400°F/Gas 6).

Bake the pie in the middle of the oven for 1 hour and 20–30 minutes until the top is golden and crisp and the middle molten.

Meanwhile, fry the bacon over a low heat (no oil needed) for around 15 minutes, until golden and crunchy. Drain on kitchen paper (paper towels) and reserve until needed.

When you are nearly ready to serve, reheat the mash and pile it into a bowl, topping with the bacon and chopped chives. Serve the pie with the mash, extra gravy and peas, if you like, but it does have a pretty good built-in gravy already.

SERVES 6-8 GENEROUSLY

700g (1½lb) marmalade
finely grated zest and freshly
   squeezed juice of 1 orange
250g (1¼ cups) golden caster
   (superfine) sugar
180g (¾ cup + 2 tsp) butter,
   at room temperature
250g (1¾ cups + 2 tbsp)
   self-raising flour
large pinch of salt
1 tsp baking powder
1 tbsp vanilla bean paste or
   vanilla extract (optional)
80ml (⅓ cup) whole milk
4 medium eggs
custard or double (heavy)
   cream, to serve

MAKE AHEAD
> You can make and bake the sponge
up to 2 days ahead and keep it in the
fridge. When you want to eat it, let
the sponge come to room temperature
before reheating.

SUBSTITUTIONS
> Go wild with your marmalade
options here – the possibilities
are endless! Jam (jelly) would also
work beautifully.
> Spice your sponge in any way you
like – I used just vanilla but cinnamon
or cardamom would be delicious, and
even some fresh ginger grated in too.

SCALING
> Halve the recipe easily to serve 4.
The recipe is easily increased too,
however, it is best not to bake a large
batch in one larger dish, or it will take
forever to cook – split the mix across
several dishes instead.

A hot sponge with custard is a very British thing I think. Steamed ones are particularly good but long-winded, so here we use a fairly standard cake batter baked on top of another very British thing – marmalade. The marmalade provides a sharp, sweet sauce for our sponge, but I recommend serving this with LOTS of hot custard for ultimate school-dinner nostalgia.

DESSERT

MARMALADE SPONGE

Preheat the oven to 170°C fan (190°C/375°F/Gas 5).

Spoon the marmalade into the bottom of a 23cm x 28cm (9 x 11in) baking dish. Add 50ml (3½ tablespoons) of boiling water and the orange juice to it and stir well to combine. Set aside while you make the sponge.

Cream together the sugar and butter until light and fluffy; this should take around 2 minutes in a stand mixer or using a hand-held electric whisk.

Combine the flour, salt and baking powder in a separate bowl, then set aside. Mix the vanilla, milk and orange zest together in another bowl and set aside.

Add the eggs, one at a time, to the creamed sugar and butter, mixing well with the electric whisk with each addition. If the mixture looks at all split, add 1 tablespoon of the flour mixture. When all the eggs are incorporated, add a third of the flour mixture and mix well, followed by a third of the milk mixture. Alternate until all the milk and flour mixtures have been incorporated and you have a smooth, fluffy cake batter.

Spoon the batter into the dish over the marmalade, aiming for a relatively even distribution. The marmalade will come up the sides of the batter but don't worry – when it cooks it sinks and the sponge rises. Pop into the preheated oven to bake for 45–50 minutes, until the middle of the sponge is springy and a skewer inserted (not as far down as the marmalade) comes out clean. If the top is getting too dark, cover it with foil.

Remove from the oven and serve immediately or keep the pud warm until needed. Or, if baking ahead, leave to cool and then reheat covered tightly in foil in the oven for 20 minutes at 160°C fan (180°C/350°F/Gas 4). Serve with hot custard or cold cream.

THE STORE CUPBOARD SAVIOUR ONE

STARTER

BROCCOLI AND CANNELLINI BEANS WITH BASIL AND LEMON

MAIN

AGLIO, OLIO AND ANCHOVY SPAGHETTI

DESSERT

CHILLI OIL AND PEANUT BUTTER KNICKERBOCKER GLORY

My pantry is my best friend in the kitchen. It has all I need to bring a dish to life or to reinvent an old classic, and is more often than not the backbone of my recipes. This dinner party menu is all about using the store cupboard to its full potential. Fresh ingredients are necessary, of course, but don't always have to be the key players in a dish, even for entertaining. The fact that these recipes use mostly dried goods doesn't make them any less impressive, in fact, I think the ingenuity is something to be celebrated. Plus, they are a whole lot cheaper and relatively quick to make, too.

This is a gorgeous dinner party for leaner months, when you need to put those hoarded ingredients to work.

GETTING AHEAD

	Broccoli and Cannellini Beans with Basil and Lemon	Aglio, Olio and Anchovy Spaghetti	Chilli Oil and Peanut Butter Knickerbocker Glory
Up to 3 days before	–	–	› Can make chilli oil
Up to 2 days before	–	–	› Can make chilli oil
Up to 1 day before	› Can make cannellini and basil cream	› Can chop garlic and chilli and keep in fridge in oil	› Can make chilli oil
On the day	› Roast broccoli › Make cream › Assemble	› Make sauce › Toss with pasta › Add chopped parsley	› Make chilli oil › Whip cream › Assemble

MISE-EN-PLACE

	Broccoli and Cannellini Beans with Basil and Lemon	Aglio, Olio and Anchovy Spaghetti	Chilli Oil and Peanut Butter Knickerbocker Glory
Up to 6 hours before	› Can make cannellini and basil cream › Can toast pecans	› Can chop garlic and chilli › Can cook garlic, chilli and anchovies	› Can make chilli oil and cool
Up to 1 hour before	› Roast broccoli	› Bring large pan of water to the boil › Chop parsley	› Warm peanut butter › Whip cream › Freeze serving bowls
To serve	› Top the cannellini and basil cream with broccoli, lemony beans and pecans; serve with warm bread	› Cook pasta; toss with sauce and combine with parsley	› Top ice cream with chilli oil, peanut butter and whipped cream

SERVES 6

For the broccoli
600g (1lb 5oz) Tenderstem
  broccoli
2 tbsp olive oil
1½ tsp dried chilli flakes
  (optional)
1 tsp flaky sea salt
finely grated zest of 1 lemon

**For the basil and
  cannellini cream**
3 x 400-g (14-oz) cans of
  cannellini beans
4½ tbsp extra virgin olive oil
freshly squeezed juice of 1 lemon
1 garlic clove, peeled
30g (1oz) fresh basil leaves
30g (1oz) toasted pecans

MAKE AHEAD
› You can make the cannellini cream
up to 24 hours ahead, but the rest of
this dish is best made fresh. It can sit
at room temperature, though, for a
couple of hours.

SUBSTITUTIONS
› If cannellini are not your bean of
choice, then feel free to use butter
(lima) beans or chickpeas (garbanzo
beans). Lentils would also work well
here too, although you might not want
to blitz them as the mix would be a
muddy brown.
› I always have pecans lying around,
but top this with whatever nuts
or seeds you have – sesame seeds,
pumpkin seeds, almonds, hazelnuts
and walnuts would all work.
› Regular broccoli can also be roasted,
just cut it into small florets, or if you
prefer you can use asparagus or thinly
sliced courgettes (zucchini).

SCALING
› You will need roughly 1 can of beans
for 2 people, just blitz half and plate
half, plus 100g (3½oz) of broccoli per
person. I like to do this as a sharing
starter, but double those quantities if
you want to serve this as a main meal.

Canned pulses are truly heaven sent when you need a quick and
delicious, robust and exciting plate of food. For years, my midweek
meals have been dominated by them, usually orienting around
a version of a bean stew of sorts, affectionately dubbed 'witches
brew' by my old housemate. With a little bit of magic and a few
tricks up my sleeve, it would always become something so much
more than the sum of its parts. This dish is more of a salad than a
stew, but it engages the same principle – take one ingredient and
think laterally with it. Then you have options, you have intrigue
and you'll have something very tasty too.

STARTER

BROCCOLI AND CANNELLINI BEANS WITH BASIL AND LEMON

Preheat the oven to 200°C fan (220°C/425°F/Gas 7).

Trim off the hard ends of the broccoli stems, then lay the broccoli
across 2 roasting trays with the olive oil, chilli flakes (if using)
and the sea salt. Roast in the preheated oven for 15 minutes – the
florets will become scorched and crunchy and the stems will wilt
and soften slightly. When they are cooked, mix them with the
lemon zest.

Meanwhile, drain 2 cans of cannellini beans, then put them in
a pan with 1 tablespoon of the extra virgin olive oil, the lemon
juice and a pinch each of salt and black pepper. Set the pan over
a medium heat; you don't want the beans to cook, you are just
simply softening and warming them (cold beans aren't nice to eat
in my opinion).

Take the remaining can of beans and drain most of the liquid,
reserving a couple of tablespoons. Pop these beans in a blender
with 2½ tablespoons of the extra virgin olive oil, the garlic clove,
basil, the reserved bean liquid from the can and another pinch of
salt. Blitz it all together to make a smooth, bright green cream.

To plate, smoosh the creamy cannellini bean and basil cream over
your serving plates, then top with the warm, lemony beans and
the charred broccoli, making sure to drizzle over all that lovely
spicy, lemony oil from the roasting trays. Scatter over your toasted
pecans, drizzle with the remaining tablespoon of oil and serve with
warm bread.

SERVES 6

2–3 tbsp fine salt

800g (1¾lb) good-quality
    dried spaghetti

160ml (⅔ cup) extra virgin
    olive oil

12 garlic cloves, thinly sliced

3 tsp dried chilli flakes

120g (4¼oz) jarred or canned
    anchovies, drained

30g (1oz) fresh parsley,
    finely chopped

Parmesan cheese, finely grated,
    to serve (optional)

MAKE AHEAD

› You can cook the garlic, chilli and anchovy mix up to 6 hours ahead and leave at room temperature if you prefer. Just reheat before you toss through the spaghetti.

SUBSTITUTIONS

› Linguine or bucatini would be lovely here instead of spaghetti. I do not recommend making this with fresh pasta as it doesn't contain enough starch to make an emulsified sauce.

SCALING

› This is a large quantity to make at one time, any more and you will need to split into several pans. You will need 2 garlic cloves, ½ tsp of chilli flakes, 20g (¾oz) of anchovies, 25ml (1 tbsp + 2 tsp) of olive oil and 130g (4½oz) of pasta per person.

This is another dish that I have made myself for literally DECADES, and I am thrilled it is getting a space in this book because it is probably my favourite pasta dish of all time. Aglio e olio e peperoncino is a classic condiment for pasta that only requires a serious amount of garlic, oil and chillies, and not much else. Once my dad had got me hooked on anchovies in my late teens, I started to put them in everything and at uni in particular, anchovy pasta became my 'thing'. This recipe might feel sparse and maybe not celebratory enough for a dinner party, but it is incredibly good and I think there's a lot of merit in boldly serving something really simple. You're saying to your guests 'trust me, I know what's good'. AND THIS IS BLOODY GOOD. I highly recommend this with Parmesan on top, although millions of Italians would fight me on that.

MAIN

AGLIO, OLIO AND ANCHOVY SPAGHETTI

Bring a large pan of water to a rolling boil and season it with the fine salt – we don't want our pasta water too salty here because of the anchovies. Drop the spaghetti in and move it all around to make sure it doesn't stick or clump together and then set a timer for 7 minutes.

Meanwhile, heat the oil in a large frying pan (skillet) over a medium heat. Add the garlic, chilli flakes and drained anchovies and let them warm up and start to cook gently in the oil, sizzling away while the pasta cooks.

When the spaghetti has had its 7 minutes it will still be fairly chewy, but nevertheless use tongs to transfer it across to the anchovy and garlic oil. Once all the spaghetti is in, add 2–3 ladles of pasta water so that the spaghetti is almost covered. Keep moving the spaghetti as it cooks for a final few minutes in the sauce, making a thick and glossy emulsion. Add a splash more pasta cooking water if it is looking too dry.

When the spaghetti is perfectly al dente, remove from the heat and toss almost all the parsley through. Serve immediately with a final flourish of parsley on top and plenty of grated Parmesan for people to help themselves.

MY PANTRY IS MY BEST FRIEND IN THE KITCHEN. IT HAS ALL I NEED TO BRING A DISH TO LIFE.

SERVES 6

For the fragrant crispy chilli oil
To be poured over:
20g (³/₄oz) dried chilli flakes
25g (1oz) Korean gochugaru
   chilli flakes or Aleppo pepper
1 tbsp soft brown sugar
1 tsp MSG
1 tbsp soy sauce
40g (1¹/₂oz) toasted white
   sesame seeds
To be sizzled:
7.5cm (3in) piece of fresh ginger,
   peeled and very finely chopped
   (do NOT grate, it won't crisp up)
2 small or 1 large cinnamon
   stick, snapped in half
2 pieces of fresh orange peel
3 black cardamom pods, bashed
   but whole
15 black peppercorns, crushed
2 cloves
6 allspice berries
1 star anise
250ml (generous 1 cup)
   flavourless oil such as
   vegetable or sunflower

For 6 Knickerbocker Glories
1.8 litre (60fl oz) tub of vanilla
   ice cream, for about 3 scoops
   per person
180ml (³/₄ cup) crispy chilli oil
   (see above) or shop-bought
180g (6¹/₄oz) crunchy
   peanut butter
300ml (1¹/₄ cups) double (heavy)
   cream, softly whipped,
   or squirty cream

MAKE AHEAD
› The chilli oil will keep for up
to 2 months in the fridge.

SUBSTITUTIONS
› Use any nut butter you like.
› Mint ice cream would be pretty wild
here, as well as banana or pistachio.
› Use any chilli oil, although the crispy
ones are the best in my opinion.

SCALING
› For each knickerbocker, you will
need 3 tsp of chilli oil, 3 tsp of peanut
butter and 3 scoops of ice cream.

Chilli oil and peanut butter are a fairly obvious pairing, but chilli oil and ice cream is not as well known. What I can say is they are SO GOOD TOGETHER, and here with the nutty, salty and creamy peanut butter, you've got a wildly delicious dessert that will wow your guests. It also relies almost entirely on ready-made stuff. If, however, you do like the idea of making your own chilli oil, then I've shared the recipe for mine. It is fragrant, spicy and doesn't contain any garlic or onion, which I think makes it better on the ice cream. Other toppings are optional, however, I do recommend the whipped cream as a bare minimum.

DESSERT

CHILLI OIL AND PEANUT BUTTER KNICKERBOCKER GLORY

I like to serve this in ice-cream bowls or glasses that have been kept in the freezer for a few hours to chill down – so, if you feel inclined, do that first.

Put all the 'To be poured over' ingredients for the crispy chilli oil into a heatproof bowl ready to go.

Put all the 'To be sizzled' chilli oil ingredients together in a small, heavy-based saucepan. Pop the pan over a medium heat and bring up to sizzling – this will take about 8–10 minutes. When the oil is sizzling, turn the heat to low, reducing the sizzle to a gentle splutter. Leave to gently simmer for roughly 20 minutes, stirring often, until the ginger pieces have turned golden and crisp. Using tongs and while still over the heat, pick out any big bits of spices like the cinnamon, orange peel, cardamom, cloves, allspice berries and star anise and discard.

Pour the hot oil over the ingredients in the heatproof bowl; they will sizzle and froth a bit but that's fine. Stir and leave to cool.

To assemble the dessert, warm the peanut butter slightly in a pan or microwave to make it easier to drizzle. Put 1 scoop of ice cream in the bottom of each (chilled) bowl or glass, then top with 1 teaspoon of the chilli oil and 1 teaspoon of the peanut butter. Add a dollop of cream, then repeat the process with 2 more scoops of ice cream for each bowl/glass, finishing with more cream and a drizzle of the chilli oil and peanut butter on top.

THE PLANT-BASED ONE

STARTERS

PUMPKIN WITH HARISSA AND DILL

RADICCHIO, APPLE AND WALNUT SALAD

MAIN

COURGETTE, KALE AND POTATO PIE

DESSERT

CLEMENTINE PUDDING

While there are vegan recipes and recipes that can be easily converted in this book, it feels important to save a space for a fully plant-based menu that truly wows. Restriction breeds creativity in cooking – if you can't use something then what CAN you use and how many ways can you use it? Not only that, but it broadens your palate and makes you taste things you might not normally eat, which is always exciting. When dreaming up my perfect plant-based menu, I wanted to be sure it would feel impressive, modern and easy, without clichés or 'vegan versions'. This is a meal that stands up on its own as delicious, regardless of its vegan status. Our first two dishes are designed to be eaten together with bread as a big sharing spread.

GETTING AHEAD

	Pumpkin with Harissa and Dill	Radicchio, Apple and Walnut Salad	Courgette, Kale and Potato Pie	Clementine Pudding
Up to 3 days before	› Can cook and marinate pumpkin	–	–	› Can make granita › Can make purée › Can freeze clementines
Up to 2 days before	› Can cook and marinate pumpkin	–	–	› Can make granita/purée/cream filling › Can freeze clementines
Up to 1 day before	› Can cook and marinate pumpkin	› Can make dressing	› Can make pesto	› Can make granita/purée/cream filling › Freeze clementines › Freeze jalapeño
On the day	› Cook and marinate pumpkin › Bring to room temperature	› Make dressing › Make the maple walnuts › Assemble salad	› Assemble pie and bake	› Blitz granita › Make cream filling › Fill clementines

MISE-EN-PLACE

	Pumpkin with Harissa and Dill	Radicchio, Apple and Walnut Salad	Courgette, Kale and Potato Pie	Clementine Pudding
Up to 6 hours before	› Can cook and marinate pumpkin	› Can make dressing › Can make the maple walnuts	› Can make pesto › Can assemble pie	› Make cream filling › Blitz granita
Up to 1 hour before	› Bring pumpkin to room temperature › Chop dill	› Prep salad ingredients	› Bake pie	› Put cream filling in piping bag
To serve	› Pile on top of coconut yogurt › Sprinkle with dill	› Assemble and dress salad	› Serve with salad and pesto	› Fill clementines with purée and cream; top with granita and jalapeño

SERVES 6

1kg (2lb 4oz) cooking pumpkin
40g (1½oz) harissa paste
100ml (scant ½ cup) olive oil
1 garlic clove, grated
1 tsp salt
1 tbsp maple syrup
1 tbsp vegan soy sauce
small bunch of fresh dill,
    finely chopped
2 tbsp shop-bought crispy
    onions, to serve
300g (generous 1⅓ cups)
    coconut yogurt

I love this method of cooking starchy vegetables and it is great when you need something that can be prepped ahead. The pumpkin, thinly sliced and dry roasted, is then marinated while still hot in spicy harissa and a couple of other good things. Served at room temperature, this is so lovely to pile onto bread or salad or hummus... or just by itself. I particularly enjoy it piled onto coconut yogurt, which is how I suggest serving here. This might seem like a lot of pumpkin, but as it has a high water content it tends to shrink when it cooks.

STARTER

PUMPKIN WITH HARISSA AND DILL

Preheat the oven to 215°C fan (235°C/455°F/Gas 8–9).

Use a mandoline or a sharp knife to thinly slice the pumpkin. To do this, I find it easiest and safest to cut the pumpkin into quarters, remove the seeds, then peel each quarter with a knife. I then cut the quarters in half again before thinly slicing each eighth into rough C-shape, 3mm (⅛in) slices, but they should be no more than 1cm (½in) thick.

Spread the pumpkin slices over three oven trays lined with greaseproof paper, ideally in one even layer on each. Put into the oven to dry roast just like this for 20 minutes. The slices are so thin that they will cook and crisp pretty quickly – you definitely want some charred bits so don't worry if that happens.

While the pumpkin is cooking, prepare your marinade in a large bowl. Mix together the harissa paste, olive oil, garlic, salt, maple syrup and soy.

When the pumpkin has got some good colour and is tender, remove from the oven and tip the slices into the marinade while they are still hot. Carefully toss the delicate slices in the marinade. Leave to cool before transferring to the fridge to chill for a few hours or ideally overnight.

Bring to room temperature before serving with the chopped dill and crispy onions sprinkled over, on top of a bed of coconut yogurt.

MAKE AHEAD
› This is best prepped ahead and will keep in the fridge for 3 days.

SUBSTITUTIONS
› Use butternut squash or celeriac instead of pumpkin, if you prefer.

SCALING
› To make any more than the recipe here, you will need to roast this in batches in the oven.

SERVES 6

For the maple walnuts
50g (2oz) walnuts
1 tbsp maple syrup
good pinch of sea salt

For the dressing
250g (9oz) walnuts
1 garlic clove, peeled
300ml (1¼ cups) plant-based
    milk, I like almond
100ml (scant ½ cup) olive oil
finely grated zest and freshly
    squeezed juice of 1 lemon
2 tsp maple syrup
¼ tsp ground cumin

For the salad
2 radicchio, roughly chopped
5cm (2in) piece of fresh ginger,
    peeled and finely julienned
small handful of fresh
    chives, chopped
2 Cox's apples, peeled, cored
    and thinly sliced
freshly squeezed juice of
    1 lemon (for the apples)
2 tbsp olive oil

MAKE AHEAD
› The dressing can be made up to
24 hours ahead, but bring it back
to room temperature before using.
› The toasted maple walnuts can
be made up to 6 hours ahead.

SUBSTITUTIONS
› If bitter leaves aren't your thing,
ditch the radicchio for some red
oak leaves and shaved fennel.
› Pears would be gorgeous here
instead of the apples.

SCALING
› Increase the recipe by half to serve
as part of a sharing spread, or keep the
same quantities if serving as a main
course for 2 with bread.

The classic combos in this salad make it seem unremarkable. Radicchio with apple? Sure. Apple and walnuts? Yeah, that's nothing new. No, we aren't reinventing the wheel, but we are making a very yummy wheel. This dressing is a great option for when you have a plant-based pal coming over but you want to serve something creamy. I love the warmth of the cumin and the ginger here, they are great against the cool bitterness of radicchio and tartness of the apple. Tossing your walnuts (OMG, is that rude to say?) in maple syrup is optional if you don't like things too sweet, but it's basically a cheat's candied walnut and I recommend you give it a go.

STARTER

RADICCHIO, APPLE AND WALNUT SALAD

Preheat the oven to 160°C fan (180°C/350°F/Gas 4).

Spread all the walnuts (300g/10½oz in total) out on an oven tray and bake in the preheated oven for around 10–12 minutes until golden and fragrant. (Tip for you: I always toast my nuts for a little longer in a slightly cooler oven as this way they are much less likely to burn; months on the pastry section throwing burnt nuts in the bin taught me that.)

Separate out 50g (2oz) of the still-hot walnuts and toss them in a bowl with the maple syrup and sea salt, then set aside.

Pop the remaining walnuts into a blender while they are still warm with the garlic, plant-based milk, olive oil, lemon zest and juice, maple syrup and cumin. Blend to a smooth, thick, glossy dressing that is a similar texture to mayonnaise – I do this in my bullet blender for best results. Set aside at room temperature.

Prep all the salad ingredients, taking care to do the apple last and immediately mixing it with the lemon juice and olive oil so it doesn't discolour.

Spread some of the dressing on the bottom of a large serving platter, then top with an arrangement of radicchio leaves and apple slices. Sprinkle over the chopped ginger, then dress with lashings of the creamy dressing, the sticky toasted walnuts, freshly chopped chives and a pinch each of salt and black pepper.

RESTRICTION BREEDS CREATIVITY IN COOKING — IF YOU CAN'T USE SOMETHING THEN WHAT CAN YOU USE AND HOW MANY WAYS CAN YOU USE IT?

SERVES 6

For the pesto

200g (7oz) chopped kale

50g (2oz) fresh basil leaves

100g (3¹/₂oz) pine nuts, toasted
in a dry pan until light golden,
then cooled

200ml (generous ³/₄ cup) extra
virgin olive oil, plus extra
if needed

2 garlic cloves, peeled

For the filling

300g (approx. 3 medium) white
potatoes such as Désirée,
peeled and thinly sliced

1 courgette (zucchini),
thinly sliced

2 tbsp dried mint

60ml (¹/₄ cup) plant-based cream

1 tbsp plant-based milk, to glaze

500g (1lb 2oz) ready-made
vegan shortcrust pastry

plain (all-purpose) flour,
for dusting

23cm x 7cm (9 x 2³/₄in)
springform cake tin

MAKE AHEAD

› The pesto can be made up to 1 day
ahead but assemble and cook the pie
on the same day or the pastry will
oxidize and the veg will leach liquid.

› You can bake the pie up to 2 hours
ahead and reheat gently at 160°C fan
(180°C/350°F/Gas 4) to serve.

SUBSTITUTIONS

› You can make a cavolo nero pesto
or even a blend of spinach and kale.

› Swap dried mint for dried oregano.

› Switch out the courgette for marrow
or squash.

SCALING

› For a pie to serve 4, use a 20cm (8in)
springform tin. Halve the pesto and
use 350g (12oz) of pastry. Reduce the
filling ingredients by ¹/₃ – use a smaller
courgette rather than lopping a bit off.

› You can double the recipe to make 2 x
23cm (9in) pies, or increase the recipe
by 1.5 times for 2 x 20cm (8in) pies.

Justice for vegan pies! That's what I cried to myself as I tested this
recipe, hoping to create something that is a fabulous centrepiece
whether you eat meat or not. Here we have it – a luxurious pie
filled with layers of flavour and not too many artificial substitutes.

MAIN

COURGETTE, KALE AND POTATO PIE

Blanch the kale in a pan of boiling salted water for about 1 minute,
then immediately transfer to a bowl of iced water to refresh. Drain,
then squeeze out as much moisture as you can before putting in a
blender with the remaining pesto ingredients and plenty of salt and
pepper. Blend until smooth – add extra oil if it's too thick. Set aside.
Put the potato and courgette in separate bowls and mix each with
1 tablespoon of the dried mint and some salt and black pepper.

Divide the pastry in half, with a slightly bigger piece for the base
and a smaller piece for the top. Keep the smaller piece covered in
the fridge while you roll the bigger piece on a lightly floured work
surface to a big circle, 0.5cm (¹/₄in) thick. Loosely fold the pastry
into a square, put it into the centre of the tin and then unfold.
It should overhang the sides of the tin no more than 4cm (1¹/₂in).
Spread 1 tablespoon of the pesto onto the pastry base. Arrange
a layer of potatoes in overlapping circles inside the tin. Sprinkle
with salt and pepper, then dollop on another heaped tablespoon
of pesto and 1 tablespoon of plant-based cream. Gently spread
the pesto and cream over the potatoes. Repeat with a layer of
courgettes, more pesto, cream and seasoning. Repeat until you have
used up all the veg. Press down the final layer before you add the
final pesto and cream – there should be a rough 1cm (¹/₂in) border
of pastry around the sides of the tin.

Roll the remaining pastry out to a thin disc that is the same size
as the tin. Carefully lay it on top of the filling, then brush with the
milk to glaze. Fold over the pastry going up the sides of the tin onto
the lid to seal the pie. Crimp with a teaspoon or your thumb to seal.
Cut a small cross in the middle of the lid to let steam escape as it
cooks, and use excess pastry and glaze to garnish. Chill for 1 hour.

Preheat the oven to 180°C fan (200°C/400°F/Gas 6) and pop a flat
baking tray in to heat up (this ensures a crisp pie bottom). Bake
the pie on the tray in the oven for 1¹/₃–1¹/₂ hours. The pastry should
be a deep golden colour and the veg tender. Leave to cool for 10
minutes before releasing from the tin. Serve with a green leaf salad,
the spare pesto and any condiments you desire!

SERVES 6

For the granita
finely grated zest and
  freshly squeezed juice
  of 4 clementines (approx.
  150ml/²/₃ cup juice)
finely grated zest and freshly
  squeezed juice of ¹/₂ lemon
35ml (¹/₈ cup + 1 tsp) water
1–2 tbsp caster (superfine)
  sugar (to taste)

For the frozen clementines
6 large, ripe clementines, with
  their leaves for extra drama
  if you can find them
1 fresh green jalapeño, frozen
  (optional)
1–2 tbsp caster (superfine) sugar

For the clementine cream
340g (1¹/₂ cups) plant-based
  cream cheese
130g (²/₃ cup) coconut yogurt
70g (¹/₃ cup) plant-based cream
100g (³/₄ cup minus ¹/₂ tbsp)
  icing (confectioners')
  sugar, sifted
finely grated zest of 2
  clementines

MAKE AHEAD
› Most of this recipe NEEDS to
be made ahead. I would strongly
recommend doing the frozen elements
the day before, and the cream can also
be made up to 2 days in advance.

SUBSTITUTIONS
› If you don't want to add the jalapeño,
leave it out, or substitute with another
surprising ingredient like toasted
coconut or even popping candy
(although this does often contain
dairy, so look out for a vegan version).

SCALING
› 1 clementine per person for plenty of
purée and a hollow vessel. The granita
can be increased by 2 clementines at a
time, always taste it to check you are
happy with the sweetness as it does
slightly depend on the fruit. For the
cream, increase or decrease by roughly
one-third at a time.

This might be my favourite pudding in the whole book. It is a
celebration of one of my favourite fruits, the clementine, and
it's great fun to make and even more fun to serve.

DESSERT

CLEMENTINE PUDDING

Make the granita the day before. Add to a pan the zest and juice
of the 4 clementines along with the lemon zest and juice, water and
sugar – use 2 tablespoons of sugar if the clementines are tart. Warm
over a low heat to dissolve the sugar – do not boil it! Transfer to a
small container with a lid, leave to cool and then freeze overnight.

For the frozen clementines, cut the tops off the clementines. Keep
the lids (and their leaves if they have them). Use a small serrated
knife to loosen the flesh inside from the edges of the fruit, before
scooping it out with a teaspoon and setting aside. Wrap the hollow
clementines in cling film (plastic wrap) individually, and put the
lids (unwrapped) onto a small tray lined with cling film. Pop in the
freezer overnight with the jalapeño (if using).

Blitz the clementine flesh in a blender until smooth, then strain
to get rid of any fibres. Put the clementine purée in a pan with
1–2 tablespoons of caster sugar – 1 if the clementines are very sweet
or 2 if they are tart. Bring to the boil, then turn the heat down
slightly and simmer for 10 minutes until reduced and thickened to
a consistency similar to a coulis, then chill in the fridge overnight.

The next day, a few hours before your dinner, remove the granita
from the freezer. Let it stand for 5 minutes before breaking it up
with a spoon and putting it in a food processor. Pulse a few times
until you get lovely small grains of ice. Place back in the freezer.

To make the clementine cream, loosen up the cream cheese in
a bowl using a spatula. Beat in the coconut yogurt, cream, icing
sugar and clementine zest until smooth and thick like cheesecake.
Transfer to a piping bag and chill in the fridge for an hour.

When it is time to serve, remove the clementine cream and
clementine purée from the fridge, and the frozen clementines
from the freezer. Put a frozen clementine on each plate, then add
a teaspoon of the purée into each. Pipe the cream mixture into
each, overfilling so the mixture comes up high. Top with more
purée. Grab the frozen jalapeño (if using) and granita. Use a fork
to scrape the granita, then pile a tablespoon on top of the cream
on each clementine. Use a Microplane to grate over a small amount
of frozen jalapeño (if using). Balance the lid on top and serve.

SERVES 6

THE BONFIRE NIGHT ONE

SNACKS
DORILOCOS
QUESO

MAIN
BEEF BIRRIA

DESSERT
CARROT AND HORLICKS TRES LECHES CAKE

Who doesn't love a bonfire party? Huddling around a crackling blaze with hot drinks, hot meat and the promise of a 6/10 fireworks display that will feel like a 12/10, thanks to the four mugs of mulled wine you put away. What an iconic moment in the winter calendar. It's also a great opportunity to do standing dinner party food, and there's no standing food better than tacos. Birria is a Mexican dish of spicy stewed meat, served shredded in tacos with its ambrosial broth on the side for dipping and sipping.

It occurred to me that this is the perfect Bonfire nightdish, it's warming, exciting, deeply delicious and great for feeding many mouths. A real upgrade from the old jacket potato and charred sausage. And if you're going to go Mexican, you might as well lean into it and make the whole menu a litany of sublime party dishes from one of the greatest cuisines in the world. Plus, it gives you a chance to exercise one of the best and most useful items in the party food cannon – the tortilla chip.

GETTING AHEAD

	Dorilocos	Queso	Beef Birria	Carrot and Horlicks Tres Leches Cake
Up to 3 days before	› Can make apricot salsa	–	› Can make birria	–
Up to 2 days before	› Can make apricot salsa	–	› Can make birria	› Can make sponge and soak
Up to 1 day before	› Can make apricot salsa	› Can make queso	› Can make birria	› Make sponge and soak
On the day	› Chop veg › Make apricot salsa › Assemble	› Make pico de gallo › Make or reheat queso	› Prep garnish › Toast tortillas › Reheat birria	› Cover sponge with cream and chill

MISE-EN-PLACE

	Dorilocos	Queso	Beef Birria	Carrot and Horlicks Tres Leches Cake
Up to 6 hours before	› Make salsa	› Grate cheeses	–	› Cover cake with whipped cream and chill
Up to 1 hour before	› Prep veg and fruit › Assemble dorilocos serving area with ingredients	› Make pico de gallo › Make queso and keep warm	› Chop onion and coriander garnish › Toast tortillas › Reheat birria	–
To serve	› Demonstrate to guests how to make; enjoy	› Serve warm queso with pico de gallo and tortilla chips	› Serve hot birria with warm tortillas and garnishes	› Decorate with sprinkles and serve

SERVES 6

1 cucumber, peeled, deseeded
    and julienned
1 carrot, peeled and julienned
1 ripe mango, peeled, pitted and
    roughly diced
6 x individual serve packets of
    tortilla chips, such as Doritos
    (I like cheese flavour)
200g (7oz) crispy coated peanuts
    – BBQ flavour works well here
2–3 limes, cut into wedges
2 small packets of pork
    scratchings, lightly crushed
    into small pieces (optional)
shop-bought hot salsas that
    you love
Tajin seasoning (chilli, lime
    and salt) (optional)

For the apricot salsa
150g (5¹/₂oz) soft dried apricots
1 red chilli, deseeded if
    you prefer
180ml (³/₄ cup) just-boiled water
1 tbsp olive oil
2 tbsp runny honey
freshly squeezed juice of 1 lime

MAKE AHEAD
› You can make the salsa up to 5
days ahead and keep in the fridge.

SUBSTITUTIONS
› Just use your favourite brand of
tortilla chips, whatever that might be.
› The mango could also be papaya or
even pineapple.
› The coated peanuts are the most
traditional here, but if you have
regular peanuts that need using
up, then use those instead.

SCALING
› Allow for 1 packet of tortilla chips
per person. The fruit/veg is easily
increased, and if you chop up too
much, then it's beautiful in a salad
the next day.
› This salsa quantity is plenty for
6 people, definitely double if you
want leftovers though.

A street food found all over Mexico; packets of tortilla chips become even more moreish with the addition of salsas, refreshing chopped veg, fruit and crunchy peanuts. Traditionally, these will also feature pickled pork rinds, which are hard to come by and hard to make, so I've given the option to add pork scratchings instead. This is SUCH a fun dish to do for a party – everyone makes their own and eats right from the packet, making it entirely portable. Having said that, I crave these so often I've taken to preparing a giant bowl of them and they work brilliantly that way too. In Mexico, these will often come with salsa chamoy, a sweet and sour salsa made from dried fruit and Tajin seasoning. I didn't want to miss out on the sweetness it gives, so I created a very easy apricot salsa that is absolutely sensational and entirely multipurpose if you accidentally make too much (do it). *Pictured on page 204.*

STARTER

DORILOCOS

To make the salsa, pop all the ingredients into a blender, adding salt to taste, and blitz until smooth. If the salsa feels too thick, add a few tablespoons more water. Check the seasoning and set aside.

Prep your veg and mango and arrange them in bowls around your packets of tortilla chips, along with separate bowls containing the peanuts, lime wedges, pork scratchings and salsas.

I suggest demonstrating to your guests how to assemble your dorilocos. Use scissors to cut one of the sides off a packet of tortilla chips – simply opening at the top doesn't leave space for good seasoning here. Next, top your tortilla chips with a handful of cucumber, carrot and mango, followed by peanuts, salsas and a squeeze of lime juice. Add a handful of pork scratchings, and a sprinkle of Tajin seasoning if you wish. Give the packet a little shake, then start to eat. You will need napkins or even little wooden forks to scoop. Writing this recipe has given me the BIGGEST craving for these, so I really must go and assemble a pack now. Goodbye.

SERVES 6

For the pico de gallo
2 vine tomatoes, deseeded
    and diced
1 small white onion, diced
1 fresh green jalapeño,
    diced (optional)
large handful of fresh coriander
    (cilantro), finely chopped
freshly squeezed juice of 1 lime

For the queso
35g (2½ tbsp) butter
1 garlic clove, grated
½ tsp ground cumin
½ tsp paprika
410ml (1⅔ cups) evaporated milk
100ml (scant ½ cup) whole milk
150g (5½oz) Red Leicester
    cheese, freshly grated
150g (5½oz) Cheddar cheese,
    freshly grated
1 tbsp cornflour (cornstarch)

To serve
plenty of tortilla chips

MAKE AHEAD
› The queso can be made up to 1 day ahead and reheated, just cover the surface of the dip with cling film (plastic wrap) to prevent a skin from forming as it cools. You can make the pico de gallo up to 2 hours before.

SUBSTITUTIONS
› I like milder cheese here, but you can swap the Red Leicester for a nuttier Monterey Jack.

SCALING
› I would advise against making huge batches of this, cooking smaller amounts in several pans will be easier to control and more successful, plus you can always keep a prepped set of ingredients waiting in the wings to make a fresh pan.
› If you are wishing to reduce, half the recipe is a perfect amount for 2–4 people.

Please let me first clarify that this is very much a Tex-Mex style queso, rather than the authentic melted, stringy queso that you would find in Mexico. That is extremely delicious, don't get me wrong, but the last thing I want to be doing is endlessly melting/reheating cold hard cheese. Instead, this version is very easy to make and keep warm on the stove next to your mulled beverages. Realistically, though, the moment anyone clocks it, it's a goner. I love to whip up a sneaky pico de gallo to have with, or it's lovely with some crumbled fried chorizo or bacon on top too. Avoid buying cheese that has been pre-grated for this, as the stabilizers will affect the consistency of the dip. *Pictured on page 204.*

STARTER
QUESO

Make the pico de gallo by mixing all the ingredients together, adding salt to taste. Set aside until needed.

For the queso, put 20g (1½ tablespoons) of the butter in a saucepan or cast-iron frying pan (skillet) over a medium heat. Let the butter melt until sizzling, then add the garlic and spices. Fry for a minute, before adding the evaporated milk and whole milk.

While the milks heat up, toss the freshly grated cheeses together with the cornflour in a bowl. When the milk is steaming and about to start simmering, add the cheese mixture in three handfuls, stirring between each one. The cheese will melt slowly at the same time as the cornflour thickens the sauce. As soon as the mix is thick, smooth and steaming again, season with salt to taste, turn the heat down to very low and stir in the remaining tablespoon of butter. Serve the delicious, melty gooey cheese hot, with the pico de gallo and tortilla chips.

SERVES 6

For the birria

3 dried ancho chillies

6 dried guajillo chillies

400ml (1²/₃ cups) water from
   a just-boiled kettle

1 large onion, peeled and
   sliced into 4 rounds

6 garlic cloves, peeled

2 vine tomatoes

2 red chillies

1 tbsp cumin seeds

4 cloves

1 cinnamon stick

1 tsp black peppercorns

1 tbsp salt

1 tbsp dried oregano

1.5kg (3¹/₄lb) beef shin, off
   the bone, cut into large chunks

1kg (2lb 4oz) beef chuck, cut
   into large chunks

2 litres (2 quarts + ¹/₂ cup)
   beef stock (broth)

To serve

large handful of fresh coriander
   (cilantro), finely chopped

1 white onion, finely diced

36 soft small corn tortillas

I actually first had birria at one of my favourite cafés in London, Bake Street. You can only sit outside, so when the birria tacos come with their steaming consommé, you are absolutely frozen and so excited to see them. The meaty tacos are superb dipped in the spicy broth and sipping it alongside is so lovely too. It occurred to me how brilliant this would be as a standing outside party dish, and so here we are. It's also so easy to make ahead and reheat, and the garnish can be stretched by adding more delicious salsas, avocado and radish if you wish. *Pictured on page 204.*

MAIN

BEEF BIRRIA

Preheat the oven to 140°C fan (160°C/325°F/Gas 3).

Start by cleaning up the dried chillies – remove their stems and seeds. Set a frying pan (skillet) over a medium heat and, when it is lovely and hot, add the chillies. Toast for about 1 minute on each side until they are shiny, slightly puffed and a richer red. Remove from the heat and leave to cool slightly before transferring the chillies to a large blender jug. Cover with the hot water and leave to soak for 20 minutes until soft.

Meanwhile, in the same pan, sear the onion, garlic, tomatoes and fresh chillies over a high heat. (You're looking to get nice blackened edges rather than attempting to cook the ingredients through – think of it as a toasting process similar to the chillies.) Tip the contents of the pan into the blender with the soaked chillies. Toast the cumin seeds, cloves, cinnamon and black peppercorns for 1 minute or so in the same pan, then add them all to the blender, apart from the cinnamon stick which you want to pull out and save. Add the salt and oregano. Blitz the mixture to make a thick paste, adding a bit more water if necessary.

Arrange the meat in one or two large, deep roasting trays or casserole dishes, adding the toasted cinnamon stick (break it in half or use 2 sticks if cooking in two trays/dishes). Pour over the spice paste and rub it in really well with your hands, coating the pieces of meat on all sides. Pour over the beef stock, splitting it equally between the trays/dishes, if using two. Cover very tightly with foil or lids, then place in the preheated oven to cook slowly for 4–4½ hours. When it's done, the meat should be fork-tender and easily shreddable.

MAKE AHEAD

› You can cook the birria up to 3 days ahead, or even make it a couple of weeks beforehand and freeze it for up to a month.

SUBSTITUTIONS

› Lamb or goat are brilliant in birria, too. Your cooking times may vary, though, depending on the cut. I would suggest using shoulder, breast or neck.

SCALING

› For smaller quantities of birria paste, reduce the chillies, spices (apart from cinnamon), garlic, fresh chillies and tomatoes, but keep the onion quantity the same.
› If you make too much paste then it keeps very well frozen until needed.
› To cook larger quantities, you will want to dice the meat up a bit smaller and cook in large stock pots on the hob, rather than in the oven. This may take a bit longer to cook but will facilitate even cooking of a large quantity at one time.

Remove the meat from the broth and shred it using two forks – this is best done while still warm as it will be so much easier. Pop a few spoonfuls of broth onto the meat to keep it moist. Keep the remaining broth separately. If you've done this part in advance, then leave the shredded meat and broth to cool completely before refrigerating until needed.

To serve, arrange the chopped coriander and onion on plates – this is the traditional garnish for the broth and tacos. Toast your tortillas, one by one, in a dry, hot pan until they puff up on one side, then flip and briefly toast on the other side before transferring to a clean tea towel (kitchen cloth) and wrapping up tightly. The trapped steam is what keeps them soft and supple, if they cool they will become brittle and tough, so do this fairly close to serving and be sure to wrap tightly.

Reheat the shredded meat and broth separately, adding a few more spoonfuls of broth to the meat if it's a bit dry, and checking and adjusting the seasoning if necessary. Bring the pots of hot meat and hot broth to the table for guests to help themselves to brimming tacos and mugs. It will be a glorious spicy hug for all concerned.

SERVES 6-8, GENEROUSLY

For the cake

270g (2 cups) plain
(all-purpose) flour

2 tbsp baking powder

½ tsp ground cinnamon

½ tsp ground ginger

1 tsp fine salt

4 eggs, separated

240g (scant 1¼ cups) caster
(superfine) sugar

240ml (1 cup) vegetable oil,
plus extra for greasing

2 tsp vanilla extract

240g (approx. 2 medium) carrots,
peeled and finely grated

For the milk soak

300ml (1¼ cups) whole milk

6 tbsp malted milk hot drink
powder, such as Horlicks

340ml (1½ cups) evaporated milk

1 x 397-ml (14-oz) can of
condensed milk

To decorate

400ml (1¾ cups) double
(heavy) cream

2 tbsp whole milk

1 tbsp malted milk hot drink
powder, such as Horlicks

40g (4½ tbsp) icing
(confectioners') sugar, sifted

rainbow sprinkles, to decorate
(optional)

MAKE AHEAD

› The sponge and soak should be done
the day before at least, ideally no more
than 2 days before. Make sure your
fridge is clean: I don't recommend
storing any onions near this cake!

SUBSTITUTIONS

› Adjust the spices to taste – nutmeg
and cardamom would also be lovely.

SCALING

› I recommend making a cake this size
and simply doubling up on the recipe
if you are looking to serve more. You
can line your tin, remove each cake
and soak them in larger tins in order
to facilitate easier, more accurate
portions or smaller squares.

› The recipe can also be halved easily.

Tres leches is a classic Mexican party cake – I dreamt of a carrot cake version, because it's my favourite cake, and then thought of adding a smidge of Horlicks (the malted hot milk that my granny used to make me on cold evenings) for a sublime toasted flavour.

DESSERT

CARROT AND HORLICKS TRES LECHES CAKE

The day before, preheat the oven to 170°C fan (190°C/375°F/Gas 5) and grease and line a 24cm x 33cm (9½ x 13in) baking tin with oil.

To make the cake, combine the flour, baking powder, spices and salt in a bowl and set aside. Place the egg yolks and sugar in a separate bowl and beat together until thick and pale using a hand-held electric whisk or in a stand mixer. Next, add the oil and vanilla and beat in until homogenous. Fold in the carrot, followed by the flour mixture, making sure it is really well combined – it will be thick.

In a separate clean and dry bowl, whisk the egg whites to stiff peaks using clean beaters. Use a large metal spoon to fold a quarter of the whites at a time gently into the carrot cake batter – you can be more vigorous with the first spoonful of whites to loosen the mix, then carefully fold the rest. When they are well combined, pour the batter into the greased tin and pop into the preheated oven for 40–45 minutes. When it's ready, the sponge will be risen, springy, and a skewer should come out clean when inserted into the middle.

Meanwhile, prepare the milk soak. Heat the whole milk gently in a saucepan over a low heat until just steaming, then whisk in the Horlicks until smooth. Remove from the heat and whisk in the evaporated milk and condensed milk. Pour into a jug and set aside.

When it's ready, leave the cake to cool for 10 minutes, then invert onto a board or rack. Remove the lining paper and then invert back into the tin. Poke holes all over the surface with a skewer. If the sponge pulls away from the sides of the tin as it cools, don't worry. Pour enough of the milk mixture over the cake to cover it completely, let it sink in as it cools, then add some more. Repeat until it is all soaked in. Leave to cool fully, then chill overnight.

At least 2 hours before serving, whip the cream, milk, Horlicks and icing sugar together to form soft peaks. Spread over the cake in a thick layer, smoothing the top with a palette knife. Chill and set in the fridge for 2 hours. Decorate with your chosen sprinkles, then cut into squares or thick wedges straight from the tin and devour.

THE ONE THAT'S A COCKTAIL PARTY

OLIVE ASCOLANE – DEEP-FRIED OLIVES

RADISHES AND TONNATO SAUCE

CHICORY, TALEGGIO AND ROASTED GRAPES

TOMATO AND BUTTER BEAN CROSTINI

ZHOUG PRAWN COCKTAIL

LAMB AND ROSEMARY POLPETTE

EGG MAYONNAISE AND CRISPS

Sometimes a sit-down dinner just isn't what is required, so here we have a 'walking dinner' in canapé/snack form. My first job in a kitchen was with an event caterer, and I learned a hell of a lot about how to create canapés that were achievable and easy during a rolling service. Something to bear in mind when you don't have staff to serve your food, is that you can create a grazing table of sorts for the items that are ambient, or simply dot them around the party room. I would then prioritize handing around hot canapés, so that they are eaten at their best, and refill the ambient stations where necessary. This menu is devised of a mix of both hot and cold options, with plenty of things you can prep in advance. It's all very chic, cute and delicious too.

GETTING AHEAD

	Olive Ascolane –Deep-fried Olives	Chicory, Taleggio and Roasted Grapes	Zhoug Prawn Cocktail	Egg Mayonnaise and Crisps	Radishes and Tonnato Sauce	Tomato and Butter Bean Crostini	Lamb and Rosemary Polpette
Up to 3 days before	–	–	›Can make sauce	›Can boil eggs ›Can make egg mayo	›Can make sauce	›Can make purée	›Can make meatballs ›Can make sauce
Up to 2 days before	›Can make and breadcrumb olives	›Can roast grapes	›Can make sauce	›Can boil eggs ›Can make egg mayo	›Can make sauce	›Can make purée	›Can make meatballs ›Can make sauce
Up to 1 day before	›Can make and breadcrumb olives	›Can roast grapes	›Can make sauce ›Can poach prawns	›Can boil eggs ›Can make egg mayo	›Can make sauce	›Can make purée	›Can make meatballs ›Can make sauce
On the day	›Fry olives	›Stuff chicory with cheese ›Warm/roast grapes	›Make sauce ›Poach prawns	›Make egg mayo ›Chop chives	›Make sauce	›Make purée ›Toast crostini	›Make and fry meatballs ›Make sauce

MISE-EN-PLACE

	Olive Ascolane –Deep-fried Olives	Chicory, Taleggio and Roasted Grapes	Zhoug Prawn Cocktail	Egg Mayonnaise and Crisps	Radishes and Tonnato Sauce	Tomato and Butter Bean Crostini	Lamb and Rosemary Polpette
Up to 6 hours before	›Bread-crumb olives	›Can stuff chicory with cheese ›Can roast grapes	›Can poach prawns ›Can prep sauce	› Can make egg mayo	›Can make tonnato sauce ›Wash/prep radishes	›Can make purée ›Can make crostini	›Can roll meatballs ›Can make sauce
Up to 1 hour before	–	›Bring chicory and cheese to temperature ›Chop tarragon › Warm grapes	›Bring sauce to room temperature	›Chop chives ›Bring egg mayo to room temperature	›Bring sauce to room temperature	›Bring both to room temperature ›Prepare toppings	›Fry/reheat meatballs ›Reheat sauce
To serve	›Fry olives and drain; serve	›Top chicory and cheese with grapes and tarragon	›Arrange prawns and dip	›Garnish with chives ›Serve with crisps	›Serve radishes on ice with sauce	›Pipe or spoon purée onto crostini ›Garnish	›Serve with sauce and extra Pecorino

MAKES 50 (SERVES 8–10)

340g (12oz) jar of pitted green
olives (50 olives), drained
well and patted dry with
kitchen paper (paper towels)
50g (generous ⅓ cup) plain
(all-purpose) flour
2 eggs, beaten
50g (scant 1 cup) panko
breadcrumbs
1 litre (1 quart) vegetable oil,
for frying

**For the meat stuffing (this makes
enough for 100, you can save
half and freeze it or use it to
make actual meatballs)**
200g (7oz) minced (ground) pork,
20% fat
40g (1½oz) Parmesan cheese,
finely grated
large handful of fresh parsley,
finely chopped
1 garlic clove, grated
1 tsp dried chilli flakes
decent grating of fresh nutmeg
25g (½ cup) panko breadcrumbs
1 egg, beaten
½ tsp salt

MAKE AHEAD
› These can be stuffed and/or
breadcrumbed and kept in the fridge
for up to 2 days or in the freezer for a
month. Fry the olives from frozen for
6 minutes at 170°C (340°F).

SUBSTITUTIONS
› For a vegetarian version, use veggie
sausage meat or ricotta, and Parmesan
that does not contain animal rennet.

SCALING
› The meat mixture above is the
perfect amount for 1 egg, and I would
avoid reducing it even if you only want
to make a few. You can use it to stuff
bigger olives or just chill or freeze the
remaining mixture.

These hail from Marche in Eastern Italy, and are one of the most
addictive canapés ever. You make a spicy meatball mix, open up a
pitted olive, stuff it in, breadcrumb it and then fry it. It's an Italian
Scotch egg in a way. I really enjoy the methodical prep that goes
into these, and love to freeze them breadcrumbed and ready to
cook. In fact, you can buy them as such in Italian supermarkets,
but I am sorry to say my petitions to the Big Five to start stocking
them have fallen on deaf ears, so you'll have to make them yourself.
Pictured on page 218.

OLIVE ASCOLANE – DEEP-FRIED OLIVES

Combine the meat stuffing ingredients in a bowl, using your
hands to knead it all together. Pan-fry a tiny bit of the mixture
for you to taste and check the seasoning. When you are happy,
pop the mixture in the fridge for 15 minutes to firm up.

Cut a slit through one side of each olive so that you can open
them up like a book. To stuff the olives, take a teaspoon of the
meat mixture and fill the hole, closing the olive slightly around it.
It will kind of look like the maritozzi on page 54. Repeat this for
all of the olives, placing the stuffed ones on trays lined with baking
parchment. Chill the stuffed olives in the fridge for 30 minutes.

To breadcrumb, set up a station with the flour in one bowl, eggs
in the middle in another bowl and panko breadcrumbs in a bowl
at the end. Toss the olives in the flour, followed by the egg and
then the breadcrumbs – I find a kitchen spider utensil is helpful
for this. Pop the crumbed olives back on the lined trays and
refrigerate or freeze them until needed. (Once the olives have
frozen, you can then take them off the trays and pop them into
bags to free up some space.)

To fry, heat the vegetable oil in a heavy-based pan or a deep fat
fryer to 180°C (350°F) – if you stick a chopstick into the oil it
should sizzle when it's ready. Fry the olives in batches for around
3 minutes until they are golden brown and crisp. Drain the excess
oil on kitchen paper, leave to sit for a minute or two and then
serve. You can keep them warm in a preheated oven at 160°C fan
(180°C/350°F/Gas 4) if necessary.

MAKES 30

200g (7oz) red grapes
2 tbsp olive oil
pinch each of salt and freshly
    ground black pepper
1 tbsp red wine vinegar
4 red chicory, stems trimmed
    and leaves separated
250g (9oz) Taleggio cheese,
    at room temperature
small handful of fresh tarragon,
    finely chopped

This is one of those brilliant canapés that makes use of good ingredients and not much more. Roasted grapes are SO delicious, as the cooking process really intensifies their flavour. The bitter, crisp chicory topped with the creamy Taleggio and sweet grapes is fabulously balanced already, but I love adding some finely chopped tarragon for a little anise kick. *Pictured on page 218.*

CHICORY, TALEGGIO AND ROASTED GRAPES

Preheat the oven to 180°C fan (200°C/400°F/Gas 6).

Line an oven tray with baking parchment and add the grapes with the oil, salt and pepper and vinegar. Toss together to mix. Roast in the preheated oven for 10–12 minutes until the grapes are just bursting and sticky. Leave to cool slightly.

Take the smaller leaves of chicory (discard any larger ones or use them in another dish) and spoon a dollop of Taleggio on each one. Arrange them on a plate, then top them all with a warm roasted grape. Drizzle over any pan juices from the grapes and then sprinkle with the tarragon.

MAKE AHEAD
› You can roast the grapes up to 2 days ahead and then warm them gently in a low oven for 10 minutes just before you are ready to serve.
› If you have time, stuff your chicory leaves with the cheese earlier in the day and keep in the fridge. Bring out an hour before you serve so they can come to room temperature.

SUBSTITUTIONS
› Any funky soft cheese will work here – Gorgonzola Dolce, Brie or Camembert or even Tunworth.
› If you don't like the bitterness of chicory, then make little cucumber cups or celery boats for this instead.

SCALING
› This recipe is easily doubled. To make it a salad to serve 6, reduce the cheese by 50g (2oz) and double the grape, oil and vinegar quantities.

SERVES 6–8 AS A CANAPÉ

900g (2lb) raw king prawns
(jumbo shrimp), shell on
2 lemons, cut into wedges

For the zhoug mayonnaise
(makes enough for 30 large
or 50 medium king prawns)
30g (1oz) fresh coriander
(cilantro), stalks and all
20g (³⁄₄oz) fresh parsley, stalks
and all
1 garlic clove, peeled
1 hot green or red chilli
¼ tsp ground green cardamom
or the seeds of 1 green
cardamom pod, crushed
½ tsp ground cumin
freshly squeezed juice of
½ lemon
½ tsp caster (superfine) sugar
3½ tbsp extra virgin olive oil
2 tbsp water
70g (¹⁄₃ cup) mayonnaise
splash of Tabasco

MAKE AHEAD
› You can poach the prawns up
to 24 hours before serving. Keep
them in the fridge until needed.
› The sauce will keep for up to 3
days in the fridge but is at its best
made on the day.
› To make this even easier, you can
use frozen cooked prawns (defrosted)
and you can make and freeze the
zhoug, defrost when needed and
mix with the mayo.

SUBSTITUTIONS
› This zhoug mayo would work well
with crudités, crisps, crispy chicken
wings or grilled squid.
› For vegans, use vegan mayo and
serve the dip with falafel, crispy
tofu or fried mushrooms.

SCALING
› If you are increasing the sauce by
one-third or half, it is fine to use a
whole small extra garlic clove and
small extra chilli to prevent waste.

The prawn cocktail is an iconic party food and looks SO spectacular. This is a new level of fun – luminous pink prawns crowded around a vibrant green sauce. It is super eye-catching, which is always good for a canapé, and tastes amazing. Zhoug is a delicious spicy Yemeni herb sauce, and I've mixed it with some mayonnaise (did I mention I am medically addicted to mayonnaise?) to make a luxurious, creamy dip for the prawns. I like to use raw, shell-on king prawns, so that I can de-shell them myself and keep the little tail ends for handles, but feel free to buy them shell-off or even buy ready-cooked and peeled prawns. *Pictured on page 218.*

ZHOUG PRAWN COCKTAIL

If you are using raw, shell-on prawns, remove their heads, legs and outer shells, leaving the little paddle at the end of the tail on. (I like to freeze the removed shells and heads in bags to use later in seafood dishes.) Run a knife gently down the back of each prawn just to slightly open it up, then scrape out the veins, leaving the prawns intact.

Bring a pan of water to a gentle boil and season it with salt. Prepare a bowl of iced water and set aside. Working in two batches, drop half of the prawns into the boiling water and poach for 1½–2 minutes, depending on how big they are. Move them straight from the pan into the iced water to stop the cooking process, then drain. Let the water come back to the boil before poaching the remaining batch in the same way. Keep the poached prawns in the fridge until needed.

To make the zhoug, put the coriander, parsley, garlic, chilli, spices, lemon juice, sugar, olive oil and water into a blender and blitz until smooth. Mix with the mayonnaise and Tabasco and season to taste with salt.

To serve, I like to find small pretty glass bowls, pop some zhoug mayonnaise in and then arrange the prawns around the rim like the best old-fashioned shrimp cocktails. You could even put the bowls in another larger bowl of ice for an incredibly dramatic effect.

SERVES 10–15 AS A DIP

8 eggs
1 tsp Dijon mustard
170g (³/₄ cup) mayonnaise
small handful of chopped
    fresh chives, to garnish
2–3 large bags of crisps – a spicy
    flavour is good here, to serve

My partner made me this once as a starter for a romantic dinner and I was blown away. I don't know why it hadn't occurred to me before, given that I am fanatical about both egg mayo and crisps, and have been known to add crisps to my egg mayonnaise sandwiches. Anyway, it's a killer combination and no party is complete without crisps and dip. My egg mayonnaise recipe is fairly classic but I like the subtle hint of mustard here. The chives are also key – they really lift it. *Pictured on page 218.*

EGG MAYONNAISE AND CRISPS

Bring a large, deep pan of water to a rolling boil. Gently lay the eggs in and boil for 8½ minutes. Transfer the eggs to some cold water and let them cool a bit, then peel them.

For the perfect egg mayo, I like to slice the eggs in half, then remove their yolks. I use a fork to mash the yolks in a bowl with the mustard and then finely chop the whites separately. Then I mix it all together with the mayonnaise and season to taste with salt and black pepper. Pile the egg mayo into bowls, sprinkle with chopped chives and serve with the bowls of crisps for dipping.

MAKE AHEAD
› The egg mayo will keep in the fridge for up to 3 days but is at its best in the first 24 hours.

SUBSTITUTIONS
› You can jazz up the egg mayo more if you like – sriracha, dill and anchovies would all be delicious additions.

SCALING
› If making for a large crowd, allow for ½ an egg per person.

SERVES 20–30 AS A CANAPÉ

700g (1¹/₂lb) mixed leafy
   radishes

For the tonnato sauce
1 x 112-g (4o-z) can of tuna
   in brine, drained
4 anchovies, drained
2 tbsp capers, drained
100ml (scant ¹/₂ cup) olive oil
120g (¹/₂ cup) mayonnaise
freshly squeezed juice of 1 lemon
ice cubes, to serve

Leafy radishes are just stunning but they also taste fabulous. I love them with this creamy, salty, fishy dip from Italy that is often served with cold roast veal (vitello tonnato). The peppery, crisp radishes are divine with the rich, savoury sauce. Plus, I love the drama of serving the radishes on a plate of ice. The sauce is great with fresh bread, too. *Pictured on page 218.*

RADISHES AND TONNATO SAUCE

Put all of the tonnato sauce ingredients into a blender or food processor, seasoning to taste with salt and pepper, and blitz until smooth. Keep in the fridge until needed.

The radishes will most likely need a good wash – soak them in some cold water to release any dirt around the roots and leaves, then give them a once over under a gentle cold tap. I always keep leafy radishes in bowls of iced water in the fridge to keep the leaves crisp.

To serve, carefully dry off the radishes and arrange on a large plate of ice cubes with a bowl of the dip.

MAKE AHEAD
› The sauce will keep for up
to 3 days in the fridge.

SUBSTITUTIONS
› The tonnato sauce will work
well with any crudités, crackers
or cold roast veal or pork cut
into canapé-size chunks.

SCALING
› Double the sauce and
radishes for a larger party.

NO PARTY IS COMPLETE WITHOUT CRISPS AND DIP.

MAKES 30

1 small baguette or ciabatta,
   sliced into 30 bite-size pieces
   (I cut thin slices down the
   baguette then cut the slices
   in half again)
4 tbsp olive oil
150g (5½oz) cherry
   tomatoes, halved
1 large garlic clove, chopped
1 x 400-g (14-oz) can of
   good-quality butter beans
   (lima beans), 2 tbsp of liquid
   reserved from the can and
   the rest drained
½ tsp smoked paprika

Optional extra toppings
olive oil plus a pinch of
   smoked paprika
finely chopped tomato
   and parsley
slices of red chilli
crispy fried capers and
   shredded mint

MAKE AHEAD
› The purée can be made and will keep
in the fridge up to 3 days ahead, just
be sure to warm it before serving.
› The crostini can be made up to
6 hours ahead and stored on kitchen
paper in a sealed container.

SUBSTITUTIONS
› Chickpeas (garbanzo beans)
or cannellini beans would work
beautifully here.

SCALING
› To use a jar of butter beans or two
cans, double the rest of the dip recipe.
This will make 60– 80 canapés.

Butter beans are just an excellent back pocket ingredient in my opinion, and I love that their name is literally exactly right – they are so buttery! Which is why I find myself using them so often in vegan food. Here, employed with sweet tomatoes and smoked paprika, they make a killer purée or even dip in a matter of minutes that looks and tastes amazing as a crostini topping. You can keep them very simple and top with more oil and smoked paprika, or you can push the boat out and garnish with some fun extras which I have suggested below. *Pictured on page 218.*

TOMATO AND BUTTER BEAN CROSTINI

Preheat the oven to 180°C fan (200°C/400°F/Gas 6).

Lay the sliced bread out over 1–2 large oven tray(s) and drizzle with 2 tablespoons of the olive oil. Bake in the preheated oven until just golden; around 12 minutes. Set aside to cool on kitchen paper (paper towels) while you make the purée.

Put the remaining olive oil in a pan and set over a medium heat. Add the tomatoes and fry for 5 minutes. Stir in the garlic and cook for a minute before adding the butter beans, their reserved liquid and the smoked paprika. Season to taste with salt. Cook for another 5 minutes until the tomatoes have broken down into the beans, then take off the heat.

Leave to cool for 5 minutes before blitzing in a food processor, bullet blender or with a hand blender until smooth. The mixture will be a deep orange colour. Place in a bowl, cover with cling film (plastic wrap) and set aside until needed.

When you are ready to serve, warm the purée through in a pan over a low heat – it doesn't need to be piping hot but it will be much more delicious warm rather than cold. You can either dollop or pipe onto the crostini – I like piping because it's a bit quicker and looks neater. Top with any of the suggested toppings and dig in!

MAKES 25-30

50g (1 cup) fresh white
     breadcrumbs
35ml (⅛ cup) whole milk
1 garlic clove, grated
handful of fresh parsley,
     finely chopped
30g (1oz) Pecorino cheese, finely
     grated, plus extra to serve
4 sprigs of fresh rosemary, leaves
     finely chopped
2 salted anchovies (from a
     can/jar), drained and finely
     chopped
1 egg, beaten
500g (1lb 2oz) minced (ground)
     lamb, 20% fat
500ml (generous 2 cups)
     vegetable oil, for frying

For the sauce
2 tbsp olive oil
1 garlic clove, grated
4 anchovies, drained
400g (14oz) tomato passata
     (strained tomatoes)
2 sprigs of fresh rosemary
1 Parmesan cheese rind (optional)

MAKE AHEAD
› The raw meatballs can be made
up to 3 days ahead and kept in the
fridge, as can the sauce.
› You can fry the meatballs ahead
of time and simply reheat covered in
the oven at 160°C fan (180°C/350°F/
Gas 4) for 15 minutes.

SUBSTITUTIONS
› Use minced (ground) pork or
beef if lamb isn't your thing.
› If you can't get hold of Pecorino,
then Parmesan is a fine substitute.

SCALING
› Double the recipe for 60 canapés.
If you want to make the meatballs
and sauce as a main course, it will
serve 4 with 4–5 larger meatballs
each. For larger meatballs, the cooking
time will be 8 minutes or so. You will
need to double the sauce if having
with pasta.

A hot canapé should be as easy as possible for the host and as
enjoyable as possible for the guest. These meatballs are full of
flavour, look beautiful and are very easy to do. The rosemary in
both the meatballs and the sauce really sings with the lamb, it's
a classic combination for a reason. In Italy, meatballs are often
deep-fried and I find it gets a really even, quick cook, and for this
party you can use the same oil for the stuffed olives too. If your
party is strictly finger food, then I would serve these with cocktail
sticks. Or if you do have a small plates vibe going, then make sure
there's some bread and serve these in sharing bowls for people to
help themselves. *Pictured on page 218.*

LAMB AND ROSEMARY POLPETTE

Mix the breadcrumbs with the milk in a bowl and leave to sit for
5 minutes, then mix into a paste. Combine the paste with the garlic,
parsley, Pecorino, rosemary, anchovies and egg. Use your hands to
squish this into the lamb, mixing them together thoroughly.

Fry off a nugget of the lamb mixture to test the seasoning – the
Pecorino and anchovies are already quite salty, so it's worth doing
this before you add any more salt.

Roll the mixture into small balls – to be accurate I like to weigh the
mixture and then divide the weight by the amount I want to make,
weighing out each portion individually. This recipe makes around
25–30 bite-size balls. Chill the rolled balls on a tray lined with baking
parchment in the fridge for a minimum of 30 minutes until needed.

To make the sauce, warm the oil in a saucepan over a medium heat.
Add the garlic and anchovies and fry for a minute or two until the
anchovies have started to dissolve, then pour in the passata. Pop the
rosemary and Parmesan rind in too, if using, and leave to simmer
gently for 30 minutes. Before serving, warm the sauce and make
sure to remove the rosemary sprigs and Parmesan rind, if needed.

To fry the meatballs, heat the vegetable oil in a heavy-based pan
or a deep fat fryer to 180°C (350°F). Fry the meatballs in batches
for around 4–5 minutes until browned on the outside and cooked
through. Drain the excess oil on kitchen paper (paper towels) and
then plate them with dollops of the warm sauce on top and a good
grating of extra Pecorino.

SERVES 6

THE FESTIVE ONE

SNACKS AND STARTERS
CHEESE PUFFS
CRAB TOASTS

MAIN
PORCHETTA AND PORK RIB GRAVY

TRIMMINGS
ROAST POTATOES WITH CHILLI, BASIL AND GARLIC

CAVOLO NERO, LEEK AND BRUSSELS SPROUT GRATIN

DESSERT
STICKY TOFFEE PUDDING

As a food stylist, you can end up cooking Christmas dinner up to five times a year. This, coupled with my frustration at the monotony of Christmas food and techniques used to cook it, make it something I have come to loathe. Every year I try to cook a 'Christmassy' meal that is less and less Christmassy because I crave change, have an innate need to rebel and also can't understand why we would waste such a celebratory and special occasion on such mediocre dishes. This menu is a selection of the recipes you WILL find me making almost every year because they are so bloody good and deserve to be repeated. It's not simplified but rather a Christmas dinner I am HAPPY to spend the time on.

GETTING AHEAD

	Cheese Puffs	Crab Toasts	Porchetta	Pork Rib Gravy	Roast Potatoes with Chilli, Basil and Garlic	Cavolo Nero, Leek and Brussels Sprout Gratin	Sticky Toffee Pudding
Up to 3 days before	› Can make dough	–	› Cure and dry porchetta	› Can make pork rib gravy	–	–	› Can make sticky toffee sauce and/or pudding
Up to 2 days before	› Can make dough	–	–	› Can make pork rib gravy	–	› Can make gratin and chill	› Can make sticky toffee sauce and/or pudding
Up to 1 day before	› Can make dough	–	› Can slow-cook porchetta overnight	› Can make pork rib gravy	› Can parboil potatoes and chill	› Can make gratin and chill	› Can make sticky toffee sauce and/or pudding
On the day	› Roll, cut and bake puffs (before or after the porchetta!)	› Make crab mix › Chop herbs › Toast bread	› Slow-cook porchetta for 7–8 hours; rest › Crisp up skin	› Make/reheat pork rib gravy	› Parboil and roast potatoes › Prep chilli, basil and garlic	› Make gratin /bring to temperature › Bake	› Make/reheat sticky toffee sauce and pudding

MISE-EN-PLACE

	Cheese Puffs	Crab Toasts	Porchetta	Pork Rib Gravy	Roast Potatoes with Chilli, Basil and Garlic	Cavolo Nero, Leek and Brussels Sprout Gratin	Sticky Toffee Pudding
Up to 8 hours before	› Can make and chill dough › Can bake puffs	› Can make crab mix	› Cook porchetta if not cooked overnight	› Can make gravy if you haven't already	› Parboil potatoes and chill (can roast potatoes if porchetta is resting) › Prep chilli, basil and garlic	› Can prep gratin	–
Up to 1 hour before	› Bake puffs	› Make crab mix › Toast bread › Chop chives	› Rest › Preheat oven › Salt skin › Roast for 20–25 mins	› Reheat gravy	› Roast potatoes while porchetta is resting › Prep chilli, basil and garlic	› Bake/reheat gratin while porchetta is resting	–
To serve	› Try not to eat them all yourself	› Top toast with crab and chives	› Carve	› Serve in warm jug	› Toss and serve	› Serve	› Reheat and serve

MAKES 40 BISCUITS

200g (1½ cups) self-raising
flour, plus extra for dusting
½ tsp salt
½ tsp freshly ground
black pepper
½ tsp garlic powder
80g (⅓ cup + 1 tsp) cold
butter, diced
30g (1oz) Parmesan cheese,
finely grated
40g (1½oz) mature Cheddar
cheese, coarsely grated
30g (1oz) feta cheese, crumbled
150ml (⅔ cup) double
(heavy) cream

MAKE AHEAD
› This dough does keep in the fridge
for up to 3 days, although because it
uses self-raising flour it will oxidize
and go a bit grey. I have baked it
though and it worked just fine, so if
you don't mind that then by all means
get ahead. Otherwise, make the dough
in the morning (it takes no time at all)
and then roll and bake later that day.
› The cooked puffs don't keep for very
long because everyone eats them.

SUBSTITUTIONS
› Play around with different hard and
crumbly cheeses – Comté, Gruyère,
Red Leicester, Caerphilly or Berkswell
would all be lovely in these.

SCALING
› Double or triple the recipe for plenty
of canapés. This recipe makes 6 cheese
scones too, by the way, just bake at
200°C fan (220°C/425°F/Gas 7) for
13–15 minutes instead.

I cannot conceive of a festive beverage being served to me without
an accompanying cheesy biscuit. It is quite simply mandatory in
my house and is a behaviour passed down by my grandfather,
who would always lay out trays and trays of cheesy biscuits, crisps
and scampi fries for us to eat while he had a whisky watching the
6 o'clock news. These are not cheese puffs in the classic way, i.e.
made with choux paste. What we have here is a puffy, flaky biscuit
that you can achieve by using a cheese scone dough cooked in a
biscuit way. It's so simple and these are the most moreish things
in the world. For any American readers, if the scone/biscuit
references are blowing your mind, just know that these taste
delicious – enjoy! *Pictured on page 6.*

STARTER
CHEESE PUFFS

Combine the flour, salt, pepper and garlic powder in a large bowl.
Add the butter and briefly and gently rub it in; you are NOT
looking to take it as far as breadcrumb texture here, rather small
shards of butter that are still very much visible. Tip in all the
cheeses and use a butter knife to stir them into the flour mix. Pour
in the cream in two batches, stirring between additions. The dough
will look very crumbly but, trust me, that's okay.

Tip the dough onto a lightly floured work surface and bring it
together with your hands to form a lump; do not knead it. Press
it out (using a rolling pin can be helpful) into a rough rectangle,
then take one half of the dough rectangle and fold it over the
top – this will not be pretty and it will definitely be messy, but
we aren't looking for perfection here. Press it out into a rectangle
again – you should notice the dough becoming a little bit more
homogenous now. Wrap it tightly in cling film (plastic wrap) and
then pop in the fridge to rest for at least 30 minutes.

Preheat the oven to 180°C fan (200°C/400°F/Gas 6). Line two large,
flat baking trays with baking parchment. Divide the chilled dough
in half and keep one half covered while you roll out and cut the
other. Roll one half out gently on a lightly floured work surface
into a square around 20cm x 20cm (8 x 8in). Use a knife to cut the
square into lots of 2cm x 2cm (¾ x ¾in) squares, then transfer them
to one of your lined baking trays. Repeat with the other half of the
dough and the other baking tray; don't worry at all if your squares
aren't perfect, these are supposed to look rough and ready.

Bake in the preheated oven for 10–12 minutes and try to resist
eating them straight from the oven because the smell is WILD.
Serve warm or cold, or not at all if you just eat them all yourself.

SERVES 6

For the toasts
6 long and thin slices
    of dark sourdough
2 tbsp olive oil
1 garlic clove, peeled

For the crab
200g (7oz) white and brown
    crab meat
80g (generous 1/3 cup)
    mayonnaise
finely grated zest and freshly
    squeezed juice of 1 lemon
1 large red chilli, deseeded
    and finely chopped
small handful of fresh parsley,
    finely chopped
small handful of fresh chives,
    finely chopped

To garnish (optional)
pea shoots or watercress

These are possibly (there are a few other contenders) the starter on my death-row menu. I have such a thing for crab and it always feels extra special and significant when I get to eat it, so it seemed like the perfect thing to pass around to your most loved ones at whichever festive event you might be partaking in. Not to mention these are bloody easy and bloody impressive, which is essential when doing that stressful C-word cooking. Crab doesn't need much, but I am a huge believer in a bit of lemon, chilli and parsley on most seafood, so that's where we have landed.

STARTER

CRAB TOASTS

Preheat the oven to 180°C fan (200°C/400°F/Gas 6).

Put the bread slices in an oven tray and drizzle with the oil. Bake in the preheated oven until golden and crisp; around 10 minutes. Immediately rub the toasts all over with the garlic clove while the bread is still hot from the oven.

Mix the crab meat with the mayonnaise, lemon zest and juice, chilli and parsley and season to taste with salt and pepper. Pile the crab onto the warm toasts, sprinkle over the chives and add a few pea shoots or watercress to garnish, if you like. Serve immediately with something sparkling and crisp.

MAKE AHEAD
› The crab mix can be made up to 6 hours before serving, just keep in the fridge and mix up again before topping your toasts.

SUBSTITUTIONS
› If crab isn't your thing, then brown shrimp, Atlantic prawns (shrimp) or hot-smoked trout would be delicious.

SCALING
› This can easily be turned into a canapé if you split the toasts into 3–4 bite-size pieces and top each one with 1 tbsp of the crab mixture. This recipe would make roughly 20– 25 canapés. For a starter to serve 2, simply halve the recipe.

**SERVES 6 (WITH PLENTY OF
LEFTOVERS), OR 8-10**

2.5kg (5¹/₂lb) piece of boneless
    pork belly (see note), ribs
    reserved for the gravy
1 tbsp vegetable oil
1 onion, unpeeled and sliced
    into 5 thick rounds
1 tbsp fine salt, kosher is best

For the rub
8 garlic cloves, peeled
1¹/₂ tbsp fennel seeds
1 tsp black peppercorns
1 tsp dried juniper berries
1 tbsp caster (superfine) sugar
2 tbsp flaky sea salt
6 sprigs of fresh rosemary,
    leaves picked
30g (1oz) fresh parsley
1 tsp dried chilli flakes

For the gravy
rib bones from the pork belly,
    separated, plus any trim
1 tsp salt
1 tsp black pepper
2 tbsp olive oil
100g (3¹/₂oz) diced pancetta
1 onion, diced
1 large carrot, diced
3 sticks of celery, diced
1 small fennel bulb, thinly sliced
200ml (generous ³/₄ cup) dry
    Marsala
1 litre (1 quart) chicken stock
    (broth)
4 bay leaves
2 tbsp butter
2 tbsp plain (all-purpose) flour

NOTE: Buy your pork belly and
ribs 3 days before your event
to leave time for the curing
process. I prefer to score the
skin myself, as I find butchers
can be heavy-handed and cut
right through to the flesh below,
which will compromise your
crackling. However, the skin can
be very tough to score without a
sharp knife, so whoever does it,
you or your butcher, it needs to
be lightly scored in a diagonal
lattice across the skin and not
too deep. Don't be afraid to
be bossy about this, as it is
important to get it right.

In the same way you might brine a turkey, we are going to give up some real time on this festive main, because it deserves it. The prep we will do will *genuinely* create a sensational and PERFECT porchetta, and it will be anything but dry. It does require a long and gentle cook but our sides can be done in the oven while it rests. We will be doing a reverse sear – cooking low and slow and then popping it into a hot oven at the very end to finish – a method which gets perfect juicy, soft meat and crispy crackling every time. Get your butcher to give you the sheet of ribs when they take off the pork belly: we'll use them to make a stunning gravy. *Pictured on page 228.*

MAIN

PORCHETTA WITH PORK RIB GRAVY

Start by deciding your serving time and work back using the 'cooking times' note (see right).

When you're ready to get cracking, pulse together the rub ingredients in a food processor to make a chunky green paste. On a clean chopping board, flip the pork belly over so it is skin-side down. Lightly score the flesh with a few cuts here and there, then rub the green paste in all over. You want the flesh to be thickly coated in the green rub, but take care not to get any paste on the skin, as moisture will make it less likely to crackle. Flip the meat over again and place onto an oven tray, skin-side up. Check that the skin is completely clean and dry, patting it down with kitchen paper (paper towels) if necessary. Put the pork in your fridge for the next 2 days, leaving it uncovered and untouched so that the skin can properly dry out and the cure can do its work.

To cook the porchetta, remove it from the fridge, preheat your oven to your chosen temperature (see the 'cooking times' note, right). Drizzle the vegetable oil in the middle of a roasting tray (one with fairly low sides), then put the onion slices on top to act as a trivet for your meat to sit on. Flip the pork belly over onto a clean board and cut away a 4cm (1½in) wide strip of the cured flesh from one of the long sides – this is so your belly can be rolled more easily. Keep the trimmed flesh for the sauce. Roll the two long sides up to meet in the middle, the side with the strip missing should be able to tuck slightly under the other. Flip the belly back over again so it is skin-side up. Use butcher's string to tie the belly into a lovely, tight cylinder. I usually do about 10 ties, with the string to the side so that it doesn't catch fire when it goes in the oven. Make sure the skin is still really clean and dry. Pop the rolled belly onto the

COOKING TIMES

› To have the porchetta ready for lunch on Christmas day, put the pork in at 90°C fan (110°C/225°F/Gas ¼) on Christmas Eve overnight for 9 hours, then remove it to rest at room temperature in the morning (leaving your oven free for the other bits). 30 minutes before serving, return the meat to an oven preheated to 220°C fan (240°C/475°F/Gas 9) for 20–25 minutes to crackle the skin and get it nice and hot.

› To have the meat ready in time for dinner, pop it in the oven at 8am at 100°C fan (120°C/250°F/Gas ½) and give it 8 hours (remove at 4pm). Then rest and cook again at a high heat to crackle the skin as above. If 7 hours is all you can give the pork, then cook it at 115°C fan (135°C/275°F/Gas ½–1) before crisping the crackling as above.

MAKE AHEAD

› Stick to my suggested timelines above for the porchetta.

› The pork gravy can be made at any point in the 3 days before your meal and will keep in the fridge. Just reheat and whisk it until smooth again when you need it.

SUBSTITUTIONS

› Use thyme in your rub instead of rosemary if you prefer.

› I like the flavour of Marsala in the sauce, but dry white wine or dry sherry would work well too.

SCALING

› You can slow-cook two porchettas in the oven at the same time, but when crackling the skin, do one at a time.

› If you want to make more gravy but don't have more pork ribs, use chicken wings to flavour the stock with the ribs.

onion trivet and then into the preheated oven for the time you have allotted. After its slow-cook, the porchetta will not look a whole lot different, in fact, it almost looks like it hasn't cooked at all, but that is completely normal. If you are concerned, use a meat thermometer to probe the centre – anything above 70°C (160°F) is perfect. Leave it to rest and get on with everything else.

To make the pork rib gravy, preheat the oven to 200°C fan (220°C/425°F/Gas 7).

Put the ribs and pork trim in an oven tray and coat them in the salt and pepper. Roast in the preheated oven for 30 minutes, until deeply caramelized; you may need to turn them over once or twice.

Meanwhile, pour the olive oil into a large saucepan set over a medium heat. Add the pancetta and fry for 10–12 minutes until starting to turn golden. Add the onion, carrot, celery and fennel and fry for 20 minutes until caramelized.

Remove the roasted ribs from their oven tray and set aside. Deglaze the hot oven tray with the Marsala, taking care to scrape up any bits of precious gold from the base of the tray. Pour the tray juices into the pan of vegetables and pancetta, along with the chicken stock. Add the bay leaves and the pork ribs. Bring to the boil, then pop the lid on and simmer gently over a low heat for 3 hours to create a deeply flavourful pork stock.

After 3 hours, strain the stock and then either cool and let it sit for 24 hours in the fridge to intensify in flavour, or finish it there and then with a roux. For the roux, heat the butter in a large saucepan, add the flour and whisk to combine. Cook the roux for 3 minutes over a medium heat until it has slightly darkened in colour. Slowly add the hot pork stock, whisking with each addition (as you would do to make a béchamel), to make a silky pork gravy. Check the seasoning and set aside until needed.

To finish the porchetta, crank your oven up to 220°C fan (240°C/475°F/Gas 9).

If you can, remove the onion slices from the tray as they are likely to burn. Without removing the string, rub the pork skin with the fine salt. When the oven is hot, put the porchetta in – this will be a bit smoky so open a window. The crackling will bubble and blister and become shatteringly crisp. Check it after 20 minutes; be careful of smoke and splatter! If it's uniformly crisp and brown, remove it and let it sit for 5 minutes before removing the string and carving.

SERVES 6

2kg (4½lb) Maris Piper (or Yukon
   Gold) potatoes, peeled and cut
   into large, similar-size chunks
600ml (2½ cups) vegetable oil
flaky sea salt

For the dressing
20g (¾oz) fresh basil leaves,
   shredded
2 garlic cloves, very finely
   chopped
2 red chillies, very finely diced

MAKE AHEAD
› You can boil and cool the potatoes
up to 24 hours ahead, just make sure
they are in the fridge uncovered so
they dry out and don't sweat.
› Roast the potatoes up to 6 hours
before your dinner and reheat if you
prefer – they hold very well.

SUBSTITUTIONS
› You can leave out the dressing, or
switch the basil for parsley and chilli
for lemon zest for a more mellow take.

SCALING
› To do tonnes of roast potatoes well
you will need two ovens and lots of
trays, so bear that in mind. 1.5kg
(3¼lb) of potatoes is enough for 4
people, for 2 people do 1kg (2lb 4oz).

Everyone says it but I don't care – my mum makes the best
roast potatoes. I learned from her the cornerstones of my
roast potato philosophy, which are:

› Fully boil, not par-boil
› Lots of salt and lots of oil
› They take as long as they take – YOU WORK FOR THE
   POTATOES, THE POTATOES DON'T WORK FOR YOU

Roasties are not an exact science – ovens behave differently and
have cold and hot spots, potatoes have different sugar contents
and cook at different rates, and some people like very crunchy
small bits, others like a crunchy-fluffy hybrid. As a rough
guideline, they should take around 1 hour 20 minutes once in the
oven if nothing else is going in and out. *Pictured on page 228.*

TRIMMINGS

ROAST POTATOES WITH CHILLI, BASIL AND GARLIC

Put the potatoes into a large pan and cover them with cold water.
Salt the water generously and bring to the boil. Carefully taste
the water – it should be salty like a soup. Once boiling, let the
potatoes simmer over a medium heat for 20 minutes, or until the
thickest ones are tender. Some will start to just crumble – that is
okay. Drain and fluff them up by giving them a gentle shake in the
colander and leave to cool completely on a couple of trays.

Preheat the oven to 210°C fan (230°C/450°F/Gas 8).

Divide the oil between 2 or 3 large, deep roasting trays and heat
in the oven for 10–15 minutes until shimmering. Remove one tray
at a time and carefully lay some of the cooled potatoes in the oil,
turning them to coat all their sides. Sprinkle with sea salt, then
pop back into the oven and repeat with the remaining potatoes
over the remaining trays; don't overcrowd or the potatoes will
steam. Roast in the oven for 20 minutes, then, one tray at a time,
remove the potatoes and turn them over. Do this every 20 minutes,
removing any that are deep golden and cooked to your liking.

Put the roasties on kitchen paper (paper towels) to drain any
excess oil. When they are all cooked, keep in a tray to reheat later
while you finish the porchetta. When the porchetta is done, pop
the potatoes back in the oven for 10 minutes to warm – they will
stay really crisp. Scatter over the basil, garlic and chilli while the
potatoes are still hot, toss really well and serve.

SERVES 6

1 tbsp olive oil

2 tbsp butter

450g (approx. 3) leeks, washed,
  trimmed and thinly sliced

400g (14oz) Brussels sprouts,
  hard ends trimmed and any
  dark or damaged leaves
  removed, finely shredded

300g (10½oz) cavolo nero,
  stems removed and discarded,
  roughly chopped

900ml (3¾ cups) double (heavy)
  cream

70g (2½oz) Parmesan cheese,
  finely grated

good grating of fresh nutmeg

1 tsp salt

1 tsp freshly ground black pepper

2 tbsp Dijon mustard

bunch of fresh tarragon, leaves
  stripped and chopped

2 garlic cloves, grated

MAKE AHEAD

› The gratin can be assembled and
kept in the fridge up to 2 days ahead.
Just bring to room temperature
before you're ready to cook.

› You can also cook the gratin up
to 24 hours before and reheat it
before serving. Reheat at 180°C
fan (200°C/400°F/Gas 6) for
30–40 minutes, covered.

SUBSTITUTIONS

› Leave any of the vegetables out and
make up their weight in more of the
others, if you prefer.

› I love doing this with Savoy cabbage
and slowly cooked onions too.

SCALING

› This makes plenty for 6 people with
other sides and leftovers, so reduce the
quantities by one-third to serve 4 as a
standalone side.

I am not a huge Brussels sprouts gal, but here in this gratin with
fragrant leeks, soft cavolo nero and plenty of cheese and cream they
are pretty irresistible. I also love the idea of bunging three types of
vegetables into one dish – it follows that weird Christmas rule of
having LOADS of different vegetable sides but requires a lot less
work and oven space. *Pictured on page 228.*

TRIMMINGS

CAVOLO NERO, LEEK AND BRUSSELS SPROUT GRATIN

Heat the oil and butter in a large saucepan over a medium heat.
Add the leeks and let them soften for around 5 minutes before
adding the sprouts and cavolo nero. Drop in a tablespoon of water,
cover with a lid and leave to cook, stirring every so often, for 10
minutes just to soften the veg.

Preheat the oven to 180°C fan (200°C/400°F/Gas 6).

Meanwhile, mix the cream with half of the Parmesan, the nutmeg,
salt and pepper, Dijon mustard, chopped tarragon leaves and
grated garlic.

When the vegetables have softened, remove them from the heat.
Drain off any excess liquid and then spoon the veg into your chosen
dish – I like a large, round, cast-iron dish, but a rectangular baking
dish will do just as well. Pour the cream mixture over the vegetables
in batches, stirring it in slightly and letting it settle and disperse
evenly. Sprinkle the remaining Parmesan cheese on top and then
cover with foil. Bake in the preheated oven for 30 minutes covered,
then remove the foil and cook for another 20 minutes uncovered.
Let the gratin rest for 10 minutes before serving.

SERVES 8, WITH LEFTOVERS

For the sauce

300g (1½ cups) dark brown
    soft sugar
2 tbsp golden syrup (corn syrup)
160g (¾ cup minus 2 tsp)
    salted butter
800ml (3¼ cups) double
    (heavy) cream
pinch of flaky sea salt

For the sponge

2 English Breakfast tea bags
580ml (2½ cups) freshly-boiled
    water
350g (12oz) soft pitted
    dates, chopped
4 eggs, beaten
80g (⅓ cup + 1 tsp) soft butter
175g (generous ¾ cup) light
    brown soft sugar
125g (⅔ cup) dark brown
    soft sugar
350g (2⅔ cups) self-raising
    flour
2 tsp bicarbonate of soda
    (baking soda)
½ tsp ground cinnamon
double (heavy) cream, to serve

You will need a 30cm x 37cm
    (12 x 14½in) baking dish

MAKE AHEAD

› You can make the sauce up to 3 days
ahead and refrigerate, or even bake the
sponge with it up to 3 days ahead and
keep covered in the fridge.

SUBSTITUTIONS

› Custard, ice cream or clotted cream
are the only acceptable substitutions.

SCALING

› Halve the recipe to serve 4–6 and use
a 20cm x 25cm (8 x 10in) baking dish.

This is an elite dessert and infinitely better than Christmas pud.
I make this every Christmas, especially as it can be baked the
day before and reheated when you need it. It is modelled on the
excellent Simon Hopkinson method, but over the years I have
tweaked it. Soaking the dates in tea gives a toasty note to the
sponge, and I love the pinch of cinnamon for warmth. I also
developed my Secret Sauce Layer, whereby you freeze some
sauce on the bottom of the dish and bake the sponge on top,
so when you dig in there's a toffee ooze at the bottom.

DESSERT
STICKY TOFFEE PUDDING

Start by making the sauce. Combine the sugar, golden syrup and
salted butter in a saucepan and melt together over a medium heat.
When the mixture has turned to a thick, dark gloop, pour in the
cream and add the sea salt. Continue to cook, stirring every so
often, until the sugar has dissolved into the cream and turned a
deep toffee colour. Bring to a gentle simmer, then remove from the
heat. Pour one-third into the baking dish and pop into the freezer
to set, ideally completely flat, for 2 hours. Leave the rest of the
sauce to cool down and refrigerate until needed.

Make a large jug (pitcher) of strong black tea with the tea bags
and freshly-boiled water. Add the dates and soak until the mixture
has cooled down to lukewarm; around 20 minutes.

Preheat the oven to 180°C fan (200°C/400°F/Gas 6).

Remove the tea bags and put the dates and tea into a food
processor. Pulse until it resembles a dark paste. If you have a large
enough food processor, add the rest of the sponge ingredients and
pulse until you have a thick, luxurious brown batter. If you don't,
transfer the tea and date paste to a bowl and beat the eggs, butter
and both sugars in with a hand-held electric whisk, then fold in
the flour, bicarb and cinnamon to make a smooth batter.

Pour the batter over the frozen layer of sauce in the dish and
bake in the middle of the preheated oven for 45 minutes, or until
a skewer inserted comes out clean (take care not to skewer as far
down as the saucy base). If you are serving straight away, reheat
the remaining sauce and pour half on top of the pud, then place
under a hot grill (broiler) for 5 minutes until bubbling. If reheating
from cold, remove the pud from the fridge and bring to room
temperature for 30 minutes, before covering with foil and heating
in a preheated oven at 160°C fan (180°C/350°F/Gas 4) for 25–30
minutes, then grill as above. Serve with hot toffee sauce and cream.

THESE ARE RECIPES YOU WILL FIND ME MAKING ALMOST EVERY YEAR BECAUSE THEY ARE SO BLOODY GOOD AND DESERVE TO BE REPEATED.

THE ONE WHERE LOVE IS IN THE AIR

STARTERS

FRITTO MISTO

WEDGE SALAD

MAIN

LINGUINE ALLE VONGOLE AND 'NDUJA FOR LOVERS

DESSERT

CHERRY AND MASCARPONE MOUSSE

In my opinion it is infinitely nicer to stay in on Valentine's, or indeed, Palentine's. Not only would a busy restaurant filled with couples be SO DISTRACTING (I am nothing if not a nosy parker), but I think cooking for another person is a much more romantic thing to do. Of course, in order to break the monotony of normal dinners at home, you need to buy some delicious not-so-monotonous ingredients as a way of marking the occasion. We have to think laterally too – what is easy and quick to cook, sexy to eat, light on the old tummy and transportive for a cold February night?

Seafood ticks all those boxes for me, although arguably, if you've ever seen me eat mussels or clams then you might say it is more along the lines of monstrous destruction... but I digress.

Also light on the tummy but a grown-up thing to eat is salad, so we have that too. And then, to mark the sentiment of the occasion, we finish with a kitschy little cherry and mascarpone mousse with the added sex appeal of squirty cream and cocktail cherries with stems. I bet you won't get any washing-up done after that.

GETTING AHEAD

	Fritto Misto	Wedge Salad	Linguine Alle Vongole and 'Nduja for Lovers	Cherry and Mascarpone Mousse
Up to 3 days before	–	› Can make dressing	–	–
Up to 2 days before	–	› Can make dressing	–	› Can make ripple
Up to 1 day before	–	› Can make dressing	–	› Can make ripple
On the day	› Prep seafood › Dredge › Fry	› Fry pancetta › Prep lettuce, tomato and chives	› Purge clams › Make sauce › Toss with pasta	› Make mousse and chill

MISE-EN-PLACE

	Fritto Misto	Wedge Salad	Linguine Alle Vongole and 'Nduja for Lovers	Cherry and Mascarpone Mousse
Up to 6 hours before	› Can prep seafood › Can weigh and mix dredge	› Can make dressing › Can crisp pancetta	› Purge clams › Cook leeks, garlic and tomato purée part of sauce	› Make mousse › Fold in ripple › Chill in fridge
Up to 1 hour before	› Chop parsley › Heat oil	› Prep lettuce, tomato and chives › Warm pancetta	› Reheat sauce › Bring pasta water to the boil	–
To serve	› Dredge seafood › Fry and serve with parsley, salt and lemon wedges	› Assemble and serve	› Finish sauce › Boil pasta › Toss pasta with sauce	› Decorate mousse with squirty cream and cherries

SERVES 2

6 raw king prawns
   (jumbo shrimp), shell on
2 red mullet fillets, scaled and
   cut into 3cm (1¼in) chunks
100g (3½oz) whitebait
100g (3½oz) squid with
   tentacles, cleaned and sliced
   into rings (you can ask your
   fishmonger to clean it for you)
1 litre (1 quart) vegetable oil,
   for frying

For the crispy coating
200g (7oz) instant polenta
1 tsp salt
1 tsp garlic powder
½ tsp freshly ground
   black pepper
2 egg whites, beaten
2 tbsp cornflour (cornstarch)

To serve
small bunch of fresh parsley,
   finely chopped
flaky sea salt
1 lemon, cut into wedges

MAKE AHEAD
› Your seafood prep can be done on
the day, but this dish has to be cooked
to order.

SUBSTITUTIONS
› If you prefer a mix of only 2–3 of the
above seafoods, then simply make up
the weight of what you take out with
everything else.

SCALING
› As this dish needs to be freshly
made to order, it is best done in small
batches, so if you do want to make
it for more people be prepared to be
frying for a while. This amount would
do 4 people as a canapé.

I think some of the most romantic food you can give a loved one
is 'holiday food'. Food that takes you back to a special place, and
which doesn't often come to mind as something you can cook at
home. A fritto misto is just that for me. Spanking fresh seafood
lightly dusted in a seasoned flour and then fried until crisp. It's
transportive, evocative and so very good. Plus it is light work, the
beauty of this dish is utterly dependent on your ingredients. Get
your lover the best seafood around for this – they are worth it.

STARTER

FRITTO MISTO

Prep your seafood where necessary, then pat dry with kitchen
paper (paper towels). Heat the oil in a large, heavy-based pan or
a deep fat fryer to 190°C (375°F) – if you stick a chopstick into
the oil it should sizzle when it's ready.

For the coating, mix the polenta, salt, garlic powder and pepper
together in a large bowl. In a separate large bowl, whisk the egg
whites until frothy and foamy, then stir in the cornflour. Toss your
prawns and red mullet first in the egg white mixture and then into
the polenta mixture, taking care to coat it all well. Set the prawns
and mullet aside on a tray, then coat the whitebait and squid in
the same way.

Add the prawns and red mullet to the hot oil first, as they take
the longest. Fry these for 1 minute before adding the whitebait
and squid. Fry for another minute until golden and crisp, then
use a kitchen spider to get everything out and drain the excess
oil on kitchen paper.

Serve the fritto misto immediately, sprinkled with the parsley
and sea salt, with lots of lemon wedges.

I THINK COOKING FOR ANOTHER PERSON IS A MUCH MORE ROMANTIC THING TO DO.

SERVES 2

75g (2²/₃oz) pancetta, diced
½ small iceberg lettuce, cut
    into 2 large wedges
1 ripe plum tomato, halved,
    deseeded and carefully diced
handful of fresh chives, finely
    chopped

For the dressing
75g (⅓ cup) mayonnaise
75g (2²/₃oz) soft blue cheese –
    I like St. Agur, Gorgonzola
    or Roquefort
1 tbsp water
5 tbsp buttermilk

A wedge salad is one of the most timeless dishes out there. It has everything I want – crunchy, creamy, sweet, savoury, sour – and it looks like a lettuce with confetti on it – cute! I like this for a romantic dinner because it's light but deeply satisfying and it's really easy to make it look good. If I'm ever stuck for a side, I often fall back on this and never regret it.

STARTER

WEDGE SALAD

For the dressing, combine all the ingredients with salt and black pepper, apart from the buttermilk, in a blender or food processor and blitz until smooth. Stir in the buttermilk, then check the seasoning and adjust if necessary. Set aside.

Put the pancetta into a cold pan over a medium heat. As the pan warms, the fat on the pancetta will render and crisp up. Fry it for 10 minutes or so, until golden and crunchy, then drain on kitchen paper (paper towels).

To assemble, place your lettuce wedges, cut-side-up, on 2 serving plates – you may want to put a dollop of dressing on the plates to hold them in place. Drape the thick dressing over the centre of each lettuce, letting it slowly seep down the sides. Sprinkle the crisp pancetta, tomato and then chives on top and marvel at this kitsch beauty. Serve immediately.

MAKE AHEAD
› The dressing will keep for up to
3 days in the fridge.
› You can cook the pancetta earlier
in the day and then reheat in a warm
oven if you wish.

SUBSTITUTIONS
› For veggies, ditch the pancetta in
favour of crispy onions and choose
cheeses that do not contain any
animal rennet.

SCALING
› Allow 1 iceberg lettuce quarter
per person and 30–40g (1–1½oz) of
pancetta per person. If doubled, this
dressing will make up to 6 portions.

SERVES 2

600g (1lb 5oz) fresh clams
   (see note)
1 tbsp fine salt, for purging
   the clams
2 tbsp olive oil
1 leek, thinly sliced
280g (10oz) dried linguine
3 garlic cloves, sliced
2 tbsp tomato purée (paste)
150g (5½oz) cherry
   tomatoes, halved
80ml (⅓ cup) dry white wine
60g (2¼oz) 'nduja
80ml (⅓ cup) double
   (heavy) cream

NOTE: Make sure you store your clams in the fridge covered in a damp cloth or newspaper – do not store them in water or they will die.

MAKE AHEAD
› You can keep the clams in the fridge for up to 24 hours before purging.
› The leek, garlic and tomato purée can be cooked up to 3 hours before you want to finish the dish, just reheat and make sure the pasta goes into the water BEFORE you add the tomatoes, clams and wine to the sauce.

SUBSTITUTIONS
› Mussels or prawns (shrimp) would work really well here in place of clams, although if using prawns, add them towards the end, and you may need a little bit more juice (wine/pasta water).
› Leave out the 'nduja if you don't eat pork, or use vegan 'nduja.

SCALING
› For up to 6 people, allow for 300g (10½oz) of clams and 140g (5oz) of pasta per person and simply scale up the recipe in thirds. You may need two pans to finish your dish in, as the linguine plus clams take up a fair amount of space.

Linguine alle vongole is deeply seductive already – lots of sucking and slurping and finger licking. Okay, maybe that doesn't sound sexy to everyone but it does to me! It's obviously an amazing standalone dish, but I wanted to make something that spoke to lovers and that means, in my book, making it red like the spaghetti and meatballs in *Lady and the Tramp* and making it a little bit spicy. And so this lovers' vongole was born – it is an unbelievably irresistible dish that will wow any date.

MAIN

LINGUINE ALLE VONGOLE AND 'NDUJA FOR LOVERS

To clean the clams, give them a rinse under cold running water in a colander. Pop them into a bowl, then cover with fresh water and add the fine salt. Discard any clams that are open or broken. Mix well and leave the clams to sit in the salted water for 30–60 minutes in the fridge – they will expel and purge themselves of any sand inside. After they have purged, pour away the dirty water. Wash the clams once more in clean water and drain them through a colander one last time.

Warm the olive oil in a large pan over a medium heat, then add the sliced leek. Sweat the leek for about 8 minutes until fragrant.

Meanwhile, bring a separate large pan of water to the boil, seasoning it well with salt. Drop in the linguine, stirring well so that it doesn't clump together. Set a timer for 8 minutes.

In the meantime, add the garlic to the leek and fry for a minute, then stir in the tomato purée and cook for another minute. Turn up the heat, add the cherry tomatoes, clams and white wine and cover the pan with a lid. Cook over a high heat for 4–5 minutes until all the clams are open, discarding any that do not open. The tomatoes will have softened and created an amazing liquor with the clam juices. Stir the 'nduja into the clams.

After the pasta has cooked for 8 minutes, use tongs to move the linguine straight into the pan of clams, along with a ladle of the pasta cooking water. Finish cooking the linguine for another 3–4 minutes in the juices of the clams so that it can soak up some of the incredible sauce. Add an extra splash of pasta water if the pan looks dry at any point. When the linguine is perfectly al dente, pour in the cream and mix well to combine. Remove from the heat and plate up with lots of good wine and napkins.

SERVES 2

For the cherry ripple
100g (3½oz) frozen
pitted cherries
1 tbsp caster (superfine) sugar
freshly squeezed juice of
½ lemon
1 tbsp amaretto liqueur

For the mousse
200g (1 cup) mascarpone
80g (2⅔oz) caster
(superfine)sugar
100ml (⅓ cup) whipping cream

To serve
75g (2⅔oz) frozen pitted
cherries, defrosted
2 cocktail cherries with stems
squirty cream (optional)

MAKE AHEAD
› Make the ripple up to 3 days ahead.

SUBSTITUTIONS
› Use frozen strawberries, raspberries
or blueberries for your ripple if you
prefer, or even a frozen berry mix.

SCALING
› If you're cooking for 6 people, this
recipe is easily tripled.

This is a very sexy pudding that looks impressive but is actually
pretty low maintenance. I think mascarpone is a wonderful
ingredient – it's very fragrant and rich but also it's essentially
cream cheese, so it is perfect for making mousse.

Fresh cherries are hyper seasonal, but frozen ones are perfect
for this, as well as mandatory cocktail cherries for the top.

DESSERT

CHERRY AND MASCARPONE MOUSSE

To make the cherry ripple, mix the frozen cherries with the sugar
in a bowl and leave to defrost for 1 hour at room temperature.
Pop the defrosted cherries in a blender with the lemon juice and
blend until smooth. Pour the blended cherry mixture into a small
saucepan, then bring to the boil and cook for 2–3 minutes until
slightly reduced. Stir in the amaretto liqueur, then remove from
the heat and pour into a small, flat tray or container. Leave to cool
slightly, then chill completely in the fridge for at least 1 hour.

When the ripple has chilled completely you can make the mousse.
Put the mascarpone and sugar together into a bowl. Using electric
beaters, whip them together until they become light and fluffy and
airy – this will take around 3 minutes. At first, the mix will get
quite liquidy, but keep going – it will stiffen up again almost like
a buttercream. Then add the whipping cream and beat again until
the mix gets to very soft, floppy peaks.

To assemble the desserts, dollop a spoonful of the mousse into two
serving bowls or glasses. Add 2 tablespoons of the cherry ripple to
each dish and use the spoon to give it one quick swirl to ripple it
into the mousse. Top each layer with a couple of defrosted cherries,
then add another dollop of mousse, more cherry ripple and repeat.
For your third and final dollop, just do a lovely pile of mousse
topped with a drizzle of cherry ripple and any remaining cherries.
Pop the desserts into the fridge to chill for at least 30 minutes, up
to 2 hours.

When ready to serve, top with some squirty cream if you like,
and drizzle over a final flourish of ripple before adding a cocktail
cherry on top of each portion.

INDEX

CONVERSION CHARTS

DRY MEASURES

	metric	imperial	spoons/cups
Biscuit crumbs	115g	4oz	1 cup
Breadcrumbs, dried	140g	5oz	1 cup
Breadcrumbs, fresh	55g	2oz	1 cup
Butter	25g	1oz	2 tbsp
	50g	2oz	4 tbsp
	115g	4oz	½ cup
	225g	8oz	1 cup
Cheese (cottage, cream, curd)	225g	8oz	1 cup
Cheese (Cheddar, Parmesan), grated	115g	4oz	1 cup
Cocoa powder	100g	3½oz	1 cup
Coconut, desiccated	90g	3¼oz	1 cup
Cornflour	140g	5oz	1 cup
Courgette, grated	200g	7oz	1 cup
Flour, plain	140g	5oz	1 cup
Flour, wholewheat	165g	5¾oz	1 cup
Mushrooms, sliced	55g	2oz	1 cup
Nuts (hazelnuts, peanuts)	150g	5½oz	1 cup
Oats, rolled	85g	3oz	1 cup
Olives, pits in	175g	6oz	1 cup
Onions, chopped	150g	5½oz	1 cup
Peas, frozen	115g	4oz	1 cup
Raisins, seedless	165g	5¾oz	1 cup
Rice (long-grain), uncooked	200g	7oz	1 cup
Rice (short-grain), uncooked	200g	7oz	1 cup
Sugar (caster)	200g	7oz	1 cup
Sugar (demerara)	200g	7oz	1 cup
Sugar (granulated)	115g	4oz	1 cup
Sugar (icing)	115g	4oz	1 cup
Sugar (soft brown)	200g	7oz	1 cup
Sultanas	175g	6oz	1 cup

WEIGHT

metric	imperial	metric	imperial	metric	imperial	metric	imperial
5g	⅛oz	125g	4½oz	500g	1lb 2oz	1.6kg	3lb 8oz
10g	¼oz	140g	5oz	550g	1lb 4oz	1.8kg	4lb
15g	½oz	150g	5½oz	600g	1lb 5oz	2kg	4lb 8oz
25/30g	1oz	175g	6oz	650g	1lb 7oz	2.25kg	5lb
35g	1¼oz	200g	7oz	700g	1lb 9oz	2.5kg	5lb 8oz
40g	1½oz	225g	8oz	750g	1lb 10oz	2.7kg	6lb
50g	1¾oz	250g	9oz	800g	1lb 12oz	3kg	6lb 8oz
55g	2oz	280g	10oz	850g	1lb 14oz		
60g	2¼oz	300g	10½oz	900g	2lb		
70g	2½oz	325g	11½oz	950g	2lb 2oz		
85g	3oz	350g	12oz	1kg	2lb 4oz		
90g	3¼oz	375g	13oz	1.25kg	2lb 12oz		
100g	3½oz	400g	14oz	1.3kg	3lb		
115g	4oz	450g	1lb	1.5kg	3lb 5oz		

TEMPERATURE CONVERSIONS

Fan / °C	Celcius / °C	Fahrenheit / °F	Gas Mark
90	110	225	¼
100	120	250	½
120	140	275	1
130	150	300	2
140	160	325	3
160	180	350	4
170	190	375	5
180	200	400	6
200	220	425	7
210	230	450	8
220	240	475	9
240	260	500	10

ACKNOWLEDGEMENTS

No one warned me about how many times I was going to have to put the word "support" in the thesaurus when writing this bit.

There are a huge number of people without whom this book would not have been possible, so this is going to be a long list.

My darling Tom – this book is for you. Your unwavering support and love throughout this process has been truly magical to receive. Thank you for helping me start the newsletter, for always shouting about me, for eating literally every single dish in this book and selflessly gaining 5kg in the process. For giving constructive, honest feedback where needed and for occasional tough love too. You have this way of making me feel powerful, strong and brave in my own right, whilst also making me feel supported and safe. Our partnership is my greatest treasure, and I will love you forever.

To my Mum and Dad, Charlotte and Muir, thank you for always encouraging me to follow my passion and my dreams and for backing me every step of the way. Mum, thank you for reminding me constantly how proud you are of me and for always picking me up when I fall. Your success and humility never cease to amaze and inspire me. YDLU. Dad, thank you for teaching me how to cook! You are the reason there is a book at all. I cherish our times together cooking, and even though I give you a hard time about food hygiene, I think you are an incredibly talented cook and I adore you.

George and Billy, my bloody annoying brothers, thanks for keeping me humble. Seriously, I love you both so much and I am so grateful to you for always having my back and spreading the good word.

Thank you to my sister-cousin India for your patience, unwavering love and encouragement and kind words. And I am so sorry I bailed on starting our catering business to write this book, thanks for not holding that against me either!

I am lucky to be blessed with a massive family and extended family, so I won't name you all, but know that I am so grateful.

To all my incredible friends who have been on the @rosiemackeanpastaqueen train longer than I have, I love you! Thank you all for just being the fucking best and for showing up every step of the way. That means you Christabel, Olivia, Hannah, Lydia, Holly, Griff, Ellie, McMorrin, members of the Lads Mags WhatsApp group and many, many more.

To my agent, Rachel Conway, thank you for getting me here. You saw this book before I did, and I am so glad we are a team. Thanks always for hearing me, for seeing my vision and for keeping me moving forwards. Long may it continue.

My flower, Holly Cochrane, our years together behind the scenes on shoots are the happiest work memories I have. Your constant love and support has been invaluable, and I truly could not have made this book without you. Thank you for your help with the recipes, particularly on the technical sweet stuff, and for being my right hand on the shoot. Your prawn is my prawn.

Huge thanks also to Rob Allison and Nicole Herft for training me up to be a halfway decent food stylist – you are the best in the biz.

Nicola Lamb, thank you for inspiring me and pushing me to start a Substack, without you, *Good Time Cooking* would just be a twinkle in my eye!

Onto the shoot team of dreams. Sam Harris, the best photographer I know. You have the most incredible talent and I am in awe of everything you do. You strike the perfect balance of warmth, approachability and honesty, making shooting with you a truly joyous process. I love every shot and I hope we get to make many more cookbooks together.

Rachel Vere, thank you for the most glorious props and styling, and your thoughtful, considerate and imaginative approach. You got my style but made it better – you're a wonder!

To everyone who worked on the shoot – Matt Hague, Sam Duff, Emma Cantlay and Emma Hatcher, you are all absolute stars and I am so grateful to you all.

To Kiron, Laura, Alice, Steph and the whole team at Pavilion – thank you for making this book with me!! Your time, energy, advice, vision and expertise are so evident across the pages and I am so grateful to every one of you. It was such a joy to create this book with you all.

ABOUT THE AUTHOR

Rosie MacKean is a chef, food stylist and food writer living in London. She writes the bestselling newsletter, *The Dinner Party* on Substack, which is what inspired this book, and has people over for dinner more than any normal person should. Rosie says she is good at two things – cooking and languages (she is fluent in Spanish and very good at Italian and French), but she is also secretly really good at karaoke, bowling and pub quizzes in her humble opinion.

Pavilion
An imprint of HarperCollins*Publishers* Ltd
1 London Bridge Street
London SE1 9GF

www.harpercollins.co.uk
HarperCollins*Publishers*
Macken House
39/40 Mayor Street Upper
Dublin 1
D01 C9W8
Ireland

10 9 8 7 6 5 4 3 2 1

First published in Great Britain by Pavilion
An imprint of HarperCollins*Publishers* 2024

A catalogue record of this book is available from the
British Library.

ISBN 978-0-00-864139-9

This book contains FSC™ certified paper and other
controlled sources to ensure responsible forest management.

For more information visit: www.harpercollins.co.uk/green

Publishing Director: Stephanie Milner
Commissioning Editor: Kiron Gill
Editors: Alice Sambrook, Laura Rowe
Editorial Assistant: Shamar Gunning
Design Director: Laura Russell
Designer: Lily Wilson
Layout Designer: Sophie Yamamoto
Production Controller: Grace O'Byrne
Photographer: Sam Harris
Photo Assistant: Matthew Hague
Food Stylist: Rosie MacKean
Food Team: Holly Cochrane, Sam Duff, Emma Cantlay,
Emma Hatcher
Prop Stylist: Rachel Vere
Proofreader: Anne Sheasby
Indexer: Isobel Mclean

Printed in Malaysia by Papercraft